Subhas Chand
and Middle Class
Radicalism

Subhas Chandra Bose and Middle Class Radicalism

A Study in Indian Nationalism, 1928–1940

BIDYUT CHAKRABARTY

BLOOMSBURY ACADEMIC
LONDON · NEW YORK · OXFORD · NEW DELHI · SYDNEY

BLOOMSBURY ACADEMIC
Bloomsbury Publishing Plc
50 Bedford Square, London, WC1B 3DP, UK
1385 Broadway, New York, NY 10018, USA
29 Earlsfort Terrace, Dublin 2, Ireland

BLOOMSBURY, BLOOMSBURY ACADEMIC and the Diana logo
are trademarks of Bloomsbury Publishing Plc

First published in 1990 by I. B. Tauris
This paperback edition published by Bloomsbury Academic in 2021

ISBN: HB: 978-1-8504-3149-7
PB: 978-1-3501-8657-6

Typeset by Columns, Reading

To find out more about our authors and books visit
www.bloomsbury.com and sign up for our newsletters.

TO MY PARENTS WHO INTRODUCED ME
TO THE WORLD OF LEARNING

Contents

Tables

Acknowledgements

This book presents the findings of my study of Bengal politics between 1928 and 1940. In the completion of this first piece of research, I owe a debt of gratitude to many.

To Professor Tom Nossiter of the London School of Economics, I am greatly indebted. His guidance which combined warm encouragement and penetrating criticism made my research in an alien country both a pleasant and an enriching experience. My thanks are also due to Professor Partha Chatterjee who initiated me into the field and always offered valuable criticism and suggestions which were of great help in reformulating some of my ideas. I owe a great deal to Dr Tapan Raychaudhuri for his comments and suggestions. It is not possible to name all those from whom I have benefited by discussion, but I should like to mention especially Professor W. H. Morris-Jones, Professor Mohit Bhatta-charyya, Professor R. I. Crane, Professor A. F. Salahuddin Ahmad, Professor Ravinder Kumar, Professor A. D. Pant, Dr Paul Greenough, Dr Philip Oldenburg, Dr Gordon Johnson, and Dr David Taylor for their comments on my draft chapters. It is a particular sadness that Professor N. C. Basu Raychaudhuri, who inspired me from my days at Presidency College, passed away before the completion of my work.

I wish to express my gratitude to Mr Patrick Davis without whose sincere efforts the book would not have seen daylight. I appreciate the assistance rendered by Mr S. Mookherjee and Mr Aloke Roychowdhury while editing the book for publication. I remember Laxmi and Swapan for typing a part of the book.

I wish to record the kind assistance of the librarians and staff of the LSE Library; SOAS Library; Indian Institute Library, Oxford; Centre for South Asian Studies, Cambridge; India Office Library, London; National Archives of India, New Delhi; Nehru Memorial

Museum and Library, New Delhi; West Bengal State Archives, Calcutta; National Library, Calcutta; Bangladesh Secretariat Record Room and University Library, Dacca.

I must finally express my gratitude to Dr Ratanlal Chakrabarty and his family, my hosts in Dacca, whose hospitality I have enjoyed thoroughly while engaged in consulting archival source materials there. All errors, of course, remain my sole responsibility.

Abbreviations

ABP	*Amrita Bazar Patrika*
ABSA	All-Bengal Students Association
ABMSA	All-Bengal Muslim Students Association
AICC	All-India Congress Committee
AISF	All-India Student Federation
AITUC	All-India Trade Union Congress
BCCO	Bengal Council for Civil Disobedience
BLC	Bengal Legislative Council
BOC	Burma Oil Company
BPC	Bengal Provincial Congress
BPCC	Bengal Provincial Congress Committee
BPSA	Bengal Provincial Students Association
BSRR	Bangladesh Secretariat Record Room
CDC	Civil Disobedience Committee
CPI	Communist Party of India
CSASC	Centre for South Asian Studies, Cambridge
CSP	Congress Socialist Party
DCC	District Congress Committee
DNB	*Dictionary of National Biography*
GKU	Girni Kamgar Union
GOC	General Officer Commanding
HMP	Hindu Mahasabha Papers
IESHR	*Indian Economic and Social History Review*
IIL	India Independence League
INA	Indian National Army
INC	Indian National Congress
IOR	Indian Office Records
JAS	*Journal of Asian Studies*
JLA	Jamshedpur Labour Association
JNP	Jawaharlal Nehru Papers

JNSW	*Jawaharlal Nehru Selected Works*
JPS	*Journal of Peasant Studies*
KPP	Krishak Praja Party
LCC	Left Consolidation Committee
MAS	*Modern Asian Studies*
ML	Muslim League
MLC	Member of Legislative Council
MR	*Modern Review*
NAI	National Archives of India
NMML	Nehru Memorial Museum and Library
PCC	Provincial Congress Committee
RPP	Rajendra Prasad Papers
RSP	Revolutionary Socialist Party
UP	Uttar Pradesh
WBSA	West Bengal State Archives
WC	Working Committee
WPP	Workers and Peasants Party

Introduction

Following the 1907 Surat split between the moderates and extremists, Bengal emerged as an important barometer of the degree to which Congress lacked ideological homogeneity. A fairly well-articulated ideological tradition opposed to the Congress High Command grew up, initially around C. R. Das, a prominent Bengali politician, and this tradition continued after his death in 1925. It was Subhas Chandra Bose who not only challenged central and regional Gandhian leadership most successfully, but also provided a broad platform for many of those who held positions opposed to Gandhi and Gandhism.

Bose's rise to political leadership was not smooth since Jatindra Mohan Sengupta, another lieutenant, also vied for Das's status and gathered different political groups around him. Unlike Bose, Sengupta was well placed in the Bengal Congress because he was one of the few of Das's recruits who had direct links with the grass-root-level political activists. Bose was at best a good organizer of urban youth. Moreover, by challenging the Congress High Command from the outset of his political career he seems to have spoiled his chances at the all-India level. Not only did Sengupta rise to prominence by organizing the workers in Chittagong during the 1920–1 Non-Co-operation movement, he consolidated his position in the Congress hierarchy by aligning himself with the Gandhi-led Congress leadership. His premature death in 1933 however changed the situation in Bengal and there was no one of Sengupta's stature to challenge Bose effectively in the provincial Congress hierarchy. There were also abortive attempts by the Congress High Command to dislodge Bose who survived because he succeeded in enlisting the support of a maximum number of factions within the provincial Congress. Although his initial success was marred by the later divisive tendencies, nonetheless he

1

projected a new ideology – radical nationalism – which might have triumphed had it been supported by a clear commitment to protect the peasants against zamindars or factory workers against the industrialists.

Developments within the Bengal Congress and its all-India counterpart between 1928 and 1940 would thus exemplify the trend of opposition. By focusing on the Bengali opposition to the Congress High Command, this study aims to analyse the nature of this opposition in a context in which nationalism underwent radical changes as a result of the link between peripheral struggles with the centrally organized Congress-led freedom movement. In organizing movements, activists with political affiliations of whatever kind faced serious challenges, based sometimes on ideological differences, sometimes on communal divisions; the latter, in fact, became decisive in causing a permanent fissure in the nationalist political platform. Not only was the Hindu–Muslim schism responsible for the 1947 'Great Divide' in the Indian subcontinent, it strengthened fissiparous tendencies as well which to some extent account for the communal riots between Hindus and Muslims in post-independence India. Although communal divisions corresponded to a socio-economic split, both Hindus and Muslims nonetheless drew on their respective religions. What seemed determining, rather unfortunately, was religion since both communities fought tooth and nail to strengthen either Islam or Hinduism and almost no significant attempt was made to change the prevalent socio-economic order.

Moreover, the deep-rooted socio-political and cultural differences between the Bengali Hindus and Muslims eased the task of the Raj in maintaining further imperial control. In such a complex situation, the application of a particular model of analysing is, in the author's view, unrealistic. The study thus purports to explain political reality with reference to the factors likely to have shaped its nature.

The middle class: its composition

Rapid socio-economic changes in a thoroughly colonized society like Bengal had a close bearing upon the formation of social strata. With the consistent decline in income from land, for instance, the upper-caste Hindus faced a severe economic crisis which they survived by seizing the new opportunities made available by

British rule. The number of careers open to the English-educated increased rapidly[1] as a result of the expansion of colonial bureaucracy; the creation of railways, municipalities and postal communication; the organization of a more bureaucratic zamindari administration; the growth of European business houses; the introduction of the Western judicial system for resolving land disputes; the build-up of Western professions; the rise of journalism; and the foundation of schools, colleges and universities. Because of their favourable response to Western education, the upper-caste Bengalis not only became widespread but also had established their hegemony over virtually every field of public life in the province.[2]

This group of people, commonly known as *bhadralok*, was drawn mainly from the three upper castes of *Brahman*, *Baidya* and *Kayastha*. Since bhadralok as a group was relatively open, in theory, at least, any men including Muslims could join its ranks.[3] Since the data about the categories of Muslim population belonging to bhadralok are not available, it is difficult to ascertain their proportion in the above group. The key to bhadralok status was education and, like the case of *Chitpavan Brahmans* in Maharastra,[4] it was English education that became the ultimate determinant of social respectability.[5] Thus bhadralok was defined by the contemporary British administration as 'despotism of caste tempered by matriculation'.[6] However clear the definition is, the term does not explicitly state the socio-economic background of those identified as bhadralok. Despite its analytical inadequacies, the concept, although not well clarified, has a cultural connotation and hence, instead of rejecting the term altogether, it will be worthwhile to use it as a general category referring to the newly emerged Western-educated professional Bengalis. In order to avoid the confusion relating to the expression bhadralok, the present study introduces the concept of *madhyabitta sreni*, or middle class, which owed its birth to a peculiar socio-economic transformation from the inception of colonial rule.

In an 1829 account of *Bangadoot* (a prominent Bengali daily) *grihastha bhadralok*, incorporating shopkeepers, small zamindars, small merchants and white-collar workers, was identified as madhyabitta sreni because they were, in terms of income, in between the *abhijata bhadralok* (aristocrats) and petty wage earners.[7] In so defining this newly emerged social group, *Bangadoot* accepted income as the sole criterion. Writing on the same concept Bhavanicharan Bandapadhyay – who was himself an upper-caste Hindu –

also labelled the middle income group as madhyabitta sreni.[8] The madhyabitta sreni, comprising principally the three Hindu upper castes, depended for their subsistence on 'English and Persian' learning (both languages existed side by side before the introduction of English as the official language in 1835), which helped earn money – the use of Bengali and Sanskrit were no longer effective as means to a livelihood.[9] With the creation of new jobs as a result of the expansion of the colonial state apparatus, English education became more and more important. Those Bengalis who accepted English education were readily identified by Bhavanicharan as an educated middle class (*sikshitya madhyabbita sreni*). Since they were engaged in white-collar professions predominantly he also called them *vishayi bhadralok*.

Socially the middle class was an open group. Although vishayi bhadralok was almost totally a Hindu group, caste as such apparently played an insignificant part in the selection: men who held a similar economic position, a similar life-style and had a similar educational background were considered members of this group. A few Muslims were identified as bhadralok in Bakerganj.[10] The low proportion of Muslims among the educated middle class may well have been caused by their belated response to Western education.[11] The above criteria setting the qualifications of the middle class clearly indicate its exclusive nature; in theory, lower casts could join its ranks, but because of their straightened economic circumstances, it was not often possible for them to satisfy the prerequisites.

Economically, a large majority of the new middle class were rent-receivers; they had no direct ties to the means of production except in some cases as suppliers of credit. Thus the Bengal Land Revenue Commission of 1940, while dealing with the emergence of the Bengali middle class, argued that they had 'built themselves up on the basis of [English] education financed by their income from their tenures or fields in the shape of rents since the mid-nineteenth century'.[12] But, with the rapid rise of the cost of living, a sharp decline in income from intermediate tenure holdings as a result of the depression of 1929, and a continued partition of landed property because of inheritance customs, they were drawn more and more to English education which provided the educated middle class with an alternative means of livelihood. Not only did the straightened economic circumstances draw the middle classes to English education, the desire to attain a better life-style by increasing income also brought them to the professional world. The economic crisis of the depression period and the desire to improve the standard of living thus contributed significantly to the formation of a new social class which was less dependent on rent incomes from landed property. In N. C. Chaudhuri's view, they were 'gentlefolk' comprising literate middle and lower classes engaged primarily in clerical posts and in the professions of journalism and law.[13]

Political currents and cross-currents, 1928–40

The changing structure of agrarian relations in Bengal during British rule contributed to the formation of new classes and strata. Although these classes owed their origin to specific changes in the socio-economic milieu, they nonetheless exhibited religious and caste dimensions; and this had a definite impact on the process of political mobilization. Thus, although the political movements were largely motivated by economic grievances, caste and religious loyalties of the participants had a decisive impact on the organizations. By concentrating on the principal political organizations of Bengal, an attempt will be made in this section to show how, in the context of a new wave of radicalization, movements were organized and strengthened both on a traditional and an economic basis.

The Swaraj Party, formed in 1923, was an example of these groupings. In order to expand the horizon of politics, it sought to incorporate new actors into the Congress through the merger of Non-Co-operation and Khilafat agitations. To understand better the changed political scenario, it will be useful to distinguish between two political domains, which may be called, 'the organized' and 'the unorganized' spheres.

Organized politics are conducted through the formal state machinery. Thus organized politics encompass activities articulated through the governmental institutions, political parties, legislatures and elections. By conforming to set rules of the political game, such actors exercise political power sometimes to challenge and sometimes to defend the existing power relationships. Organized politics as an explanatory category incorporate the activities of both the opposition and those favouring the status quo. Thus a fair understanding of this type of politics requires study of the processes which surround the state. With the council entry decision in 1922, organized politics were principally centred around the Bengal Legislative Council, Calcutta Corporation and various local administrative units, introduced under the 1919 Montague–Chelmsford Reforms for self-rule.

The domain of unorganized politics lies outside the institutionalized state structure. This type of politics is called unorganized because it lacks formalized structure. What exist as organizational networks, although transitional because they appear at specific junctures of history, are well-rooted in the consciousness of the participants. What is crucial here is the sense of community maintained by activities connected with various economic, religious or cultural institutions. Thus it was not anachronistic to find that *ulemas* drawing the attention of the Muslim masses to the wrongs of the *caliph* were more effective as organizers than the Congress volunteers in the 1921 Non-Co-operation–Khilafar movement. This indicates the autonomous nature of the unorganized world where political idioms are interpreted from an altogether different perspective.

The distinction between organized and unorganized worlds of politics is useful in the understanding of Bengal politics of the period, 1928–40, because there were serious attempts by the political activists, irrespective of ideological commitments, to link the unorganized and the organized together. By drawing the local leaders, whatever their religion, to the provincial Congress hierarchy in the wake of the Non-Co-operation–Khilafat movement, and supporting the 1921 Chandpur strike, C. R. Das initiated a new political trend involving a new set of actors. Contemporaneously the revolutionary terrorists also endeavoured to extend the boundary of nationalist politics by organizing political movements on issues relating to the agrarian and industrial economy. An Intelligence Bureau report of 1927[14] made clear that a substantial section of revolutionary terrorists had come to the view that, unless peasants and workers were involved in the anti-British struggle, the nationalist movement would never be strong enough to achieve India's independence. Evidence of growing discontent, the report continued,

was to be found in the proceedings of Political Sufferers' Conference at Gauhati [in Assam] and was voiced by Bhupendranath Dutta [brother of Vivekananda] in his presidential address. This speech was openly communistic and it [was] said to have created a profound impression on the minds of the youths to whom it was addressed. Dutt advocated the organization of the peasants and workers and the formation of a people's party.[15]

In his personal recollections Tridib Chaudhuri, an Anushilan member who later became a leader of the Revolutionary Socialist Party, has corroborated this. According to him, by the early 1920s the Anushilan party in particular adopted definite policies and programmes along socialist lines in order to reach beyond 'the world of bhadralok politics'.[16] Side by side with the indigenous movement designed to include hitherto neglected political actors, there were also attempts by the Communist International through its emissaries, such as M. N. Roy, Abani Mukherjee or Gopen Chakrabarty, to spread socialist ideas. Although the Third International succeeded in attracting a sizeable section of the revolutionary terrorists, there was opposition too.[17] Judugopal Mukherjee, himself a revolutionary terrorist, has recollected in his memoirs that the majority of the Anushilan members never liked the idea of launching a nationalist movement under the direction of a foreign country.[18]

Whatever the principal reason for this ideological change in Bengal, the above evidence indicates the awareness among the revolutionary terrorists, who increasingly dominated the Congress after the days of Das, of the importance of building an organization involving the peasantry and workers. In a programme of action published in 1931 by the Chittagong revolutionaries, the aim was clearly stated:

> The Congress platform is to be availed of. Then follow orders for the capture of trade unions, the formation of ryot associations, secret entry into social and philanthropic organizations and the formation of unity to offer armed resistance to troops and police. Revolutionary students should join university training corps for observation of military methods. A women's committee should be coopted for the duty of revolutioning the women folk and selecting from them active members for direct service.[19]

Though declaring that the Congress was dominated by 'selfish commercial interests' and that 'the creed of ahimsa' was futile as a means of achieving independence, the above document appreciated

Gandhism because 'it count[ed] on mass action. It [had] paved the way for the proletarian revolution by trying to harness it, however selfishly or crudely to its own political programme. The revolutionary must give the angel his due.'[20]

This awareness of linking the peasant and working-class movement with the wider anti-British struggle was manifested in Congress's decision to incorporate the peasants' and workers' demands in its policies and programmes adopted in the 1929 Rangpur session of the Bengal Congress.[21] The Congress's failure to adopt a concrete agrarian programme[22] and the fact that the majority of east Bengal peasantry were Muslims enabled the non-Congress and communal organizations to flourish at its expense. Among the workers, the Congress had built a support base, but its national democratic line of maintaining an amicable understanding between the workers and the native industrialists prevented any consolidation of its position.

As long as C. R. Das was alive, the Bengal Congress was an umbrella organization integrating all types of political forces against the British. With his death, the unity was disrupted and there emerged not only several splinter groups within the Congress but also a separate Muslim organization, the Krishak Praja Party (KPP), with the sole purpose of protecting the interests of Muslim peasants. The arrival of the KPP divided rural Bengal in communal terms which, by dissociating the Muslims from the Hindu-dominated Congress, weakened the nationalist movement as such.

With this necessary background, we will look at the organized political forces in Bengal in order to show the variations in organization and ideology.

The Bengal Congress as an institutional structure was ill-developed in the pre-Das period. It was only during the Swadeshi Movement of 1905 that there were attempts by the Congress to popularize the nationalist cause at the district level. But the movement, though a success from the point of view of its object of annulling the Bengal partition, was not as popular as the organizers expected because its Hindu character alienated the Muslims. The anti-partition agitation was, as Gordon Johnson has said, a Bengali high-caste Hindu affair.[23] Nonetheless, it permeated throughout west Bengal and created the possibility of an organization having root in the localities. It was C. R. Das who first felt the harmful effects of city politics on Congress as a fighting platform. Moreover, the militancy he perceived in different movements at the local level led him to realize the necessity of projecting local political actors to provincial level so as to widen the organizational base. Das, therefore, recruited district leaders into the provincial Congress hierarchy: B. N. Sasmol who in 1919 led an effective campaign in Midnapore; Anil Baran Roy who also directed a successful anti-Union Board movement in Bankura in 1921; and J. M. Sengupta who came to prominence after having organized the labourers of Bullock Brothers in Chittagong in 1919. Das was also instrumental in bringing the revolutionary terrorists into the Congress. He did not believe in terrorism, yet he decided to work with them. His decision was conditioned by his desire to utilize their organizational strength for the Congress cause. In the case of Bengal, the formation of two groups, Anushilan and Jugantor, roughly corresponded to the geographical division of the province. Anushilan was east-Bengal based while Jugantor was west-Bengal based. Although both groups had their roots in different circumstances, organizationally, in terms of internal structure and even to a large extent philosophically, they were the same.[24] Their philosophy was derived from Hindu religious scriptures, such as the *Bhagavadgita*, and their message was conveyed through Bankim Chandra Chattapadhyay's *Anandamath* and Aurobindo's *Bhavani Mandir*.[25] By concentrating on Hindu philosophy, revolutionary terrorism was unable to attract the Muslims.[26]

The year 1921 was crucial in the development of broad-based Congress organization: Das, in the wake of the Non-Co-operation–Khilafat movement, skilfully seized the opportunity to mobilize the Muslims by incorporating the new line Muslim leadership.[27] This paved the way for a joint Hindu–Muslim political venture. An erstwhile congressman, Tamijuddin Khan,[28] who later joined the KPP, appreciated Das's efforts in taking such a cause to build a united anti-British platform.[29] In order to strengthen the unity between the two communities, Das seems to have drawn on the Swadeshi ideological tradition of 'composite patriotism'. The Bengal Pact of 1923 for which he was largely responsible incorporated the educated Muslims in the world of bhadralok. Muslims, according to the Pact, were to be given 55 per cent of government jobs and 60 per cent of membership in local bodies in Muslim majority districts.[30] Das's liberal initiative toward the Muslims was commendable but, given the depth of communal animosities in rural areas, it is by no means certain that had he lived longer the history of the subcontinent would have taken a different course. Tamijuddin Khan has argued:

> Hindu–Muslim differences were . . . of such a radical character that the influence of one single man, however strong, could provide a temporary diversion of the natural [sic] course of history, but it could hardly lead to a different destiny unless some social upheaval uprooting the causes that divided the two people intervened.[31]

Das's achievement was indeed short-lived and in 1926, within a year of his death, the Bengal Pact was rejected at the Krishnanagar session of the Provincial Congress.[32] Faced with organized opposition from the majority of the Bengal Provincial Congress Committee (BPCC) members, the arrangement proved fragile. Das had failed to foresee the 'adverse effects of excessive dependence on the terrorists',[33] who had a clearly defined Hindu ideology in view. His reliance on them was determined by the pragmatic consideration of 'utilizing those groups for building up an organization of full-time cadres'.[34] For their part, the terrorists joined because by that time they had realized 'the advantage of taking political activity under the Congress as a cover'.[35] This arrangement was conducive to both parties, but damaged the possibility of establishing Congress as an organization representing the interests of both the Hindus and the Muslims. Das, despite his initiatives, had failed 'to integrate in his dominant Bengal party the Bengali Muslim politicians',[36] thus creating the possibility that the Muslims would build an organization of their own to fight 'the two enemies, the British and the Hindus'.[37] With the abrogation of the Bengal Pact in 1926 the possibility became a probability if not a certainty, and the first sign was 'the parting of Muslims from the Congress in the Calcutta Corporation during the 1927 election'.[38]

The Krishnanagar Conference of 1926 was significant in another respect. As mentioned earlier, Das, by recruiting the leaders of the localities, attempted to link the localities with the province – B. N. Sasmol, J. M. Sengupta and Anil Baran Roy were the recruits under that scheme. Sasmol, a barrister with a strong support base in Midnapore who presided over the Krishnanagar Conference, launched an attack on those championing terrorism without the customary obeisance to patriotic motivation. He was hounded out of the pandal.[39] This was Sasmol's last appearance as part of the BPCC. He resigned and thereafter concentrated on his Midnapore base.

The removal of an 'effective mass leader', as Sasmol was characterized by a staunch terro-communist,[40] caused significant damage to the Bengal Congress from which it never recovered. Das's hope of strengthening the Congress by incorporating the local leaders into the provincial hierarchy was, therefore, aborted. Anil Baran Roy of Bankura, who was imprisoned for his political activity in 1924, left politics after his release in 1926 and joined Aurobindo in Pondicherry for his 'spiritual uplift'.[41] So among Das's recruits, the only leader left with a local political base was J. M. Sengupta.

Sasmol's overthrow was clearly engineered by the Karmi Sangha, a revolutionary terrorist platform, numerically preponderant within the BPCC;[42] and so it is difficult to agree with J. Gallagher who accepts Sasmol's son's contention that 'abhorrence of Calcutta upper caste elites for a mofussil Mahisya (low caste) was responsible for his father's overthrow'.[43] Given Sasmol's anti-terrorist stance and the Karmi Sangha's numerical strength within the BPCC, Gallagher's explanation may seem too simple; but since provincial politics was still dominated by bhadralok, constituted by the three Hindu upper castes, Sasmol's relatively low-caste background might have had a role in consolidating his opposition.

The removal of Sasmol, the dissociation of Anil Baran Roy from politics, the incarceration of Subhas Bose and the strong backing from the most influential and numerically strong Karmi Sangha made Sengupta's rise as the undisputed leader of the post-Das Bengal Congress easier. But a challenge came in 1927 when Bose was released. Bose found ready support among the Big Five[44] and the Jugantor group, including the Karmi Sangha, because a majority of its members were affiliated to Jugantor.[45] Big Five support can be explained in terms of both personal equations and ideological homogeneity with Bose. Both B. C. Roy and Nirmal Chunder, two of the Big Five, were aligned with the extremist section,[46] while Sarat Bose was Subhas's elder brother. Similarly, Jugantor's decision to back Bose was determined, to a large extent, by the militant image Bose projected in the 1928 Calcutta Congress, first at the GOC of the Bengal Volunteers, and secondly as an active supporter of the 'Independence Resolution'.[47]

The polarization between two prominent Bengali leaders, though corresponding to a rough ideological division, was clearer after the 1928 Calcutta Congress in which Sengupta, by opposing the young militant group led by Jawaharlal Nehru and Subhas, became identified as a Gandhian, and Bose, by rejecting the 'dominion status', consolidated his radical image. Whatever the explanation, the schism between two top provincial leaders was manifested in the fight for the control of the provincial Congress machinery.

The consequences were significant for the Bengal Congress in particular and for the freedom movement in general. The first consequence was the separation from the BPCC of district-level Congress hierarchy and the complete dissociation of Anil from politics. Moreover, Bose's and Sengupta's explicit desire to use the urban-based revolutionary terrorists for the Congress cause alienated, to a large extent, the rural Gandhians. In the following years, therefore, the unity Das had forged between the provincial and district level was lost. Instead, some of the district centres, Midnapore, Bankura and Arambag for instance, launched movements entirely on their own and, even during the Civil Disobedience movement, the BPCC failed to organize a united movement. There were two different sets of leadership in the BPCC. In the post-Das period the Bengal Congress never operated as a unified whole; on the contrary, its activities at different levels were scarcely ever co-ordinated.

The second consequence was still more serious. The BPCC stalwarts failed to gauge the adverse effects of the separation of Muslims from Hindus. Das's Bengal Pact, however fragile it appeared, temporarily gave Congress a secular character. The abrogation of the Pact as well as the submission of both Bose and Sengupta to the 'terrorists', whose faith in Hinduism was well known, gave the communal Muslims an opportunity to prove to the Muslim masses that Congress and Hinduism were synonymous. The British administration, capitalizing on this, encouraged *The Star of India*, a Muslim newspaper and the sole mouthpiece of the anti-Congress–terrorists combination, 'to continue and intensify the production of articles against the combination written from its own point of view'. The government was so certain about the impact of this newspaper on the nationalist movement that it was decided that 'the paper would be supported in case of financial difficulty and would be encouraged to start a vernacular edition for the *mofussil* [small town].'[48]

The existing social distance between the two principal communities was enough to alienate the Muslims from the Hindus in general. 'Socially', as Tamijuddin remarks, 'Muslims were in most respects untouchables to the Hindus . . . and if therefore a Muslim somehow happened to enter the cook-shed of a Hindu, even if he did not touch food or utensils, all cooked food stored in the house along with the earthen pots were considered polluted and thrown away.'[49] In addition to this, the perception that because the landlords were Hindus they exploited the Muslim tenants[50] exacerbated the situation, given the composition of zamindars and cultivators in east Bengal. Moreover, the humiliating treatment of Muslim tenants by Hindu landlords did not escape notice. As Tamijuddin has narrated,

> Muslim tenants, most of whom were cultivators, while visiting the landlords' offices were to squat on the gunny clothes spread on the floor or planks or on *piris* [low stools not higher than an inch or two] placed on their floor, while Hindu peasants of similar status were allowed to sit on the raised *farash* [knee-high platform covered with *staranj* or sheets] on which the officers of the landlords used to be seated. Muslims, not allowed to smoke from the same *hookas* as the Hindus, were to smoke from inferior hookas meant for them or from the *chhillims* [cone-shaped earthen containers of tobacco prepared for smoking placed on the perpendicular cylinder of a hooka] with the help of their fingers and folded palms.[51]

The socio-economic segregation of the two communities was so pronounced that they felt that they were 'two distinct peoples in spite of fraternization in certain fields of activity'.[52]

Given the socio-economic and cultural differences between the communities it is understandable why the abrogation of the Bengal Pact in 1926 and the nature of Congress voting in the 1928 Bengal Tenancy (Amendment) Act led to the view that it would no longer be possible to rely on Congress to maintain either Muslim interests or the Praja interests.[53] By this stage Muslims realized, as Abul Mansur Ahmad, an erstwhile Congress member, notes, 'where mere number counts, they must necessarily be a power'.[54] These factors provided the basis of a new Muslim political movement, known as the Praja movement – though it owed its origin to 'protests against the refusal to give Muslim peasants a seat in the *kachhari* [zamindar's administrative block] and the use of colloquial *tui*, instead of the polite *apni* in addressing Muslim elders by Hindu zamindars and naibs'.[55] The idea of a separate Praja organization was put forward before 1929 when its political platform, the All-Bengal Praja Samiti, was founded, in the form of *krishak samitis* (peasant organizations) in almost all districts in east and north Bengal.

The newly formed Praja Samiti represented the interests of certain emerging socio-economic groups – *jotedar* (landowner), *sampanna praja* (cultivator), professionals – in Muslim society.[56] At a conference in Dacca in April 1936, over which Fazlul Haq presided, the Praja Samiti became the Krishak Praja Party which strove to unite the activities of the samitis throughout the province.[57] The east Bengal Muslim landlords reacted instantly and in May formed a United Muslim Party under the presidentship of Nawab Habibullah of Dacca in alliance with the New Muslim Mazlis, a Calcutta-based political group of Muslim business interests.[58] Referring to the composition of the Muslim Party, Fazlul Haq argued that any Muslim unity, forged in 'Nawab's *ahsan manzil*' and not in '*krishak*'s hut' would never last long.[59] Haq's popularity as a leader and the non-Bengali dominance in the Muslim League and its elite character were the reasons why the Muslim League did not penetrate into the areas where the KPP had strongholds.[60]

Although in August 1936 Jinnah attempted to bring all Muslim political forces under the Muslim League Parliamentary Board, his move was abortive and the Bengali Muslims went to the first provincial polls deeply divided. The election results showed that the KPP had won forty and the Muslim League thirty-nine of the Muslim constituencies and the KPP polled 11 per cent more votes than the Muslim League.[61] Soon after the elections, the KPP initiated negotiations with the Congress over the formation of a coalition or a Congress-backed KPP ministry. But the Congress High Command's decision not to accept office and a disagreement between the Congress and the KPP on economic and political programmes provided the League with an opportunity to share power with the KPP.[62] On being offered the chief ministership, Haq agreed to form a coalition with the Muslim League, compromising on fundamental issues. For instance, all the major promises made in the KPP election manifesto regarding the abolition of zamindari without compensation, free primary education and the release of political prisoners[63] were put aside. In an eleven-member ministry, Haq accommodated eight zamindars and was a minority within the ministry because out of eleven ministers, four were Muslim Leaguers, three non-Congress caste Hindus and two non-Congress scheduled caste nominees.[64]

Haq's failure to comply with the election pledges and the composition of the ministry caused dissension within the KPP. At one stage, in March 1938, a majority of the KPP Members of the Legislative Assembly (MLA) sat with the opposition in order to strengthen the anti-coalition bloc.[65] The internal schism within the KPP appeared irredeemable when a dissident KPP group led by Nausher Ali broke away in protest against Haq's consent to the idea of issuing certificates to the defaulter to realize the rents due to the government.[66] The Haq faction thus became a minority within the coalition and his position untenable – caught, as he was, between two strong and formidable forces: the Muslim League within the coalition; and the combined opposition of the Congress and the KPP in the legislature. These currents and cross-currents presumably influenced Haq's decision to join the Muslim League at its 1937 annual session in Lucknow.

The period between 1937 and 1940 saw Haq attempting to champion the Muslim cause. In 1939, he declared that he was 'a Muslim first and Bengali afterwards'.[67] To establish himself as a genuine Muslim leader he also agreed to introduce the famous Lahore Resolution demanding a separate homeland for Muslims. According to a recent work on the KPP, Haq did not endorse Jinnah's 'two nation' theory, yet he supported the resolution as the only alternative to safeguard Muslim interests.[68] This indicates how calculating he was as a politician. Whatever Haq felt, the fact remains that the outcome of his involvement with the All-Indian Muslim League helped Jinnah favourably in two ways: (1) the task of mobilizing the Bengali Muslims was made easier as they found that their leader, Haq, was a supporter of a separate homeland for the Muslims; (2) in order to shape his stipulated Muslim homeland, Jinnah brought the powerful Muslim leaders from both Bengal and Punjab within the fold of the League. This was a significant step in the formation of a separate state in 1947 as it ensured a merger of national and regional Muslim power bases, a merger consolidating the organizational strength of Muslims in India. The 1940 Lahore session was thus a grand success for Jinnah: he succeeded in projecting the demands of Muslims through the leader of a Muslim majority province.

The above summary dealing with the emergence of Muslims, not merely as a community but also as a political force in the wider struggle for independence, demonstrates that Muslim separatism owed its growth to the realization initially of the aristocratic Muslims and later of an English-educated Muslim middle class of their insigificant role in the power structure. The situation was further complicated with the extension of the franchise, the penetration of formal governmental institutions into rural areas, and the opening up of governmental appointments to a relatively larger section of people. With the arrival of new Muslim groups on the political scene, there developed simultaneously a strong pro-Haq ministry support base in the 'unorganized' world. Despite his association with the zamindari-dominated League, Haq pressed hard for the adoption of a series of executive and legislative measures (Bengal Tenancy (Amendment) Act, 1938; the work of the Debt Settlement Boards; the Money Lenders Act, 1940), which increased Haq's popularity among the Muslim peasants. In east Bengal any effort to bring down the Haq ministry was interpreted as a betrayal not only of 'the Muslim cause' but also of 'the peasant cause'.[69] Further, the fact that the chief minister was a Muslim led them to think that they should not be afraid of the police.[70] The interaction between the 'organized' and 'unorganized' worlds, based obviously on different perceptions of the actors involved, illustrates a general ideological change among the Muslims.

Hindus underwent similar types of changes after the days of C. R. Das. As already shown, the Bengal Congress adopted programmes involving the peasants and workers. The most noticeable change in the Hindu-dominated Congress occurred among the revolutionary terrorists who decided to operate under the Congress platform after 1919. In the early 1920s, the revolutionary terrorists were reported to have changed their strategy because they realized that 'a handful of terrorists, however determined they might be, could never win swaraj for India unless they had the support of the mass of populace.'[71] Das's decision to include them in the Congress provided the revolutionary terrorists with an opportunity to work among the masses in the Non-Co-operation movement. This involvement with a mass movement led a group of revolutionary terrorists to realize, as Gopal Halder, himself a Jugantor member, notes, how strong a movement involving the people could be if it was properly organized.[72] With this new realization, they searched simultaneously for new ideologies. One of the sources which shaped their thinking was certainly the influence of the Moscow-returned Bengali revolutionary terrorists, Nalini Gupta and Abani Mukherjee, who sought recruits from among their old acquaintances to their new ideology aimed at a mass revolution following the Russian model. Though they failed to attract their friends in large numbers, they did draw Gopen Chakrabarty and Jatin Mitra, who were instrumental in the mass conversion of the revolutionary terrorists to Marxism in the early 1930s. Chakrabarty played a more decisive role than Mitra who left the newly converted Marxists as a result of his personal differences with M. N. Roy and was reported to have resumed terrorist activity.[73] By convincing the Anushilan members of the importance of building organizations among the students, workers and peasants, Chakrabarty contributed to a shift in their ideological orientation. The conversion of Dharani Goswami was, according to the British Intelligence Report, 'a landmark in the history of terrorism in Bengal'.[74] Though Goswami did not accept all the tenets of Marxism, he believed firmly in linking the sporadic mass struggle with the organized national movement under Congress leadership.

The ideological shift, which started in the early 1920s, was manifested in the formation of new organizations involving workers and peasants. The Labour-Swaraj Party is an example. Founded in 1925, this party became in 1926 the Workers and Peasants Party (WPP)[75] which united both these Anushilan and Jugantor members who were deviating from 'terrorism' on the same platform.[76]

In order to improve the conditions of the factory workers, the WPP proposed the following programme of immediate demands on a national scale:

(1) Eight-hour day (two weeks holiday with pay per year); (2) abolition of child labour; (3) abolition of system of fines; (4) minimum living wage; (5) state support for unemployed, old-age pensions, maternity benefit and sickness benefits; (6) improvement of laws regarding workmen's compensation and that of employers; (7) installation of modern safety appliances in factories, mines etc.; (8) abolition of the system of sirdars.[77]

These demands drew the attention of the jute workers. An official note records that 'Reds are prominent and active . . . in most of the jute workers' union.'[78] The WPP had, as will be shown, a decisive role in the 1928–9 strike of jute workers. Although its militant section, the Bengal Jute Workers Association, led the strike, the WPP always provided organizational support. The strike was not a success because the workers returned on the conditions proposed by the jute mill owners. Nevertheless, the strike and the WPP's role in it demonstrated a new phase of working-class history signifying new dimensions in working-class militancy. In his study of the Bengal jute mill workers, Dipesh Chakrabarty has shown how the communist influence became decisive in the jute workers' defiance of authority during the period 1928–40.[79]

The WPP also strove to mobilize the peasantry. As early as 1928, the party put forward the following demands, aimed at the amelioration of peasant conditions:

(1) Elimination of all mid agencies between the peasant and the state; (2) direct representation of the peasant on the state apparatus, through an adult franchise, working through peasant *panchayats* [village administration]; (3) immediate provisions of land from big estates; (4) substantial reduction in rent; (5) review of the debt and interest obligations through peasant courts with a view to their extinction; (6) state credit to the peasants.[80]

In comparison with its organizational strength among the jute workers, the WPP was less significant among the peasantry, in part because of the popularity of the krishak samitis, indigenous peasant platforms, founded by the grass-root congressmen. Although it had influences in all east-Bengal districts, the Kisan Sabha had strong organizational networks in two of them, Noakhali and Tippera. The krishak samitis were affiliated to the DCCs, but with the foundation of the All-Bengal Praja Samiti in 1929, a majority of the samitis shifted their allegiance to the new organization.[81] By associating with the Praja Samiti which became the KPP in 1936, the krishak samitis provided adequate organizational support to their provincial political wing in the first provincial elections.[82]

Although the role of the WPP was marginal among the peasants, the Kishan Sabha, the genesis of which could be traced back to the WPP, contributed significantly to the peasant organization. Though the Sabha was formally inaugurated in the 1936 Lucknow Congress, it had its roots in various sporadic peasant movements in the districts of Mymensingh and Tippera in east Bengal. It also included activists who owed their allegiance previously to the Congress, the KPP or the revolutionary terrorists. As a Bengal wing of the Kishan Sabha, the Bengal Provincial Kishan Sabha (BPKS) was constituted in August 1936. Its composition indicates that it comprised, like other mass organizations, 'the ex-detenus whose main object was more to unite the cultivators and labourers with a view to [organizing] a mass revolution than to perpetrate any act of immediate violence'.[83] Within three years of formation, the BPKS registered 50,000 members, an increase of 80 per cent between 1937 and 1940.[84]

In the 1937 provincial elections, the Kishan Sabha played a prominent part in organizing the peasants for the KPP on anti-zamindari slogans.[85] In this respect, the Sabha was not unique because the anti-zamindari sentiment was also utilized by the KPP which pledged to abolish the zamindari system. But the KPP's desire to keep the intermediary landed interests safe stood in the way of its espousing the cause of peasants in general. Fazlul Haq's order to issue a certificate to appropriate rent from the defaulters exemplifies this. Moreover, in their zeal to fight the zamindars in east Bengal, a majority of whom were Hindus, the KPP also undermined the broader anti-imperialist struggle. The Sabha, unlike the KPP, pledged to secure 'complete freedom from economic exploitation of the peasantry and workers, and the achievement of full economic and political power for the peasants and workers and all other exploited classes.[86] Its ultimate aim was not only to eradicate the roots of economic exploitation but also to give full economic and political power to the peasants and workers so that they could successfully combat the exploiters. Whatever its ultimate aim, the Kishan Sabha was not organizationally as strong as the KPP and thus never became a decisive political force in provincial politics.

The above summary indicates that a general ideological transformation in the world of 'organized politics' was intimately connected with a simultaneous change in the process of political mobilization. By incorporating new actors in the anti-British and anti-zamindar movements, the political activists of this era introduced new dimensions to the broader political struggle. In general, the period thus saw an unprecedented development in unorganized politics which assumed different forms in different parts of Bengal. For instance, since to the Muslim peasants of east

Bengal the immediate oppressor was the Hindu zamindar, the anti-landlord feeling was expressed in communal animosity; on the other hand, in west Bengal, the introduction of new taxes through the establishment of the Union Boards led the peasants to identify the British as solely responsible for such exaction. The difference in the perception of those involved in the local struggles helps to explain the nature of both the participants and the movements. Since politics was neither an exclusively bhadralok affair nor confined to Calcutta only, the post-Das Bengal Congress leadership strove to incorporate the hitherto neglected actors to strengthen the anti-British platform.

Among Das's direct disciples, Subhas Chandra Bose, in his relatively short political career, exemplified Congress's attempt to search for new constituents in the nationalist movement. When he began to get involved in the Das-led nationalist movement, Bengal Congress, as an organization, was more widespread than ever; but he failed both to maintain the previous party unity and to prevent the secession of a large number of Muslim members from the Bengal Congress. So the situation became far more complex. On the one hand, the Bengal Congress was divided into a number of groups with different ideological commitments; on the other, Muslims, by forming a separate political organization, not only weakened the anti-British struggle but also strengthened the separatist tendencies which were soon to be consolidated in the demand for a Muslim homeland. Amid these pulls and pushes from within as well as without, how the Bengal Congress shaped its ideology, designed to reach beyond the Calcutta-based bhadralok, will be discussed in detail in the following chapters.

1 Constraint and Tension in Middle-Class Leadership

The Indian National Army (INA) connection and the 'springing tiger' image of Subhas were well known; but equally interesting was his political career in the pre-INA days which has not been adequately addressed in the available literature. Most of the biographies have adopted a 'life and times' perspective,[1] and none specifically deals with Bose from the perspective either of ideology or as a regional leader seeking to compete at the all-India level. The aim of this chapter is to focus on his political life to show that he was one of the significant political actors in many of the events of Bengal and Congress politics between 1928 and 1940.

Compared with other nationalist leaders Bose had a relatively narrow span of political life because, during the nineteen years 1921 to 1940, he was in gaol for more than six.[2] He was however considered one of the most dangerous of the freedom fighters, in part because of his radical stance within the Congress, but mainly because of his intimate association with 'revolutionary terrorism'. With his entry into nationalist politics, the Bengal Special Branch police were often preoccupied with 'the tiresome business of Bose', whom the British administration compared with 'a leopard changing its spots according to convenience'.[3] In the same vein, Charles Tegart, the Calcutta Police Commissioner of 1930–2, had also instructed his fellow officers to maintain a strong vigil on Bose; he believed that a person like Bose, with no scruples about political means, was more dangerous than Gandhi.[4] In his reminiscences, M. O. Carter (who became secretary to the Bengal Governor in 1942), corroborated the fear and anxiety of the British when Bose decided to organize civil disobedience in Bengal after the failure of the 1931 Gandhi–Irwin Pact to ensure the release of political prisoners in Bengal.[5]

Bose's reputation was such that he also caused alarm to the

India Office when he came to Europe in 1933. He was denied permission to come to England on the ground that he would instigate 'destructive activities',[6] according to Lord Zetland, the Secretary of State. In view of his involvement with 'subversive activities in Vienna' he was warned that 'if he returned to India he could not be permitted to retain his liberty.'[7] In fact, Lord Zetland had a point because Bose in his *Indian Struggle*, which was published in London in 1934, had justified application of physical force on the grounds that (1) it alone would bring a response from the Western people, and (2) recourse to it was an apt answer to Macaulay's characterization of Bengalis as cowards.[8] The manifesto which he wrote for the *Samyabada Sangha* in 1933[9] and his interview in Budapest on 9 May 1934[10] suggest that Bose, unlike other principal Congress leaders, was far from devoted to the doctrine of non-violence.[11]

The administration was so apprehensive that R. S. Peel, Secretary to the Public and Judicial Department, requested the Secretary of State to cancel the validity of his passport for India permanently by applying his discretionary power, even though he knew that 'in principle, admission [could not] be refused to nationals in their own country.'[12] By encouraging close ties with the revolutionary terrorists, Bose attracted the attention of the administration and incurred serious restrictions on his political activity. Although the British police officials expressed fear and anxiety about many nationalists, their view of Bose was qualitatively different.

Background

Subhas Chandra Bose came to Calcutta, then a centre of revolutionary activity in India, in 1913 at the age of sixteen. At this stage, he was more an ascetic than a political activist perhaps owing to religious instructions he received from his mother. As a result, his attachment to Shaktism and Vaishnavism was clear.[13] At the same time as his introduction to the Hindu epics, he developed by the age of thirteen interests in the Vivekananda's idea of worshipping God through service to the poor.[14] At sixteen, Bose involved himself in a village reconstruction programme which, he later wrote, led to awareness of the social distance between the bhadralok and the villagers. Recollecting his experience, he noted:

God has given us good physique but we look upon labour as behoving only inferior classes because we are of the class of *babus*. For all sorts of work we cry out for servants – we have difficulty in working our limbs – because after all we are *babus*. Though born in a tropical country we cannot bear the heat because we are *babus*. We are so scared of the cold that we cover ourselves up with the heaviest possible clothing because we are *babus* . . . we are animals in the garb of humans devoid of human attributes.[15]

The study of philosophy as his main subject at Presidency College, Calcutta, intensified the inner struggle which led him to find a guru who could direct his way to the 'ideal' towards which he had long been striving. In 1914 without intimation to his parents he left his college hostel to search for a 'spiritual master', travelling widely in north India. His mission was not a complete success, but it at least brought him in close touch with social reality, opening his eyes to discrimination based on caste rigidity. He was refused food in one place and water in another because he was born to Kayastha caste (ritually inferior to Brahman).[16]

Bose's fascination with spiritualism was short lived. By the time he returned to Calcutta in August 1914 he claimed to have realized that 'guru-hunting [was] a wild-goose chase'[17] and became a serious college student. Hugh Toye asserts that Subhas became politically active from this time;[18] but Bose himself later wrote that he was still groping politically and his involvement in college activities was only aimed to gain 'wisdom, intellectual discipline and a critical frame of mind' through emancipation from preconceived notions.[19] This led him to form a (non-political) college debating club which, he told his friend D. K. Roy, would promote quick thinking and self-reliance.[20]

The year 1916 was a landmark in Bose's life which he later identified as the turning point of his career. His alleged involvement with the Oaten incident at Presidency College gave him 'a foretaste of leadership, though in a very restricted sphere, and of the sacrifice that it involve[d]'.[21] The controversial Oaten incident had its root, as E. F. Oaten (then a history professor of Presidency College) himself has confirmed, in Oaten's speech in the Eden Hindu Hostel in which he drew 'a parallel between the Hellenization of the Middle East by the Greeks after Alexander the Great and the Anglicization of India by the educated classes of

England'.[22] He mentioned that the Hellenes called the Persians and other subjects 'barbaroi' and explained that it meant 'non-Greek speaking'. This comparison led some students, as Oaten recollected in his memoir, 'to twist this historical statement into an allegation that I had called Indians barbarians'.[23] On 10 February, Oaten had an encounter with the students in the main building corridor when he was reported to have insulted the students.[24] In response, a strike was called, but by 15 February the majority of the students came back. In his address to the sixth-year students, Oaten condemned the strike. On the same day J. W. Holmes, a teacher of English, abused a first-year student who was reported to have been violating a college rule by 'playing and larking in the corridor'. In the general suspicion and unrest, Holmes's action, as Oaten's memoir corroborates, was ascribed to Oaten 'by some if not all and helped to make the dissident section come to the conclusion to assault [him]'.[25] He was attacked by a body of men whom he 'never saw . . . and was brought to the ground in the middle of about ten pairs of kicking feet'.[26] It is however not clear whether Bose had a direct role in it. In his reminiscences he mentioned that he was merely 'an eyewitness'[27] and the immediate victim, E. F. Oaten, was not certain as to who assaulted him.[28] Although there was nothing definite to prove Bose guilty, he accepted the responsibility as the leader and was expelled from Presidency College.[29] This incident, his close associate in the college D. K. Roy recollects, 'transformed [Bose] into a hero overnight'.[30] Subhas wrote that the Oaten controversy led him to realize the incompatibility of Sankaracharyya's *maya* with the stern reality of practical life: 'It was quite impossible to persuade myself that to be insulted by a foreigner was an illusion, i.e. maya, that could be ignored.'[31]

The nationalist Subhas accepted the sentence of the college authority as the price for fighting against racial prejudice. He went back to Cuttack and devoted himself to 'strenuous nursing, social work and the process of mental discipline' which he called 'self-analysis'.[32] He came back to Calcutta in 1917 to resume his study and with the help of Asutosh Mukherjee, Vice-Chancellor of Calcutta University, he got a place in Scottish Church College. At this time, he expressed an interest in military training, but his attempt to join the college military corps failed on medical grounds. In 1918 he fulfilled his mission and became a part of the university unit of the India defence force. Involvement with this unit was a gain to Bose because he felt that the training 'further enhanced the feeling of strength and of self-confidence'.[33]

The year 1919 was another turning point in Bose's life. He finished his BA with a first-class honours in philosophy. This gave him tremendous mental turmoil because his father offered to send Subhas to England to sit for the Indian Civil Service Examination (ICS) which was, according to young Bose, 'the heaven-born service'.[34] He was in a dilemma because he thought that successful completion of ICS meant 'giving up of [his] goal in life'. Rejecting his father's advice at the outset, Bose later accepted the offer in order to prove, as he explained, 'his superiority over the British'.[35] Bose's zeal to prove his worth may well also have been a direct result of his interview with the Provincial Adviser for Studies who did not think that Bose was competent to compete for the ICS and argued that taking the examination meant throwing away Rs10,000.[36] Bose believed that the Adviser's opinion arose from the fact that he was an 'expelled student'; but he went primarily to gather information about Cambridge since the Adviser himself was a Cambridge product.[37] Possibly the reported attempt to discourage Bose strengthened his ever-present tendency to prove his worth in competition with 'other non-expelled students'.[38] Explaining the decision at the age of forty when he was a well-established national leader, Bose might have looked back with a different point of view. For instance, his decision may well be an illustration of loyalty to his father or sheer opportunism on his part. Given the paucity of evidence, it is very difficult to be sure of the specific reason.

Bose arrived in Cambridge in 1919 and worked hard for the ICS examination. Between 1919 and 1921 he was so busy with the preparation for ICS that he did not take the Moral Sciences Tripos papers seriously. Among his teachers in Cambridge were Professor P. Sorley (Ethics), Professor T. Myers (Psychology) and Professor W. McTeggart (Metaphysics).[39] His bad performance in the Tripos (Class III) and the fact that he was not involved in any of the Fitzwilliam Hall activities[40] suggest that Bose gave priority to the ICS. But he was keen to do military training. Thus when he was denied a place with the University Officers' Training Corps, on allegedly racial grounds he went as far as to the Under-Secretary of State for India to argue his case.[41]

The young Bose who fought, as the Oaten incident shows, against real or imagined racial prejudice, and who believed in

Vivekananda's teaching and service to humanity, expressed his joy in a contemporary letter at having an English college servant serving him and cleaning his shoes.[42] Bose failed to distinguish between the English ruling class and the people who were as oppressed by them as their Indian counterparts.

Resignation from the ICS and after

After having secured fourth position in the ICS, Bose resigned because he could not serve the country and British bureaucracy simultaneously.[43] He felt that 'he [could] not sign a covenant for a foreign bureaucracy which . . . [had] no moral right to be there.'[44] Bose also questioned the moderate means of political struggle. Observing he preferred 'the uncompromising idealism of Hampden and Cromwell' to what he called Burke's philosophy of expediency,[45] Bose gave a general idea about the type of ideology he was championing then. Whether this particular preference was an opportunistic rationalization or a sincere attempt to grope for a particular type of ideology may be a matter of debate. But his political views on India during this period seem to have been largely shaped by his continuous correspondence with C. R. Das whom he considered as 'the high priest of the great movement of national service'.[46] In fact long before Bose resigned he had written to Das, introducing himself as a son of Janakinath Bose and brother of Sarat Bose,[47] about the type of job he could take up as a Congress member. Bose's suggestions included: (1) teaching in the National College which was founded during the Non-Co-operation days as an alternative to English education; (2) working for an English-language journal; (3) participating in the suggested research department of the Congress; (4) spreading education among the people; and (5) social service.[48]

Initiation into politics

In Cambridge, Bose's brother Sarat and a number of friends, like Hemanta Sarkar and Charu Chandra Ganguly, wrote to him about events in India.[49] When Bose sailed for India, Non-Co-operation was at its peak. The All-India Congress under Gandhi's guidance, according to Bose's biographer, N. G. Jog, entered a new phase in which 'mass meetings, processions and demonstrations on an unprecedented scale fired the spirit of nationalism. The cry of

Mahatma Gandhi Ki Jai [victory to Gandhi] reverberated through the length and breadth of India.'[50] Bose had thus sought an interview with Gandhi once he arrived in Bombay. The meeting with Gandhi on 16 July 1921 caused bewilderment in Bose who failed to understand how 'Mahatma expected a change of heart on the part of the British Government leading to an acceptance of India's demands.'[51] His political baptism thus delayed, Bose left Gandhi disappointed. But he was enthused by C. R. Das who impressed him so much that, after his first meeting, he acclaimed Das as a leader who was conscious of his exact role, that of a practical politician.[52]

Bose and Bengal

The visit of the Prince of Wales to Calcutta in 1921 gave Bose the first opportunity to prove his ability as a political organizer. The *hartal* (strike) of 17 November 1921 organized by Bose in protest at the visit was a success which to the British administration, as Sir Algernon Rumbold has confirmed, looked like 'a concerted threat to their existence'.[53] He was given a six-months gaol sentence. During this period, Bose was actively associated with the National College as its principal and with the nationalist English-language newspaper *Forward*. Bose's success as a political organizer and an intellectual through his activities in the college and the Congress publications impressed Das so much that he took him as his secretary to the 1922 Gaya Congress. This was Bose's first opportunity to associate himself with the all-India Congress leaders. At this sitting, the national Congress was split between the 'pro-changers' and 'no-changers' over the question of council entry.[54] Das, the leader of the 'pro-changers' defended council entry as the most effective strategy. According to him, the 'reformed councils are really a mask which the [alien] bureaucracy has put on. I conceive it to be our duty to tear the mask from their face.'[55] By deciding in favour of council entry, Das associated the Congress with institutional politics, a line vindicated by Congress's success in the 1923 Council and Calcutta Corporation elections. In the Council, the participation of the Swaraj Party members in the discussion, Das argued, enabled the people to know what was going on inside the council and the Congress's role in it.[56] Moreover, he utilized the Calcutta Corporation resources to further the Congress cause. By providing jobs in the Calcutta Corporation to those who suffered in the country's cause, Das consolidated, as C. Tegart, the Police Commissioner recollected, the bond between the 'terrorists' and the Bengal Congress.[57] By distributing the spoils of institutional power to the Muslims through the Bengal Pact of 1923, Das ensured active Muslim co-operation. Subhas as the Chief Executive Officer of the Corporation provided 75 per cent of the vacant Corporation jobs to the Muslims[58] and for this he received much praise from them.[59] Bose also seems to have largely accepted Das's political strategy of council entry.

Like his guru, Bose maintained a close link with the revolutionary terrorists. In fact, he was reported to have been instrumental in the acceptance of a resolution by the Corporation 'eulogizing an assassin, Gopinath Saha', who was hanged for the murder of a European in Calcutta.[60] This attracted the government's attention[61] and in October 1924 he was detained without trial for three years.[62] His absence from the political scene possibly made him a late entrant in the struggle for power within the Congress which had important implications for his political career.

Between 1924 and 1927 when Bose was away from the scene the Bengal Congress underwent radical changes. Upon Das's death in 1925, factional schism within the Bengal Provincial Congress (BPC) surfaced. Two groups began to exert their influence: the Karmi Sangha, comprising principally the released Jugantor political activists, imprisoned after the 1919 Rowlatt Satyagraha; and the so-called Big Five, consisting of professionally successful Bengali bhadralok, B. C. Roy, Tulsi Goswami, Nalini Sarkar, Nirmal Chandra Chunder and Sarat Bose. Both these groups backed J. M. Sengupta in his fight for the 'Triple Crown' – presidency of the BPCC, leadership of the Congress in the Legislative Council and Mayoralty of Calcutta Corporation.[63] But in the 1926 Krishnanagar session of the BPC, the split between Sengupta and the Karmi Sangha who opposed the Pact on the ground that it was, as Upendranath Banerjee of the Karmi Sangha claimed, 'not merely a device to snatch a few votes for the Swaraj Party but also [a] one-sided undertaking [because] it forbade music in procession before any mosque ignoring altogether the existence of temples, churches and other places of worship'.[64] The Big Five suggested modification of the Pact because it failed to prevent the Calcutta riot of 1926. Subhas, who was in the Mandalaya gaol, communicated his approval by referring to C. R. Das who, if alive, Bose thought, would have done the same under those circumstances;[65] but it hardly affected the outcome of the Krishnanagar session in which the Karmi Sangha, with its numerical preponderance within the BPCC, pushed forward the rejection of the Pact.[66] Amarendranath Chattapadhyay, Karmi Sangha's president, denounced the Congress for its attempt to solve a problem which had its root in rural Bengal. He thus suggested that instead of a 'shilly-shally Pact' which aimed at 'bribing the urban Muslims by giving them jobs, [congressmen] should go to the villages and serve Muhammadans as well as untouchables with a view to improving their lot.[67] Given the pronounced Hindu orientation of the revolutionary terrorists, the above justification seems a tactical move to defend their opposition to the Pact. Once the Pact was rejected, the Muslim members of the Swaraj Party, as Tamijuddin Khan has confirmed, felt threatened and the majority of them left the Swaraj Party by 1927–8.[68]

So in 1927, when Bose was released, the Bengal situation was more complicated than ever. The Congress was split and according to Sengupta's widow, Nellie Sengupta, neither the Karmi Sangha nor the Big Five liked Sengupta. This eased Bose's bid to capture the BPCC presidency in 1928.

The divisive factional rivalry between Sengupta and Bose was yet to unfold. Neither Sengupta nor Bose was strong enough to hold the 'Triple Crown' which Das had held as long as he was on the scene. When Bose became a candidate for Mayor of Calcutta in 1928, Sengupta withdrew his candidature and agreed to campaign for Bose.[69]

Bose's election to the BPCC presidency in 1928 elevated him to the top of the provincial Congress hierarchy. But he was still a student-youth leader. Bose now endeavoured to consolidate and develop his support base. In view of his active support for the 1928 Bengal Tenancy (Amendment) Act, the peasantry was hardly a possibility. What was thus left was the working class which was equally in ferment because of the growing trade depression and their perception that the capitalist selfish desire to maintain profit was responsible for their distress. As will be shown in chapter 3, Bose was only temporarily successful in organizing the workers for the nationalist cause in otherwise favourable circumstances. By conforming consistently to a role of 'secondary organizer' in the 1928 Liluah Railway strike and the 1929 strike of the jute workers, Bose failed to include the working class as a new constituency of

Congress support. The 1928 TISCO strike, which he had a chance to lead from the beginning, revealed that none of the Congress leaders including the militant Bose would champion the workers' cause at the cost of the indigenous capitalists.

In 1928, not only had Bose assumed the BPCC presidency, he also associated himself with the All-India Congress leadership. At the request of Motilal Nehru, Subhas agreed to accept[70] membership of the Nehru Committee which presented its report asking for 'dominion status' at the 1928 Calcutta Congress. Although the 'dominion status' resolution was approved by the majority of the delegates, Jawaharlal Nehru not only opposed but also formed the India Independence League (IIL), to advance the cause of India's independence.[71] Realizing the weight of the IIL as an important pressure group within the Congress, Subhas immediately changed his affiliation and joined Nehru, sustaining his radical image in the public eye.[72] While in April he insisted on 'complete independence',[73] within three months he became one of the signatories of the Nehru Report.[74] But he very soon changed his stand when the young progressive section of the Congress led by Jawaharlal Nehru categorically rejected the concept of 'dominion status' and announced the formation of the IIL, which became instrumental in the acceptance of the 'independence resolution' at the 1929 Lahore Congress.

Another example of Bose's opposition to the All-India Congress leadership could be seen in two amendments he proposed to the Subject Committee at the 1929 Lahore Congress. The first urged an all-round boycott of British goods and a simultaneous constructive programme. The second proposed the substitution of the prevalent norm of forming the Working Committee through presidential nomination with direct election by the AICC.[75] Both these amendments, as Bose wrote to Basanti Das, widow of C. R. Das, were calculated to fight the 'tyranny of the majority',[76] but they were lost and Bose now followed Das in forming the Congress Democratic Party within Congress. Unlike the IIL, the new party failed to draw much support. Some members of the Bengal Provincial Congress Committee (BPCC) and Punjab PCC joined Bose who was the only all-India leader in it. Since the party owed its origin to Bose and depended very much on him for its survival, it disintegrated when Bose was imprisoned in 1930.[77]

In order to clarify his opposition to the 'saintly politics' of Gandhi, Bose now paid attention to the shaping of his own ideology. At the outset it must be made clear that Subhas was born and nurtured in a changing socio-political environment, which saw new waves of political radicalization encompassing a mass movement with a complex and differentiated structure and many layers of effectivity in organization and in ideology. Although Bose realized the usefulness of mass organization, he never attempted it seriously. In terms of political practice, he seemed to have preferred 'revolutionary terrorism' which itself lost its significance to a large extent as a result of Congress's professed attempts to extend 'organized politics' to the masses after the 1921 Non-Co-operation–Khilafat merger.

This was the context in which Subhas emerged as a political leader. From the outset, there had been attempts by Bose to arrive at a synthesis of political ideologies incorporating both egalitarianism and revolutionary terrorism. For instance, in his opening speech as the Mayor of Calcutta in 1930, he spoke of a synthesis of socialism and fascism. In his words, 'we should endeavour to combine the justice, the equality, the love which is the basis of socialism with the efficiency and discipline of fascism' – a surprisingly early reference to fascism.[78] From now onwards, he began talking about the idea of synthesis which was, he believed, adapted to the Indian conditions and traditions.

On such an ideological foundation, Bose sharpened his anti-Gandhi attacks. He had already denounced Gandhi at the 1929 Students' Conference at Lahore for his policy of banning student participation in politics. In his presidential address he mentioned that, since all national activity was in reality political in character, the ban imposed on the students was inconceivable.[79] Further, the Bengal Volunteers, organized by Bose in 1928, illustrated Bose's attempt to mobilize youth support on the basis of what he called 'modernism' and not 'passivity'. By drawing attention to the defects of the 'Sabarmati School' of Gandhi and the 'Pondicherry School' of Aurobindo, Bose substantiated the point about the inadequacies of 'metaphysical speculation' which constituted the basis of these two schools of thought:

The actual effect of the propaganda carried on by the Sabarmati School of thought is to create a feeling and an impression that modernism is bad, that large-scale production is an evil. [It is as if] we must endeavour to the best of our abilities to go back to the days of the bullock cart ... The actual effect of the

propaganda carried on by the Pondicherry School of thought is
to create a feeling and an impression that there is nothing higher
or nobler than peaceful contemplation, that *yoga* means *pranayama*
[breathing exercise] and *dhyana* [meditation], that while action
may be tolerated as good this particular brand of *yoga* is
something higher and better.[80]

Bose condemned the philosophies of both Gandhi and Aurobindo
as they would breed 'passivity'. Hence he urged students and
youth to follow the life of Kamal Pasha and De Valera.[81] This was
'a philosophy of action'. Given the failure of Bose to back his
statements by concrete steps, this prescription was, however,
criticized by his contemporary political adversaries as 'efferves-
cence'.[82] But one may doubt how justified it was. Bose might not
have clarified his views sufficiently; but it would be going too far to
suggest that they were without any substance.

Bose on the national scene

As soon as he came out of prison following the Gandhi–Irwin Pact
of 1931, Bose spearheaded his attack against Gandhi on the basis
of the flaws of the Pact. He accused Gandhi at the 1931 Karachi
Congress of a blunder in making peace and not securing the release
of all political prisoners.[83] In his presidential address at the 1931
Karachi Conference of the All-India Naujawan Bharat Sabha, a
Youth organization in Punjab, Bose denounced the Congress
leadership and put forward an alternative view of the way the
organization ought to function. His goal was the establishment of
'a socialist republic', designed to achieve, 'complete, all-round and
undiluted freedom', the antithesis of the Congress programme
based on 'adjustment between landlord and the tenant, between
the capitalist and the wage-earner, between the so-called upper
classes and the so-called depressed classes, between men and
women'.[84] To achieve the stipulated goals, Bose suggested the
following steps:

(i) organise the peasants and workers on a socialist basis;
(ii) organise the youth into volunteer corps under strict discipline;
(iii) organise the women; (iv) convince the people of the futility
of social and religious superstitions; (v) in order to convey the
message to the masses, create new literature; and (vi) organise

an intensive programme for boycott of British goods in order to attack the British economic interests.[85]

What he developed with this address was extended further in his 1933 London address on the anti-imperialist struggle and *samyabada* (egalitarianism).[86] Bose regarded the Gandhian civil disobedience campaign as an effective means of paralysing the administration, but he did not think it adequate unless backed by guerrilla warfare which, he believed, had already brought success to the Irish freedom fighters. He thus urged the anti-Gandhi section of the Congress to organize under the platform of Hindustani Samyabadi Sangha, an organization striving (1) to provide a correct line to the Congress, and (2) to fight the alien power by violent means.[87] The British authorities naturally showed extreme concern at Bose's plans to achieve 'samyabada',[88] which revealed that he, unlike Gandhi, was thinking in terms of a political movement aimed not merely at India's political independence but also social revolution.[89]

The anti-Gandhi line continued with the Bose–Patel statement issued from Vienna in 1933.[90] Bose and V. J. Patel, elder brother of Vallabhbhai Patel, criticized Gandhi for suspending the civil disobedience campaign in 1933. They agreed that in so doing Gandhi exposed the inadequacy of a strategy based on the principle of maximum suffering for the Indians and minimum suffering for the British. They thus argued:

The latest action of Mr Gandhi in suspending the civil disobedience is a confession of failure. We are clearly of the opinion that, as a political leader, Mr Gandhi has failed.

The time has therefore come for a radical reorganization of Congress on a new principle and with a new method. To bring about this reorganization a change in leadership is necessary, for it would be unfair on Gandhi to expect him to evolve or work on a programme and method not consistent with his life-long principles.

If the Congress as a whole can undergo this transformation it would be the best course; failing that, a new party would have to be formed within Congress composed of its radical elements. Non-co-operation cannot be given up, but the form of non-co-operation would have to be changed to a more militant one and the fight for freedom waged on all fronts.[91]

Bose's theme was undoubtedly anti-Gandhian. Despite his personal admiration for Gandhi as a man who 'by his pure and lofty character could attract the Indian more than anyone else',[92] he took every opportunity to criticize Gandhi as a political strategist. Gandhi was 'a spent force' and thus incapable of achieving the goal for which he was striving.[93] He was reported to have said that Gandhi would die soon and he was the one who could take his place;[94] but there were occasions, such as in his 1936 Paris speech,[95] when Bose was publicly loyal to Gandhi and his tactics and denied that Gandhi was a spent force. These apparently contradictory statements implied the following: (a) Bose was trying to provide an alternative to 'saintly politics', but was too weak politically to accomplish this; and (b) Bose found that Gandhi was very popular in India and abroad and thus thought it expedient to balance his criticism by toning it down on occasions.

Bose in Europe, 1933–6

Bose came to Europe for treatment for tuberculosis. The India Office agreed to let him come out of prison once it was confirmed that he was seriously ill.[96] Both his brothers, Sarat and Sunil Bose who financed the trip to Europe, insisted on sending Sabhas to Denmark or Austria to convalesce.[97] The government of India did not object to Bose coming to Europe but refused him permission to visit Calcutta and his parents because, according to the director of Intelligence Bureau,

> there were very good reasons to suppose that while he was lying ill at Madras in custody Bose was actively organising terrorism. The Government of India are . . . frightened of Bose getting into dangerous touch with the old terrorist friends in Bengal if he were allowed to go back there before he sails.[98]

Though M. Clawson of the India Office believed that 'there [was] apparently no idea of his [Bose] having been associated with communism or with revolutionary intrigue outside India', he objected to the idea of sending Bose to Denmark because, 'given his terrorist connection, he [may] use two foreign lines (Hausa and the others) which maintain links between Scandinavian and the Indian ports to smuggle arms.[99] So he was allowed to go to Austria.

As 'an Indian ambassador'[100] to Europe, Bose allotted to himself the task of a spokesman for Indian nationalism and culture. Like V. J. Patel who raised the question of propaganda abroad, Bose used the opportunity to undertake propaganda for the Indian cause. In order to achieve this objective, Bose advocated cultural exchanges between India and abroad, and urged Indian schools to write about their country in the international journals, deliver lectures and participate actively in the international forum. He believed that such propaganda would counter anti-Indian propaganda that 'India [was] a place of uncivilized people'.[101] Though Bose was keen to create propaganda for India on these lines, he was handicapped financially. In a personal letter to Mrs Wood, Bose narrated how he was denied access by the AICC to the money which the late V. J. Patel left for foreign propaganda because 'the official party [seemed] to be opposed to the idea that I should undertake the work.'[102]

He was very successful in countries like Austria, Czechoslovakia, Poland, Ireland and Italy in meeting important statesmen. Mussolini, for instance, saw Bose several times.[103] What disappointed Bose was the lukewarm attitude of the German government towards him. Hitler was utterly indifferent to the Indian independence movement: in *Mein Kampf* he wrote that 'a German would far rather see India under British domination than that of any other nation.'[104] Bose explained Hitler's characterization as an attempt 'to curry favour with England'.[105] He also felt that Hitler had 'a severe as well as a dangerous psychopathic personality in whom Satan dominated'.[106] Though Bose was disappointed in 1936 as he was denied an interview with Hitler, he saw him in 1942 when he was organizing an Indian Legion in Germany from the Indian prisoners of war.[107] This meeting was encouraging to Bose because Hitler accepted the idea of fighting the British from outside.[108]

In publicizing the meeting of Bose with Mussolini and his attempt to seek one with Hitler, the *Chicago Tribune* on 30 November 1937 alleged, 'Bose had convinced Gandhi and other Congress leaders that the surest guarantee against the Japanese and other aggression' was to win the support of the bellicose fascist powers.[109] It is very difficult to say whether the report was accurate since, according to the Intelligence Bureau Records, the idea of joining the Axis Powers, which he did only in 1941, did not dawn on him until 1940.[110] The nationalist newspaper *Advance* characterized the *Chicago Tribune* report as 'a stupid suggestion'.[111]

Given Hitler's racist bias and Bose's failure to persuade him to disavow the derogatory remarks about Asians in *Mein Kampf*,[112] the 1941 alliance with the Axis Powers was still an impractical proposition. Mussolini, unlike Hitler, did not explicitly formulate the 'race ideology'; he espoused the 'idea of establishing cordial relations' between East and West as a stepping-stone towards 'world peace'. He thus declared that 'an essential condition of such cooperation was that we should free ourselves from every idea of superiority or inferiority, from every selfish motive, from every narrow sense of *race* and *creed*.'[113] Bose's increasing contact with Mussolini attracted him more towards fascism in which he already had found several good points (sic). In an interview in Italy, Bose declared how 'greatly he was interested in fascism', although to him fascism and 'hot nationalism', to use Bose's own expression,[114] were identical.

Compared with Bose's trip to Germany, his visit to Italy was a greater success in a number of ways. Here he met Mussolini who provided him with constant support during the INA campaign. He established contact with Indian students there, attended the inauguration of the Italian Oriental Institute in Rome in 1933 where, he noted, Mussolini made a fine speech,[115] and also found a congenial atmosphere in which to express his political opinions. In an interview, Bose applauded the concept of pan-Asianism which his mentor, C. R. Das, had already cited in his 1922 Gaya Congress presidential address.[116] Bose's admiration of the idea of pan-Asianism as evinced by the Japanese was not unqualified: he supported their fight against European domination, but he condemned their attacks on China which, according to him, smacked of imperialism.[117]

His European sojourn was on the whole very productive. He published *Indian Struggle* in 1934 in London, although it was instantly proscribed in India. The book indicated much of Bose's future political ideology. He rejected outright the Gandhian method of winning hearts as well as the Congress decision to co-operate with the new constitution. Instead he sought a synthesis of communism and fascism as suitable to Indian conditions. Unlike Nehru who rejected the synthesis formula as nothing more than a 'crude and brutal effort of the present capitalist order to preserve itself at any cost',[118] Bose saw it as the only appropriate means towards India's salvation.[119] Though he was impressed by fascism while he was writing his book, he later changed his opinion considerably. In an interview with R. Palme Dutt in 1938, four years after the publication of the book, Bose admitted that fascism as an expression was not a happy one but defended his position by saying that while he was writing fascism had not started 'its imperialist expedition' and, to him, fascism meant 'an aggressive form of nationalism'.[120] In his 1938 presidential address at the Haripura session of the Congress he criticized strongly the leadership principle of the fascists as it eroded democracy from the party.[121] His critical appraisal of fascism indicates his constant search for an appropriate political ideology for India, which in turn reveals his sincerity for the national cause.

The growing disillusionment with fascism led Bose to turn to the goal of national reconstruction along socialistic lines.[122] In order to benefit the 'have-nots', Bose sought a comprehensive scheme of industrial development under state ownership and control.[123] In contrast to Gandhi who was opposed to industrialism of any kind, Bose reiterated his faith in massive industrialization as the only means for India's economic development. He did not reject the 'cottage industry' formula altogether. In fact, he wanted the revival of cottage industries where they might survive the inevitable competition of factories.[124] Not only was he interested in industrialization, he was also aware of the importance of agriculture in India's economy. He believed that to improve the plight of those involved in agriculture the state had to adopt a radical land-reform programme, involving abolition of the zamindari system. In his prescribed economy, the state was vested with all powers and responsibilities: 'the state, on the advice of a planning commission', would, he argued, 'have to adopt a comprehensive scheme for socializing our entire agricultural and industrial system in the spheres of both production and appropriation.'[125] In suggesting these methods towards India's modernization, Bose was not different from Jawaharlal Nehru.

At the same time that he insisted on a modern industrial state, Subhas emphasized the founding of a new social structure entailing abolition of discrimination on the basis of 'religion', 'sex', 'caste' and 'creed'. In his 1929 Rangpur address, the idea was hinted at but not elaborated. At the 1929 Midnapore Youth Conference, Bose argued:

> To achieve *samyabada*, i.e. social-political equality, caste must be abolished and women should be freed to enjoy equal rights and

responsibilities with men in every walk of life. Economic inequality must not be tolerated any longer and every individual irrespective of caste, creed, and sex should be given equal opportunities for education and advancement.[126]

In his Haripura address (1938), he re-emphasized his commitment to building a society in which 'all citizens are equal before the law, irrespective of religion, caste, creed and sex'.[127] By challenging the foundation of traditional Hindu society Bose provided a scheme for a new society. He nonetheless did not escape from caste prejudices because as late as 1937, in his autobiography, he referred to his high-caste affiliation.[128] In other words, though he was opposed to caste,[129] he emphasized his own caste background to highlight his relatively higher position in the social hierarchy. Similarly, as regards Hindu–Muslim discrimination, Bose was equally ambivalent. As will be shown in chapter 2, none of the Congress leaders, including Bose, succeeded in evolving a concrete solution to the Hindu–Muslim problem in Bengal. The Congress, in order to protect the Hindu rentier interests, never allowed the peasants, the majority of whom were Muslims, to pursue the anti-zamindari cause. In such a complex situation, where the Hindu–Muslim division largely corresponded to that between zamindars and peasants and the Congress committed itself to protect the former, Bose's declaration to achieve samyabada seemed pious.

The Haripura address stipulated the policy of live and let live – 'a policy', as Bose himself characterized it earlier, 'of complete non-interference in matters of conscience, religion and culture . . . The Muslims have, therefore, nothing to fear.'[130] His view of the Hindu–Muslim question followed exactly C. R. Das's idea of 'composite patriotism', and thus he repeatedly argued for Muslim support when he became powerful enough to influence the Congress's decision. Like his mentor, Das, instead of looking at the roots of the problem, he tried to win over bhadralok Muslims by securing their demands through concessional pacts, such as the Bose–League Pact of 1940.

Though Bose was generally in favour of concessional pacts, he opposed the Communal Award of 1932 which he viewed as nothing but a concession to the minorities and the Muslims in terms of legislative seats in Bengal and Punjab. It is well known that, with the adoption of the Award, Hindus in Bengal were marginalized as a political force and the Muslims, by being demographically preponderant, secured control of institutional resources as given under the Government of India Act (1935). Having foreseen the bleak future, Bose argued strongly against the Award. The two pacts, the Bengal Pact of 1923 and the Bose–League Pact of 1940 in which Bose had an active role, were arrangements initiated by the bhadralok Hindus aimed at distributing spoils of institutional power between high status Hindus and Muslims. In both cases, Hindus had the major say in implementing the facts. The Award, however, altered the balance in favour of the Muslims and thus the Bose-led Hindu-dominated Bengal Congress was reduced to a minority party with no real power at its disposal. The Congress's fear of being politically eclipsed was one of the reasons why Bose questioned the Award, though it was a concessional pact biased strongly in favour of the Muslims.

While rejecting the communal concessions, Bose was equally critical of the federation scheme as enunciated in the Government of India Act (1935). In a letter to Mrs Wood, he argued that though the 1937 election results signified the 'strength of the Congress Party in spite of divide and rule . . . the Congress should not accept office until the governors [of the provinces gave] an assurance that they [would] not interfere in the work of the ministers'.[131] He also believed that even if the governors agreed not to intervene, the possibility of achieving the Congress's goal was remote because 'the central (federal) government [was] as reactionary as ever.'[132] In an article, 'Federation in India', published in *The Tribune* (Lahore), he elaborated his arguments further.[133] According to him, the arrangement of the Government of India Act (1935) was something like 'democratic government' in the provinces, while at the centre there was 'unbridled autocracy'. He criticized the idea of 'transferred' and 'reserved' subjects as this vested *de facto* authority in the British bureaucracy inside and outside India and thus left little power and meagre funds with the provincial ministries. Moreover, the prescribed composition of the federal legislature was likely to provide an incompatible team as it would draw its members from British India and the princely states; the legislature would therefore be, Bose argued, a forum in which the nominees of the princes would join the British to oppose the 'progressive policies' of the Congress.[134] What is revealing in Bose's criticism is that he was still under Das's influence. Though he was aware of the nature of limited provincial autonomy, he was willing, like his guru, to accept office on an experimental basis. For instance, although Bengal Congress refused to form a coalition with the KPP in 1937, Bose in the very next year made an attempt to arrive at an agreement with the dissident KPP over ministry formation (see chapter 4).

The Haripura address and his article in *The Tribune* constitute what we may roughly call Bose's ideology. Bose hinted that a federal arrangement was futile and thus he emphasized again and again the founding of a strong and centralized state as the instrument of ensuring the well-being of the people. What was in embryo became clear in his 1944 Tokyo speech. 'We must have', Bose insisted, 'a political system – a state – of an authoritarian character.'[135] By authoritarian political system, he meant a strong state. This perhaps indicates an element of confusion in Subhas's political thinking since authoritarianism and the survival of a strong state do not necessarily go hand in hand. Thus in the *Hindustan Standard* he remarked, '[since] no other constitution can flourish in India and it is to India's good that she should be ruled by a dictator to begin with . . . She suffers from so many ills that only a ruthless dictator can cure her.'[136] He also argued for the creation of a well-organized and disciplined all-India party to accomplish India's goal.[137] One might recall that while Bose was in Europe he was impressed by the organizational strength of the fascist and Nazi parties,[138] and this may well have convinced him of the importance of a well-disciplined party as an instrument of bringing about the regeneration and all-round advancement of India. Bose's faith in the national centralized party was firm. He, like other Congress leaders, never approved of Gandhi's idea of disbanding the Congress after independence; instead, he insisted that the Congress Party should 'take over power, assume responsibility for administration and put through its programme of reconstruction', because he held that 'only those who had won power could handle it properly'.[139] Though he was in favour of a strong state centrally controlled by a well-organized party, he was aware that this could lead to 'totalitarianism'. In order to avoid the possibility, he insisted on (1) the internal democracy of the Congress Party, and (2) the existence of more than one party.[140] But at the same time, there is an element of contradiction in Bose's suggestion for the containment of totalitarianism: a strong state centrally controlled by a well-organized party was likely to escape the reins he proposed.

Crisis of leadership, 1939

The political philosophy of Bose differed substantially from that of the Congress High Command led by Gandhi. This formed a background to the leadership crisis of 1939. Bose's election to the Congress presidency in 1938 was AICC recognition of his contribution to the national cause and enjoyed the support of Gandhi and an overwhelming majority of the PCCs.[141] During his presidency, Subhas formed the planning commission to co-ordinate developmental plans of the provincial governments.[142] Although he received Gandhi's criticism for his insistence on industrial development as the means to achieve economic strength,[143] he more or less conformed to the High Command in major political decisions; for example, he supported the 1938 Bombay Trade Dispute Bill which ensured protection to the industrialists against strikes, and he did not find fault with the AICC verdict against N. B. Khare of the Communist Party, who challenged the right of the Patel-led High Command to intervene undemocratically in the PCC's operation.[144] Since he was, as Pattabhi Sitaramiah contends, 'one of the silent presidents',[145] in the sense that he did not differ from the High Command on fundamental issues, he got on well with a Working Committee like Nehru's composed principally of Gandhians.

But difficulties ensued once Bose decided to seek re-election. Two terms of presidency was not unprecedented since Nehru held the office three times.[146] Gandhi disapproved and felt that given the acute communal rivalry between Hindus and Muslims, Maulana Azad was the most suitable person.[147] Azad declined to accept the offer on the ground that the contest with another Bengali would make it inelegant and even distasteful from more than one point of view. Further, he thought that he could more effectively ease communal tension as an ordinary congressman than a president burdened with administrative responsibilities.[148] With Azad's refusal, Gandhi recommended Pattabhi Sitaramiah, an Andhra Congress leader. Accordingly, the AICC issued a press communiqué just five days before the election requesting Bose to withdraw because:

> the matter is not one of persons or principles and not of left or right. The sole consideration is what is in the best interests of the country ... Pattabhi was the only choice since we [Gandhi,

J. Nehru, J. B. Kripalani, Maulana Azad, Bhulabhai Desai, and Rajendra Prasad] were clearly of the opinion that it was unnecessary to re-elect Subhas babu.[149]

Nehru personally appealed to Bose to avoid a split within the Congress camp. 'What [was] far more important [was] the policy and programme of the Congress . . . and the President himself [could] not make much difference to this policy laid down by the Congress itself or the AICC.'[150] Nevertheless Subhas stuck to his decision to contest the election. This put Nehru in an awkward position because he could not afford to ignore the Gandhian influence over the Indian masses. He believed that it would not only be impossible for Bose to function without Gandhi's co-operation but his re-election would also cause disunity within the Congress. These considerations led Nehru to oppose Bose's candidature.[151] Subhas, however, interpreted Nehru's action as an illustration of an absence of a clear-cut political stand since his 'head pulled him to the left but his heart to the right (i.e. Gandhi)'.[152]

To Subhas, the 1939 presidential election was a fight between left and right, although to him left meant opposition to Gandhi. That his determination to fight the Gandhian nominee was not a question of ambition is indicated by Bose's willingness to withdraw in favour of Narendra Deo of the Congress Socialist Party (CSP).[153] Two days before the election, Bose made an appeal to the pro-Gandhi AICC members 'to accept as president somebody who [would] command the confidence of the left'.[154]

The controversial 1939 election provided the left forces with an opportunity to unite under a common platform. In a joint statement, J. P. Narayan of the CSP and Swami Sahajananda of the Kishan Sabha urged the delegates to vote for Bose as a left winger and also a person most eminently fitted for this high office.[155] A press statement was also issued by M. N. Roy requesting support for Bose.[156] The National Front group (Communist Party of India) never expressed its view clearly but, P. C. Joshi later reported, an instruction was given to their delegates to vote for Subhas in order to strengthen left unity.[157] Rabindranath Tagore too wanted Bose's re-election because he felt that without 'a modernist' in the Congress High Command, India's economic development would be in jeopardy.[158]

In spite of High Command's opposition, Subhas defeated Pattabhi

Table 1.1 Vote distribution, 1939 Congress presidential election (in percentage)

	Subhas	Pattabhi
Ajmer	32	66
Andhra	11	72
Assam	57	37
Bengal	74	14
Berar	31	60
Bihar	22	66
Bombay city	46	54
Burma	28	72
Delhi	67	33
Gujrat	4	87
Karnataka	65	25
Kerala	78	18
Mohakoshal	46	47
Maharastra	44	50
CP (Maharatta)	39	55
NWFP	33	42
Punjab	64	30
Sind	33	54
Tamilnad	48	37
UP	54	37
Utkal	30	66
TOTAL	48% (1580)	41% (1377)

Source: Adapted from AICC, G/45(i)/1939, delegates for Tripuri Congress

by a margin of 203 votes (see table 1.1). Bose won a comfortable victory. Although 11 per cent of the total delegates of 3319 were absent,[159] the result showed a swing against the High Command. Thus Bose's victory symbolized not merely left unity but also consolidation of dissident congressmen who, according to Nehru, voted not against Gandhi but 'against the dictation of the Patel group'.[160] Nehru's contention may well have been justified in the case of Bombay and Central Provinces where Bose gained remarkably because of the explicit opposition of the respective PCCs to Patel who, having discarded the democratically elected PCCs leaders, imposed his own candidate. Patel's choice of B. G. Kher against K. F. Nariman who was nominated by a majority vote of the Bombay PCC, and of R. S. Shukla against N. B. Khare in the Central Provinces, annoyed a sizeable section of the PCC members,[161] who were reported to have requested the AICC members to vote for Subhas.[162] In the Lahore *Tribune*, the Punjab PCC members condemned Patel's action and asked the electorate to cast their vote in such a way as to express their opposition to the Patel-led Congress High Command.[163]

Bose's lead in the radical strongholds of Bengal, Kerala, Punjab and Uttar Pradesh (UP) was substantial.[164] It is likely that the resentment at the High Command's non-committal stand on the Communal Award may partly explain the swing in Bengal and Punjab. Bose failed to make any inroad in Pattabhi's home province, Andhra; and in Gujarat and Bihar Patel's and Prasad's influence respectively held against Bose.

Pattabhi's defeat, which Gandhi characterized as his own defeat,[165] polarized the pro- and anti-Gandhi forces more clearly than ever. The incompatibility of the two wings became apparent on 21 February 1939 when twelve of the fifteen Working Committee members resigned on the ground that Subhas had criticized them for their acts of 'omission and commission. This state of affairs', they continued, 'had been tolerated long enough and now that the leftists [had] a majority, they should be given a free hand in running the Congress.'[166] In addition, Nehru also resigned on different grounds. Given the resignation of twelve Working Committee members, he thought that Bose as president would prevent there being 'a united and determined front to political opponents, to the external authority with sway over the country'.[167]

The Tripuri session (8–12 March) started with a major split within the Congress. Bose was seriously ill and the pro-Gandhi members led by Patel were determined to force Bose's resignation long before the session began. According to the Lahore *Tribune*, a concerted effort was made by the congressmen in the seven provinces where they constituted the provincial governments to ensure votes against Bose in the following session.[168] The device used was a resolution moved by Govindballabh Pant, UP premier, reiterating faith in Gandhian leadership and asking Bose to nominate his new executive 'in accordance with the wishes of Gandhiji'.[169] The resolution was carried by 218 to 133 votes in the Subject Committee,[170] where Gandhians dominated.[171] Apart from some communist members from Bengal,[172] none of the left allies opposed it for fear of a complete split in the Congress camp.

Gandhi disliked the Pant resolution[173] but did not reject it. He allowed Bose to have his own Working Committee[174] but said at the same time that 'he [could] not guarantee approval by the AICC of [his] cabinet and policy.'[175] Though Gandhi was silent about the merit of the resolution, by denying his support in the formation of the Working Committee, he seemed to have upheld its spirit. Having realized this, Subhas attempted to bridge the gap between him and Gandhi:

> I shall resign automatically if you [Gandhi] feel that the Pant Resolution signifies no-confidence. You know well that I don't follow you blindly in all you say or believe as so many countrymen do. Why then should I resign if you opine that the Resolution signifies no-confidence? The reason is plain and simple. I feel it as galling to my conscience to hold on to office if the greatest personality in India today feels – though he may not say so openly – that the passing of the Resolution should automatically have brought in my resignation. This attitude is perhaps dictated more by personal regard for you and your opinion in this matter.[176]

Nehru, who had not supported Bose's re-election, sought to settle the differences between Gandhi and Bose. On the eve of the Calcutta session (29 April) he told Gandhi that 'to try to push [Subhas] out seems . . . an exceedingly wrong step', in view of its adverse impact on the Congress organization.[177] Gandhi however stuck to his earlier decision – to let Bose choose his own Working Committee, and the impasse continued.

The post-Tripuri crisis reveals that the differences between Gandhi and Bose were not only based on personal incompatibility but also on principles. Gandhi did not object to the Pant resolution even though it was *ultra vires* in the sense that it deprived the duly elected president of his power to nominate the Working Committee. That he backed the resolution indirectly, as expressed in his letter to Subhas, on the grounds that Bose's electoral victory 'was not so much confidence in [him] as censure of the old horses especially the Sardar [Patel]',[178] suggests the extent to which he was keen to push Bose out. The conflict, Linlithgow told R. N. Reid, the Bengal Governor, in May 1939, was much more a cleavage between different ideas and different points of view than between two important personalities.[179] One can however speculate whether, by opposing Subhas, Gandhi was also tactically checking the rise of the left within the Congress. To a large extent, Gandhi might have been correct because Bose failed to ensure the support of the Congress left when the question of forming an anti-Gandhi platform came to the fore. It was the era of popular front and the CPI General Secretary, P. C. Joshi, for instance, argued that the interests of the anti-imperialist movement demanded not the exclusive leadership of one wing but a united leadership.[180] Having failed to soften the language of the Pant rsolution, the CSP, as its spokesman Jay Prakash argued, felt it correct to remain neutral.[181] The Royists supported the resolution to put Bose down. Their opposition to Bose may have been due to Bose's refusal to accept M. N. Roy as the general secretary of the proposed Working Committee.[182]

The AICC met in Calcutta on 29 April. Bose failed to constitute the Working Committee and, in the light of left disunity, the chances were remote. In view of a determined effort by Gandhi and his followers and the schism within the left bloc, it was highly improbable that Bose would have succeeded as president. He thus resigned.[183] Without his choice of Working Committee, he would certainly have been outflanked. Rajendra Prasad was selected as an interim president on the same day, even before Bose's resignation was accepted formally by the AICC. With Bose's exit, a new Working Committee was formed without difficulty which included B. C. Roy and Prafulla Ghosh, two of the prominent High Command supporters from Bengal.[184]

The Forward Bloc and Left Consolidation Committee

Shortly after his resignation Bose announced the formation of the Forward Bloc within the Congress to expose the limitations of the Patel-led High Command and to unite different left groups on its platform.[185] However, since the CSP, CPI and Royists declined to submerge their identities in the new organization, Bose formed the Left Consolidation Committee (LCC) in June 1939, which included all leftist groups within the Congress. This new organization was nothing but a pressure group within the Congress. It sought to provide a general platform for the left: it was to endeavour to win over the majority within the Congress to its viewpoints; it proposed to mobilize for the resumption of the national struggle under the Congress banner.[186] So long as Bose agreed to operate under the Congress banner, the alliance survived; but once he called for an all-India protest day on 9 July against the recent AICC resolution banning civil disobedience without prior permission of the PCCs, the split became apparent. The CPI and the socialist leader Jay Prakash accorded first priority to Congress unity; it was, they thought, in jeopardy as a result of Bose's call.[187] And thus they decided to stay away from the LCC. Roy felt that in the light of the national movement, Bose's decision to hold an anti-AICC campaign was 'a great blunder'. Explaining his hostility, Roy argued that Bose's only motive was personal ambition.[188] Having seceded from the LCC, he pressed Nehru to persuade the CSP to dissociate itself from it.[189] By 6 July 1939, all the major constituents had left the LCC with the exception of Sahajananda's Kishan Sabha and a few Anushilan Marxists from Bengal.

Congress High Command was determined to finish Bose as a force within the Congress. There were protest resolutions against the AICC decision banning civil disobedience (CD) from a number of subordinate Congress committees but that did not amount to a breach of discipline because they had been arrived at by a majority vote.[190] Since Bose's decision to organize a protest day was rejected by the majority of the BPCC members,[191] the action was not only 'unconstitutional' but also seen 'as an open breach of discipline'.[192]

Defending the 9 July demonstration to the Congress President Rajendra Prasad, Bose argued that it was an attempt to exercise the 'democratic right of the members of a democratic organization':

> It is a strange situation if we have the right of freedom of speech and expression against the British government but not against the Congress or any body subordinate to it. If we are denied the right to criticize adversely resolutions of the AICC which in our view are harmful to the country's cause, then it would amount to denial of a democratic right.[193]

To the High Command, the explanation was unsatisfactory. Subhas was not only removed from the BPCC presidency but also debarred from holding any Congress office for three years: 'As ex-President, he should have realized that having received peremptory instructions from the President it was his duty as the servant of the nation to obey them implicitly even though he differed from the ruling of the President.'[194] By appointing an 'Ad hoc' Committee to run the Bengal Congress, the AICC endeavoured to weaken Bose politically. Though his opposition to the AICC-controlled Bengal Provincial Congress continued unabated, he was never able to enlist the support of the majority of the BPCC or District Congress Committee (DCC) members. Thus the fight between the centre and periphery, unfolding with Bose's resignation in 1939, went on until he left India in January 1941.

Concluding comments

Compared with other national leaders, Subhas Bose had a relatively short active political life. During a period of nineteen years, Bose was away from the Indian political scene for more than nine years: three years in Europe and more than six years in gaol. Except for a few months in Mandalaya gaol, Bose had always been granted first-class prison facilities. His internment in Madras gaol, prior to his departure for Europe in 1933, for instance was, according to Edgar Hyde, Assistant Commissioner of the Central Provinces, 'very comfortable: [he] was given the whole of the women's compound, allowed special furniture and his own possessions, given a privileged dietary (Bose even having fish from Bengal), and allocated five servants from amongst ordinary prisoners.'[195] In an otherwise favourable atmosphere in prison, Bose could thus concentrate on personal reading and writing. Between 1924 and 1927 when he was in Mandalaya gaol, he was introduced to Marxist literature by Jibanlal Chattapadhyay, one of the first Indian communists. Bose himself organized several discussions in which Jibanlal explained, as Suren Ghosh, a co-prisoner of Bose in Mandalaya, has confirmed, the Marxist approach to history.[196] Though he was impressed by the egalitarian content of Marxism, he questioned the idea of class struggle as the only means of socio-political emancipation. As a national democrat, he deprecated the idea of class confrontation and in practical situations like the TISCO and Tinplate strikes of 1928 and 1929 he, like other Congress leaders, insisted on the idea of class collaboration which eventually led the Bengal Workers and Peasants Party to secede from the Congress fold (see chapter 3).

In his political career of ten years, Subhas rose to the top position of the national as well as regional Congress hierarchy. Whatever he achieved he did independently. Unlike Nehru who was shrewdly unquestionably loyal to Gandhi, he was neither a satellite nor did he represent the reflected glory of Gandhi. The 1939 presidential election results illustrate Bose's rise and fall at the same time. Having established himself at the top of the AICC despite Gandhi's opposition, Bose, lacking an organizational backing, failed to retain the presidency. His victory was less the result of an ideological homogeneity between Bose and other Congress dissidents than the opposition of a majority of congressmen to the Patel-led High Command. Bose's failure to draw support against the Pant Resolution of 1939 further indicates that the Congress would never allow the 'consolidation of the anti-Gandhi forces'.

Ideologically, Bose claimed to have represented the 'left wing' within the Congress. Though he frequently used the term *left*, his concept of 'left wing' was exasperatingly vague and confusing. To him, criticism of Gandhi and rejection of Gandhism came to be the hallmark of his variety of 'leftism'. Thus Bose agreed, as Madhu Limaye, a socialist worker, has recollected, to co-operate with the Kesari group of Maharashtra in spite of its pronounced Hindu Mahasabha symapthies.[197] Similarly, his friendship with K. F. Nariman of Bombay and N. B. Khare of the Central Provinces, whose credentials as congressmen were equally questionable in view of their association with the Hindu Mahasabha,[198] shows the degree to which their criticism of Gandhi determined Bose's choice. This seemed to have puzzled Nehru who thought that Bose's characterization of Gandhi and his group in the Working Committee as rightist was wrong and confusing in view of Bose's association with extreme communalists, like Nariman and Khare.[199]

Though Bose failed both as a national and regional leader, he projected through his opposition to Gandhi the nationalism of the periphery – Bengal, Maharashtra and Punjab – which had its ideological roots in the 'revolutionary terrorism' of the pre-Gandhian days. Had he been a co-worker of Aurobindo or Tilak, he might have achieved success. But with the emergence of Gandhi, 'revolutionary terrorism' itself seems to have lost much of its significance. Bose, championing an earlier ideology of action in an age which tended to widen the basis of nationalist struggle by incorporating new actors in it, became, in one sense, as N. C. Chaudhuri has rightly observed, an anachronistic personality[200] who worked in adverse circumstances.

2 The Hindu–Muslim Question

The beginning of the twentieth century witnessed the interplay of the three major political forces on the Indian scene: the Hindu nationalist/communalist; Muslim separatist/nationalist; and the British. In terms of organizational affiliation, the nationalists from both the communities had their place in the All-India National Congress: the Muslim separatist stream flowed through the Muslim League and their Hindu counterpart through the Hindu Mahasabha.

By 1916, with the adoption of the Lucknow Pact, it was fairly clear that without the approval of the Muslim League no scheme aiming at Hindu–Muslim unity would succeed. The Non-Co-operation–Khilafat agitation of 1921, demonstrating Hindu–Muslim amity at the all-India level, is illustrative. Even with its strong religious overtone (because to the Muslims, it was more a *jihad* than a political struggle), this movement was the last instance of an understanding between the principal communities on the national plane. Unlike the League, the Hindu Mahasabha was never able to build a strong support base; it had a chance to consolidate Hindu opinion when the Congress High Command indirectly accepted the 1932 Communal Award. But the Bengal Congress's opposition to the AICC on this issue ruined that possibility. Although, in rejecting the Award completely, the Bengal Congress leadership achieved Hindu unity, it simultaneously identified itself with a sectarian ideology. Given the polarization of political forces on communal grounds at the level of 'organized politics' and deep-rooted socio-economic differences between the two communities, it is not hard to discern why Hindu–Muslim rivalries became a significant issue in the inter-war period. The aim of this chapter is to analyse the Bengal Congress's attitude and policies towards the Hindu–Muslim question and so to understand better the nature of communal animosity which culminated in the 1947 partition of the subcontinent.

We must, however, begin with some general observations on the Hindu–Muslim issue. First, until the 1935 Government of India Act was promulgated, the Hindus were the dominant forces in all institutional bases of power in Bengal, and so Hindu hegemony developed throughout the province, thus alienating Muslims from Hindus and aggravating communal animosities. The 1935 Act changed the situation radically by recognizing the numerical majority as the likely source of political power at the provincial level. As a result, the Muslims in Bengal and the Punjab, by sheer demographic preponderance over the Hindus, captured the institutions of power, patronage and influence.

Second, having achieved this, the Muslim leadership (the KPP and the Muslim League in Bengal and the Union Party in the Punjab) adopted policies and programmes to counteract Hindu preponderance in all walks of life. These policies aimed ostensibly to redress the grievances of the Muslim masses as well as the educated Muslims. The legislative acts and their implementation during the period are illustrative of this. For instance, the adopted tenancy legislations were aimed at protecting the Muslim intermediary landed interests. Similarly, in the urban areas, the Muslim leadership sought to ensure jobs for the newly emerging educated middle-class Muslims.

Third, since the days of C. R. Das, the Bengal Congress had consistently upheld the interests of Hindu rentiers and urban professionals. In the post-Das period, the bhadralok orientation of the Congress continued to influence its policy decisions; therefore, whenever there were attempts by the new Muslim leadership to adopt apparently pro-peasant legislation, vehement objections were raised suggesting the extent to which Congress was constrained by its ideological limitations. No Bengal Congress leaders overcame this; and by its opposition to these initiatives, Congress led the Muslim peasants to identify it with vested interests in land.

Fourth, the one Bengali politician who could have changed the general orientation of the Congress was Subhas Chandra Bose. But he rose to prominence in institutional politics long before – and helped to impede – the creation of a widely based support at the grass-root level.

Bose's involvement with institutional politics, a follow-up of C. R. Das's strategic calculation to 'wreck the council from within', is a good point to start because most of his actions relating to the Hindu–Muslim question were taken either as part of an institution (Calcutta Corporation, for instance) or as one who championed the Pact-type concessional arrangement at the institutional level. Therefore, the discussion will be pursued in the following way: the Hindu–Muslim question and (a) the Calcutta Corporation; and (b) the Holwell Monument agitation.

Calcutta Corporation and the Hindu–Muslim question

When Subhas arrived on the Bengal political scene, C. R. Das, in the wake of Non-Co-operation–Khilafat movement, had already brought a much wider section of Muslim leadership on to the mutually agreed organizational platform. Das sought to reach beyond the Calcutta-based 'Westernized' aristocratic Muslim leadership. As a result, men like Abdullahahel Baqi of Dinajpur, Maniruzzaman Islamabadi of Chittagong, Akram Khan of Twenty-four Parganas, Shamsuddin Ahmad of Kusthia and Ashrafuddin Ahmad Chowdhury of Tippera,[1] who had strong links with the localities, emerged as members of the Bengal provincial leadership.

In order to consolidate this unity, Das effected the Bengal Pact in 1923, which provided that 55 per cent of the government jobs and 60 per cent of membership to local bodies in the Muslim majority districts would be reserved for Muslims.[2] Ideologically he was following the Swadeshi tradition of composite patriotism, a mental construct which blended religious-communal consciousness with the institutional forms of representative politics. The idea seems to have had its origin with Bipin Chandra Pal, an extremist Swadeshi leader, who had visualized the political unity of India in the form of a federation in which the units were to be religious communities.[3] Rabindranath Tagore's Swadeshi Samaj headed jointly by a Hindu and a Muslim, was a follow-up of the same tradition. Commenting on this the *Bangabasi*, one of the powerful dailies during the Swadeshi agitation, suggested in 1908 that 'different religious groups should form a party of their own and then co-operate among themselves.'[4]

The Pact, apart from being a short-cut measure to win the support of the newly emerging Muslim educated middle class by incorporating them in the bhadralok world, illustrated Das's awareness of the distinct identities of the two religious groups. What separated Das from other contemporary Congress leaders was his serious effort to redress the grievances of the new social groups within the Muslim community. He realized, as his discussion with the novelist Sarat Chandra Chattapadhayay shows, that 'by sheer demographic strength, the Muslims are soon going to oust the Hindus from the positions of power and influence.'[5] Das was far-sighted.

This was the background when Subhas took charge in 1924 as chief executive officer of the Corporation. In order to implement the provisions of the Pact relating to jobs, he appointed '25 Muslims against 33 vacancies in subordinate services'[6] on the grounds that

> the claims of the different sections of the people have to be considered in making appointments . . . In the past the Hindus have enjoyed what may be regarded [as a] monopoly in the matter of appointments. The claims of Mahammadans, Christians and the depressed classes have to be favourably considered, though it is sure to give rise to a certain amount of heart burning in the ranks of Hindu candidates.[7]

Commendable though the step was on the part of Subhas and the Swaraj Party, it did not avert the Calcutta riot of 1926. If the riot was confined to the 'up-country Hindus and Mahammadans',[8] it nonetheless indicated the inadequacies of the Pact-type concessional arrangement in neutralizing 'communal frenzy'. The Bengal Pact might have been operational had all the constituents supported it, but from the beginning the Karmi Sangha, a revolutionary terrorist group, numerically preponderant within the Swaraj Party, 'ideologically committed to Hindu orthodoxy',[9] was opposed and eventually contributed to its total rejection in the 1926 Krishnanagar session of the BPCC. An explanation as to why Das, having known the ideology of the terrorist group, recruited them to the party, lies in his strategic calculation of utilizing the terrorist organization for the Congress.[10] In the face of Karmi Sangha's strong opposition, Subhas acquiesced to the idea of modifying the Pact, justifying this by saying that C. R. Das would have done the same. To Das the Bengal Pact, in Bose's interpretation, was one of the probable steps towards communal amity. 'He was agreeable to a revision of individual items or clauses in the pact . . . [Thus] it is perfectly clear that a staunch follower of Deshbandhu [as Das was called] can ask for a revision or modification of the pact.'[11]

Bose did not try to revive the Pact later when he became the mayor of the Corporation in 1930; he displayed no desire to offer Corporation jobs to Muslims. On the contrary, 'he secured positions in the Calcutta Corporation for active terrorists on the teaching staff of the Corporation schools, thus facilitating recruitment for the Terrorist Party.'[12] Unlike C. R. Das, Bose was not a constitutionalist and his terrorist connection was well known. Because of Das's stature both as a regional and a national leader, he was able to control the terrorists who were increasing in numbers within the BPCC by the last year of his office and to guide the Congress according to the agreed non-violent formula. Bose however never achieved such ascendancy: the BBPC 'divided on the leadership issue in the post-Das period'[13] and fell gradually under terrorist control. By 1939–40, the Executive Committee of the Bose-led BPCC was dominated by ex-detenus or state-prisoners.[14] Ideologically the terrorist parties in Bengal (especially the Jugantor) were pro-Hindu; and the Muslim leadership utilized this bias in the Congress to alienate the Muslims. In the Muslim majority areas the district leadership that had emerged at the provincial level during the Non-Co-operation days was no longer evident; Congress organization was confined to Calcutta and heavily involved in the factional rivalry between Subhas Bose and the Gandhian leadership led by K. S. and B. C. Roy.

While Das lived, the political demands of the Muslims for a separate electorate consisted of embryonic and concessional schemes, such as the Bengal Pact which temporarily appeased them; but the emergence of an educated middle class among the Muslims led to a realization that, though a majority, they were politically and economically backward.[15] The Communal Award of 1932[16] and its adoption in the Government of India Act (1935) recognized numerical majority as the basis for separate electorates. As a result, Muslims for the first time fought provincial elections at an advantage. In the case of Bengal, the failure of an agreement between the KPP and the Congress contributed to the formation of a coalition ministry led by the KPP and the Muslim League. This ministry continued in one form or another until 1941.[17]

Once in power, the coalition ministry took some legislative steps ostensibly to ameliorate the conditions of the Muslims. Here we will concentrate on the Calcutta Municipal (Amendment) Act (1939) in order to show how the Muslim ministry was determined to weaken the Hindus in the Corporation. In a letter to Lord

Linlithgow, R. N. Reid, Bengal Governor, made it clear that 'the real question at issue [in the Calcutta Municipal Bill], under all the verbiage that has surrounded it, is how far Muslims will succeed in ousting Hindus from strongholds of political power, amongst which Calcutta Corporation is one of the most important.'[18]

The main aim of the bill was to amend the original 1923 Municipal Act which gave thirteen seats to Muslims, increasing to fifteen in 1927 and to nineteen in 1932. Election to these seats was based on the principle of joint electorate[19] in order, firstly, to enhance the number of Muhammadan seats in the Corporation to twenty-two, and secondly to establish the principle of separate electorates in the election for these seats. The bill created consternation in the Legislative Assembly. The debates during the pasage of the bill show the rival calculations of the Hindus and Muslims in relation to this important piece of legislation.

The Muslims defended the share of twenty-two seats as legitimate, 'because 22 out of 84 elective sets for the Muslims is in accordance with the proportion which the population of the community bears to the total population'.[20] Fazlul Haq, the premier, justified the bill on communal grounds. He felt that 'a separate electorate is an absolute necessity in consequence of the fact that [Hindus and Muslims] are in watertight compartments. The watertight compartments are not the results of separate electorates but rather separate electorates are the results of watertight compartments that already exist.'[21]

Both the Congress and Hindu Mahasabha leadership opposed the bill vehemently. Sarat Bose, the leader of the Congress Party, characterized it as 'anti-national and anti-democratic' and he argued that 'the bill is opposed to all reason, common sense, to all ideas of justice and fair play and is calculated to prejudice the growth of the civic freedom.'[22] The representative of the Mahasabha, S. P. Mookherjee, expressed his opposition to the bill because he thought that 'the effect of the bill will be to deprive the Hindus who form 70 per cent of the total population of Calcutta and 76 per cent of total tax payers and 80 per cent of total voters of the Corporation of their legitimate claims.'[23]

Among the Muslims there were dissenting voices too. Nausher Ali, who was originally a member of the KPP but quit later as a result of a controversy over his appointment as a minister in the Haq cabinet, believed that the bill 'will do nothing but increase the acrimoniousness between different sections of the citizens of

Calcutta'.[24] Maulvi Abu Hossain Sarkar (himself a KPP member), while opposing the bill, exposed the logical flaws of Haq's demand for a separate electorate as the only means of securing the Muslim interests. He argued that 'Fazlul Haq himself was elected when the joint electorate system was introduced in the Calcutta Corporation on a Congress ticket. Is there anybody in the House who can say that the Honourable Mr Haq did not represent the Muslim community in Bengal?'[25] Maulvi Hossain Sarkar was anxious as the bill would secure

> the interests of the Urdu-speaking non-Bengalis, the Iranis, the Suhrawardys, the Siddiqis, the Adamjis and the Currimbhoys who are in a majority in Muslim Calcutta . . . whose forefathers came to exploit Bengal alone, but seeing it now impossible, have joined the Campbells and the Morgans, the representatives of the European interests in Bengal.[26]

In spite of the opposition from the Hindus and a group of Muslim leaders, the bill was passed and the new statute Calcutta Municipal (Amendment) Act (1939) provided forty-seven seats to non-Muslim voters, including four reserved for Scheduled Castes in a House of ninety-three councillors. The principle of a separate electorate was also introduced.[27]

The Corporation election under the new arrangement commanded public attention. Subhas, who was trying to regain the strength he had lost as a result of his virtual removal from the Congress in 1939, came forward. Realizing that in the changed circumstances an electoral alliance with the contending forces was the only way of maintaining his influence inside the civic body,[28] Bose forged an alliance with the Hindu Mahasabha on the understanding that 'the election would be run in the name of the Joint Congress Corporation Election Board, and that all those who would be elected would join the Congress Municipal Association'.[29]

The agreement (see below) shows that both the Hindu Mahasabha and Bose-led Congress agreed to work on the same platform only in so far as the Corporation election was concerned.

> (1) Six members from the Hindu Mahasabha to be nominated by that body to be co-opted as members of the Congress Corporation Election Board. One of the six will be secretary of the Board.

(2) A selection committee consisting of Sjts Sarat Chandra Bose, Rajendra Chandra Deb and Subhas Chandra Bose and three nominees of the Hindu Mahasabha to select the candidates.

(3) Any candidate objected to by three members of the selection committee shall be automatically dropped.

(4) The election will be run by the joint Congress Corporation Election Board as above constituted.

(5) After the election all candidates returned shall join the Congress Municipal Association and work in accordance with its rules and regulations. The Congress Municipal Association will be an autonomous body.

(6) If and when any communal question comes up before the Corporation, the Congress Municipal Association will not make it a party question but members shall have liberty to vote as they like.[30]

The terms and conditions of the pact suggest:

1   It was primarily an electoral arrangement aimed at ensuring the Corporation for the Indians. In other words, both the parties were keen not to let the Europeans control the civic administration. Bose, the leader of the Congress, justified the alliance on the ground that 'if the Indian members of the Corporation . . . do not join hands, the Corporation will pass into the hands of the British.'[31] The Hindu Mahasabha also saw an electoral pact with the Congress (then suspended) as the only way to save the Corporation for the Indians. In his press statement B. C. Chatterjee of the Mahasabha emphasized the utility of the pact as a means to keep the Corporation free from the British influence.[32]

2   Not only was the pact a temporary device, it was also inadequate to create a homogeneous whole. In fact, from the very beginning, it was clear that the pact because of its in-built weaknesses would soon collapse. The third condition (see above), for instance, indicates one area likely to cause controversy. Within nine days, disagreement had appeared between the constituents and one of the major reasons that led to the disintegration was the selection of candidates.[33]

3   The pact failed to evolve a unity. As the sixth condition (see above) shows, on the communal question the members of the Congress Municipal Association could vote independently ignoring the general overtone of the collectivity (here the Association). This

meant that the signatories of the pact allowed the communal identity of the members to prevail without recognizing the consequences. Given the ideological commitment of the Mahasabha it is not hard to explain why this condition had a share in the collapse of the pact. From the very beginning, the pact was fragile. No wonder that it did not last long.

However, the pact, though short lived, illustrates interesting trends in Bengal politics. First, on the part of the Mahasabha, conclusion of a pact with the Congress was sheer opportunism because the Mahasabha expressed disgust at the inclusion of the congressmen (B. C. Roy and Sarat Bose) in a conference, called by Fazlul Haq, Chief Minister of Bengal, for the settlement of communal differences. The objection, as B. C. Chatterjee, a Hindu Mahasabha representative, explained, was based on the ground that 'the Congress does not represent any community and therefore it has no moral right to participate in talks dealing with the settlement of communal differences.'[34] This was opportunism in view of the fact that what drove the Mahasabha to agree a pact with the Congress was not a principle but a consideration based on an assessment of how to secure Mahasabha's role within the Municipal administration.

Second, the agreement intensified communal feelings; Muslim opinion characterized this electoral deal 'as another instance of Congress and the Mahasabha being the same under diffrent guises whenever a question affecting Muslim interests is at stake'.[35] Subhas countered the allegation by saying that he effected the pact with a real Hindu Mahasabha (meaning non-political religious face of the organization) and not with an organization that sought to utilize Hindu orthodoxy for political mobilization.[36] The pact collapsed;[37] and the official Bengal Congress ridiculed it 'as a nine days wonder'.[38]

The election took place on 28 March 1940, and as a result of introducing a 'separate electorate' the Muslims secured their chances of winning more than the Hindus. Of a total of 47 seats allotted to the Hindus, the Bose group secured 21 out of 42 sets contested and the Hindu Mahasabha 16 out of 33 contested. The Muslim League won 18.[39] There was a controversy over the number of seats captured by the respective groups because, according to the *Ananda Bazar Patrika* (organ of the Bose group), the suspended Congress had secured 26 and the Hindu Mahasabha 15; the *Bharat* (newspaper of the official Congress) attributed 22 seats to the Bose group and 16 to the Hindu Mahasabha.[40] In any case, none of the contending groups attained a majority. Bose tried to effect a second agreement with the Hindu Mahasabha over the selection of candidates for the posts of aldermen. That broke down too because the Hindu Mahasabha did not agree with the 'principle of electing the aldermen by the councillors; instead, the Mahasabha insisted on fixing a quota of two of the five aldermen for the Hindu Mahasabha'.[41] The fear of being outnumbered by the Bose group, as expressed above, is understandable because had there been an election, the Bose group would have captured all the posts (as they had 22 councillors).

After this failure, Bose turned to the Muslim League which responded readily and the Bose–League pact was concluded. The willingness of the League to come to terms is readily explained in view of what preceded. Once the election was over, the Muslim League started talks with the European councillors for an agreement; that was not possible because the European members of the Corporation, sceptical of the Coalition Ministry, especially its soft attitude towards the militant Bengal Congress, 'had partly committed themselves to the right-wing Mahasabha and declined to co-operate with the Muslim League'.[42] Though justifying the agreement with the (suspended) Congress by referring to the possibility that the pact 'will ensure smooth-running of the civic administration of Calcutta',[43] the Muslim League leadership had the primary intention, as John Herbert, Bengal Governor, wrote to the Viceroy, of utilizing Subhas to create further dissension within the Bengal Congress.[44] Not fully convinced, the Bengal Governor noted that the Muslim League, in so doing, 'have taken a risk in trying to outwit so clever and slippery an opponent'.[45]

According to the agreement, a Muslim Leaguer would be chosen as the mayor with two aldermen from his party and the remaining three aldermen from the Bose group. Accordingly, the following five were elected: (1) B. C. Chatterjee, (2) Hem Chandra Naskar, (3) Subhas Chandra Bose (from Bose group), (4) Adam Osman, (5) Taj Mohammed (from the Muslim League). The aldermanic election was followed by the election of Abdur Rahaman Siddiqui, MLA, as the new Mayor of Calcutta; Phanindra Nath Brahma of the Bose group was elected Deputy Mayor.

The agreement, Bose wrote, was 'a great achievement not in its actuality but in its potentiality'[46] and he thought that it would ensure 'amicable relations between the two communities'.[47] This is rather doubtful. It might have set the beginning of an understanding between the two communities, and if that was followed up it might have subsequently laid the basis of an agreement involving participation from both the communities on a wide scale; but by itself this agreement was certainly feeble, especially when Hindu–Muslim animosity penetrated deep into rural Bengal.

What the pact did achieve was the isolation of the Europeans from the Corporation. The Bengal Governor, John Herbert, in his letter to Lord Linlithgow, the Viceroy, resented the fact that the failure to achieve an agreement with the Muslim League not only removed the Europeans from the power nucleus of the Calcutta civic administration but also ensured the right of Subhas 'to keep fingers on some of the resources of the Corporation'.[48]

The pact raised controversy and criticism. Congress High Command deplored the pact because by this act Subhas became 'a cheap purchasable commodity . . . and sold himself for aldermanship in the Calcutta Corporation'.[49] The Hindu Mahasabha opined that 'the Bose group has sold the interests of the Hindus for a mess of pottage'.[50] *Forward*, the organ of the official Congress, condemned Bose for not fulfilling his promise of an orgnized campaign against the iniquitous Calcutta Municipal Amendment Act (1939).[51] By this opportunistic device, *Forward* suggested, Bose had severely damaged the anti-imperialist platform only to serve his 'narrow careerism'.[52] *Advance*, a daily run by the Sengupta followers, expressed utter surprise at the pact and sarcastically commented that 'Subhas has bartered away the larger interests of the nationalist Bengal for the dubious honour of being elected alderman in the Corporation.' Bose had become 'a pliant tool in the hands of the Muslim League and thus helped consolidate the League in Bengal'.[53] The *Modern Review*, a monthly journal of Hindu nationalist tone, criticized Bose bitterly because, instead of waging a relentless war against the discriminatory Calcutta Municipal (Amendment) Act, he himself 'has walked into the parlour of the Muslim League which has humiliated the Congress and the Hindus'.[54] Clearly Bose wounded the Hindu nationalist feelings and diminished his credibility as a leader among the Calcutta bhadralok.

Another view is that the drive to sign an agreement with the Muslim elite over the question of sharing spoils of institutional power followed C. R. Das's ideological tradition. Like his guru, Bose also held the view that Hindus and Muslims were two distinct socio-political entities and the pact-type concessional arrangement, recognizing that distinctiveness, would bring them together. Although he believed in agreement at the elite level to amicably settle Hindu–Muslim differences, he never pursued it until 1940.

The pact is suggestive of another trend in Bengal politics. The 1923 Bengal Pact was concluded at a time when Das's leadership was accepted unanimously by both communities, and the concessions provided to the Muslims were those granted them by the Hindus; but in 1940, because of their hold over the legislative machine, the Muslims were better off politically and hence they were able to bargain with the Congress. The appointment of Abdur Rahaman Siddiqui as mayor illustrates that.

Bose, according to the Bengal Governor, conceded the pact because he thought that this would ensure his political freedom.[55] In fact, the Governor was not sure whether this deal would stand in the way of arresting Bose. He was convinced neither by the strategic considerations of the Muslim League, nor by the assurances of Suhrawardy (the League leader, who took a prominent part in the negotiations). His view was that 'this would make no difference in Ministers' political attitude towards him and despite any pact of this sort relating to the Corporation, the Government would arrest him tomorrow if they so chose.'[56] In fact, there was a disagreement among the ministers over the question of Bose's detention on the Holwell Monument agitation issue. The reason why the Ministry was reluctant to arrest Bose was explained by the Home Minister, Nazimuddin, who argued that Bose's freedom and his anti-High Command activity meant disintegration within the Bengal Congress and was thus a great help to the Muslim League.[57] The vacillation may well have been ascribed to the apprehension of agitation by the Muslim students who actively participated in the removal of the Monument under Bose's leadership. This was again evident in December 1940, when there was a sincere attempt on the part of the Muslim League to release him in order to revive the Bose–League pact. This move was, as the Intelligence Report suggests, 'deliberately taken by the Government to avert a settlement of the Bengal Congress dispute, as Congress consolidation meant trouble for the Cabinet'.[58]

The pact, nonetheless, raised hopes among the bhadralok Hindus that it might be a stepping-stone towards communal amity. A former Hindu Mahasabha member and an alderman in the newly constituted Corporation, B. C. Chatterjee requested the

Government of India to release Bose so that he could be given 'a chance of consecrating the coming years of life to the achievement of Hindu–Muslim understanding on which the future destiny of India depends'.[59]

To the Bengal administration, the pact was 'a remarkable piece of opportunism true to Bose's past history'.[60] The interpretation may appear to be valid in view of his negotiation with different types of political forces (Hindu Mahasabha/Muslim League) irrespective of ideological considerations. It can be attributed to his desire to be within the power-caucus of the civic body. His pact with the Muslim League after an abortive attempt to come to an agreement with the Hindu Mahasabha confirms this. It could now be argued that the nationalist Subhas did not believe in 'the differences based on religion'[61] as soon as the situation demanded. This is rather one-sided because, to a Machiavellian like Bose, what was important was to keep power in Indian hands rather than risk having power pass into British hands due to the failure of Indians to co-operate with each other. The Bengal Governor, John Herbert, was himself unsure of the impact of the League–Bose pact and apprehended that 'the pact might be extended to the question of the formation of the ministry of Bengal.'[62] This is rather doubtful given the fact that the Muslim League leadership (especially Jinnah) was hoping 'to use Bose as a means of weakening the Congress'.[63]

It is more probable that the pact was indicative of a change in Bose's mind. He had never recognized the Muslim League as 'the authoritative representative organization of the Mussalmans of India',[64] but once he was out of the Congress hierarchy, he was keen to open a dialogue with the Muslim League in order to bring about communal unity and felt (in contrast to his earlier stand), that, 'without the League, no one could do it'.[65] The pact, therefore, seems to be a stepping-stone towards that at the all-India level. That was a remote possibility since Bose's attempt to negotiate with Jinnah at the national level, in October 1939, was abortive because the latter refused on the ground that 'there could be no question of negotiating with S. C. Bose as a rebel but only as a possible representative of the Congress.'[66] Having failed here, Bose met Jamiat-Ul-Ulema leaders and wanted an assurance from them that they would 'support Forward Bloc' and its effort to fight relentlessly against the British 'irrespective of what the Congress may decide hereafter'.[67] He thought that through his commitment to fight the British he could gain the Jamiat-Ul-Ulema's support.[68] Emphasizing the need for unity among all the political organizations aiming to achieve national freedom, the Jamiat leaders declined to co-operate with Bose.[69]

The pact certainly paid political dividends to the Muslim League leadership in Bengal because (a) politically it was a recognition by a powerful section of the Bengali Congress leadership even when it was quite clear (especially after the Lahore Resolution, 1940), that 'the Muslim League wants partition of India';[70] and (b) the fissure among the Bengal congressmen appeared unbridgeable after Bose was suspended formally from the Congress, which was interpreted by the Muslim League as a gain because now 'Subhas can be left without friends if and when the League chooses to desert him.'[71]

Holwell Monument agitation, 1940

Along with his attempt to have friendly arrangements with the Muslim League leadership, Subhas Bose endeavoured to consolidate Muslim support in his favour in Calcutta. His efforts in this direction began with the agitation to remove the Holwell Monument which was erected by G. Holwell 'at his cost during the short tenure of his Calcutta Governorship in 1760 . . . to commemorate those deceased in the Black Hole'.[72] To Subhas, the monument was a symbol representing the alleged savagery of the last Nawab of Bengal, Sirajuddowla, and the bravery of the British soldiers who sacrificed their lives. Thus, he argued, 'the monument must go because it is not merely an unwarranted stain on the memory of the Nawab, but has stood in the heart of Calcutta for the last 150 years or more as the symbol of our slavery and humiliation.'[73]

The selection of Holwell Monument as the main issue for the agitation reflected Bose's strategic sense. By itself anything that related to the past glory of the Muslims was likely to draw the attention of the Calcutta Muslims. The Muslim ministry was in a dilemma. In principle, they suported the movement. Fazlul Haq and his Home Minister in particular, sought an agreement with the Bose brothers on this particular issue because 'there should be no opportunity on Subhas' part to start any form of direct action in which he could claim and obtain Muslim sympathy.'[74] Hindu opinion was also in favour of the removal of the monument. Both

the *Hindustan Standard* and *Amrita Bazar Patrika* not only approved
the movement but urged everybody irrespective of religion to
support it in order to strengthen the joint Hindu–Muslim effort.[75]

At a meeting at the town hall on 3 July 1940, resolutions pay-
ing homage to Sirajuddowla, condemning the falsity of foreign
historians and urging deletion from school textbooks of matter
derogatory to Sirajuddowla were adopted. It was agreed as well
that if there was no ministerial decision on the Holwell Monument
by 15 July, satyagraha by the council of action would start on 16
July.[76] Subhas could not attend the meeting because he, along with
other Forward Bloc activists, Hemanta Bose, Pannalal Mitra and
Krishna Chatterjee, was arrested the same morning.[77] The meeting
was definitely illustrative of a unity in the sense that not only was it
attended by the Hindus and anti-government Muslims, but the
Muslim League Student Organization was also there. Nazimuddin,
the Home Minister, in particular, was disturbed by the participation
of the students and he pressed for a quick cabinet decision on the
Monument question and the release of Subhas Bose.[78] This put
the ministry in an awkward situation. Both Haq and Nazimuddin
agreed to set Bose – imprisoned as a result of the Holwell Monument agitation – free as early as possible. When D. A. Brayden,
Central Intelligence Officer, emphasized that 'as S. Bose was an
all India figure . . . the Government of India would be interested
in his fate', Nazimuddin in his reply argued that the government of India would take no action against Bose 'as they had
already allowed J. Nehru to make speeches as objectionable as
S. Bose's'.[79]

As regards the removal of the Monument, neither the ministry
nor anybody from the *de facto* ruling authority objected. On the
question of Bose's release, however, both the Bengal Governor and
the Intelligence Branch refused to concede. Herbert, the Governor,
for instance, attributed Bose's rise and the alliance between him
and the powerful Calcutta Muslims like Isphani, Siddiqui and
Nooruddin

> to the obduracy and shortsightedness of the comparatively petty
> Europeans in the Calcutta Corporation which created the
> occasion for the pact between the League and S. Bose . . . a pact
> which both enhanced the power of the Calcutta trio [Isphani,
> Siddiqui and Nooruddin] and tied the hands of Nazimuddin to
> curb S. Bose's openly defiant and anti-war attitude.[80]

The Bose-led anti-Holwell Monument agitation and the consistent opposition of 'the Calcutta trio' to European business reveal that 'there is no greater common factor in their efforts than common antagonism to European vested interests.'[81] He thus suggested to Linlithgow that the agitation 'has to be stopped . . . which would remove the last of the immediate causes of conflict in which revolutionary Hindus and Muslims can be banded together against the Ministry and Europeans'.[82] The Central Intelligence Officer of the Government of Bengal, D. A. Brayden, was also reluctant to accept either of the ministry's suggestions: he felt that the removal of the Monument and the release of Bose 'will greatly enhance S. Bose's popularity and prestige and he will then be enabled to launch his campaign for the release of political prisoners with the assistance of the students whose enthusiasm [has already been] aroused'. Having shown the necessity of putting Bose behind bars, he requested W. N. P. Jenkins, Deputy Director of the Intelligence Bureau (Home Department, Government of India), to issue orders, if necessary, 'to detain Bose under section 26 (i)'.[83]

The Holwell Monument was finally removed, but Bose remained in prison until December 1940. So, in terms of achievement, the movement was successful not only because its goal was realized but also because it created a unity, however fragile and short-lived, between the Hindus and Muslims in the 'organized world of politics'.

Concluding comments

Analysis of the theme of the Bengal Congress and the Hindu–Muslim question reveals interesting dimensions relating to the social composition of the Congress. Neither in the case of 'job reservation' nor in that of the 'Money Lenders' Bill', was Sarat Bose as the Assembly leader of the Bengal Congress able to support these acts as firmly as was expected because of the pulls and pushes from within the organization.

What is evident is the heterogeneity of its composition. The Muslim leadership, especially the KPP, by its direct link with the 'unorganized world' gained remarkably out of the Congress opposition to the 1928 Bengal Tenancy (Amendment) Act, indifference to another amendment to it in 1938 and vacillation on the Money Lenders Bill (1939). By its almost exclusive confinement to Calcutta, the Bengal Congress practically failed to mitigate the

KPP–Muslim League efforts which sealed its prospects in the 'unorganized world'. It should however be noted that none of the Bengal Congress leaders by themselves created this situation. They inherited it and could not or were unable to force a decision that could have changed it. The Congress in Bengal had for a long time been dominated by urban middle-class Hindus, many of whom had interests in land rents. For many reasons, long before Subhas came into politics, the *raiyats* (cultivators) – Hindu or Muslim – had little or no role in or influence upon the nationalist leadership. Bose did not change this political fact and the Congress continued to be dominated by middle-class people with rentier ties, mostly urban Hindus.

Bose, like most other Congress leaders – including those who saw clearly what the aims of the Government of India were – was incapable of devising a strategy that would undermine or counter the 'divide and rule' policy of the government. In part, at least, this was true because, as has been noted, the Bengal Congress had for long been dominated by Hindus of rentier mentality. When these nationalists were forced to choose between their opposition to foreign rule and the loss of their long-standing social and economic class interests, most of them opted for 'protection' of those class interests. Presumably, this would have held true even had the tenants and raiyats been fellow Hindus. The fact that most of them were Muslim merely made it *easier* for government to use its 'divide and rule' strategy. As a leader, Subhas failed to rise above the limitations of the dominant groups within the Congress.

3 Ambivalence to the Working-Class Struggle

When Bose came out of Mandalaya gaol in 1928 the succession struggle in the wake of C. R. Das's death was in full swing.[1] Late on the scene,[2] Bose had considerable ground to make up if he was to inherit Das's mantle as provincial Congress chief. After a period of initial frustration, using skilful political manoeuvres Bose forged an alliance with the Calcutta-based urban clique known as the Big Five[3] and succeeded in capturing control of the Bengal Provincial Congress (BPC). However, if he was to consolidate this dominance, it was imperative that he build a solid grass-roots base.

In effect there were two alternative possibilities: the peasantry or the working class. A bid for the backing of the cultivators was hardly realistic in the light of his stand on the 1928 Bengal Tenancy (Amendment) Act[4] and his dependence on the Big Five which included notable zamindars.[5] What was thus left was the working class which was equally in ferment, due first to the adverse impact of the trade depression, and secondly to their belief that the selfish desire of the owners to maintain profit was responsible for their distress. Bose, like other Congress leaders, endeavoured to mobilize the working class as a constituent of nationalist struggle. He supported the labour cause in his public speeches, but his active participation in the actual struggle was partly the result of the High Command's instruction and partly in order to develop and consolidate the Congress support base among the workers. While reviewing his role, an attempt will be made to show how far he succeeded in organizing the working class on the basis of a national democratic ideology for the freedom struggle.

We have already seen that Bose's role as a Bengal leader[6] was confined to Calcutta. Unlike B. N. Sasmol, a potential contender for the provincial leadership, who led an agitation against the imposition of the Union Board Tax in Midnapore,[7] Bose had not directly participated in mass mobilization despite his eloquence in favour of popular causes. Instead of being one of the participants from the outset and thereby helping the movement to grow organically, Bose preferred to take on the responsibility of leadership once the movement achieved some prominence.[8] He was in gaol for more than six years and abroad for three years in a political career of nineteen years. Even when he was very much on the provincial scene, he did not take part in any of the strikes from the beginning.

Historically the period between 1928 and 1931 was very sensitive and provided Bose with ample opportunity to try mobilization 'from above'. Economically, Bengal was undergoing a critical phase of unprecedented hardship. Both the peasantry and factory workers especially in the jute industry were hard hit. We will leave out the peasantry from our discussion as we have already seen that at that time Bose was not in favour of upholding the rights of the peasantry against landlords and intermediaries.[9] So in the following paragraphs attention will be drawn to his career as a labour leader. First we will take up his role in the context of the 1929 strike in the jute mills.

Jute in Bengal

Jute had a special importance for Bengal, both as an agricultural commodity and as an industry. By 1928–9, a paid-up capital of Rs16.15 millions (£1.2 million)[10] was invested in 89 jute mills,[11] the majority of which were sited in the towns along both banks of the Hooghly in 24 Parganas, Howrah and Hooghly districts.[12] Of the 62,404 looms in India 97.6 per cent were in Bengal[13] and the Europeans controlled 81.2 per cent.[14] In terms of the work force, the jute industry was peculiar. Out of a total of 279,854 workers in 1921, '32.25% came from Bihar, 23.23% from the United Provinces',[15] while the share of the workers born in Bengal was only 23.38 per cent;[16] though the number of the Bengali workers was remarkably low, they constituted 31.3 per cent of the skilled workers,[17] while the share of the Bihari workers was 38.76 per cent of the total.[18] The jute provide employment to 64.60 per cent of the total industrial work force.[19]

Profits in the jute industry were normally high. The 1939 *Fawcus Committee Report* shows that, though the profit during the depression period was not as high as before, the industry never ran

Table 3.1 Percentage of profits in the Bengal jute mills, 1929–31

Year	No. of companies	Paid-up capital (Rs millions)	Net profits (Rs millions)	Net profits (as % of paid-up capital)
1927–28	46	16.21	6.61	40.8
1928–29	47	16.15	6.86	42.5
1929–30	47	16.15	4.50	27.4
1930–31	47	16.40	1.21	7.4

Source: Fawcus Committee Report, 1939, vol. I, p. 80

at a loss (see table 3.1). The sudden decrease of profit adversely affected the harvest price of jute. Between 1927 and 1931, the harvest price of jute per ton fell by 56 per cent.[20] It is evident from table 3.2 that all the items except cotton experienced a set-back and the decrease of jute price was most dramatic.

The harvest price of jute was low in part because of the unsecured economic position of the growers. In the face of pressure from the credit agents (landlord, *mahajan* (money-lender), credit bankers and local authorities), 'the grower brings all the jute he has for cash money . . . and all at once.'[21] The onslaught of the depression reduced the market of commercial crops in general as well as the harvest price of jute.

Table 3.2 Value of marketable crops obtained by cultivators according to harvest price (Rs millions)

Crop	Average for 10 years, 1920–1 to 1929–30	1930–1	1931–2	1932–3
Food grain	20.83	21.22	17.07	13.64
Tobacco	4.57	3.30	2.44	2.13
Cotton	0.37	0.21	0.21	0.20
Jute	37.72	17.60	10.29	8.62

Source: Finlow Committee Report, vol. I, Minority Report, p. 69

Jute and the depression of the late 1920s

In order to maintain the profit rate, the industrialists adopted a policy of 'restricted and limited production', which meant reduction of the working hands. In fact by 1931 25 per cent of jute workers had lost their jobs,[22] and the averge wages of jute workers had fallen. In 1925, a jute worker earned Rs19.2 per month, while the corresponding figure in 1930 was just Rs14.3.[23] A double-shift system was replaced by a single-shift system and the workers were required to work sixty hours a week without a proportionate increase in their wages. In 1928 the mills secured large profits because of the limitation of production. Here the lack of an organized trade union among the Bengal jute workers explains the failure of the workers to protest to the extent they might have done had there been a strong platform. The only registered union of the jute mill workers at the time of the inquiry by the Royal Commission of Labour (1931) was Kankinarah Labour Union, founded in 1920 by the Khilafatists.[24] Its registered membership in 1930 was 1000,[25] although it claimed to represent 50,000 mill hands in the jute mills in the Bhatpara municipality.[26] The major jute mill strike of 1929 was led by the Bengal Jute Workers Union, which claimed to represent all the jute mill workers, but given that 'not more than 4 per cent of workers in jute mills were organized in any trade union',[27] it is difficult to accept the claim. On the other side, because of the location of all the jute mills in a small area arond Calcutta and concentration of ownership in European hands, organization among the employers was easier than in other industries. The Indian Jute Mills Association (IJMA) thus arose earlier and had a determining role in the jute industry from the very outset.

We have seen in chapter 2 that in the 1920s a new politically active group irrespective of its ideological commitment showed concern for the 'subaltern groups'. By the mid-1920s this group had, as the recent work of A. J. Mackenzie illustrates, 'achieved a point of influence in the labour movement'.[28] In the case of Bengal in particular, Edward Benthall of the Bird company reported, by 1921–2, 'the Swarajist politicians have discovered that labour is another whip with which to beat the government.'[29] The Bengal Congress officially adopted resolutions supporting the cause of the jute workers. At a meeting on 10 August 1929, J. M. Sengupta characterized the 1929 strike as nothing but 'a fight between labour and capitalistic government' and urged the congressmen to help the labourers 'when the government and police went to the help of the capitalist'.[30] By the end of August 1929, the government was certain that the Congress was going to support 'the General Strike in order to harass the government'.[31]

The 1929 strike of the jute workers

The trouble first started in the Jagatdal group of mills when they reverted to a sixty-hour week schedule on 1 July 1929. With the introduction of the new system, the mill owners withdrew *khoraki* (a maintenance allowance to the labourers when they did not work) on the ground that since they were working extra hours, they were getting more. They also refused to grant a bonus proportionate to the extra six hours work.[32] Begun as a result of refusal to work extra hours, the strike soon spread to other mills and by the second week of August, B. C. Roy reported to the Council, 'more than 30,000 looms were idle'.[33] Even so the IJMA chairman, R. B. Laird, was reluctant to call it 'a trade dispute' and justified his explanation by referring to the fact that, since 'the jute worker was a contented person . . . and was likely to remain so, if not interfered with . . . the strike situation was', he believed, 'engineered by outside interference'.[34] One of the active participants in the 1929 strike of the jute workers, P. Saha, has confirmed that the communists and other leftists played a role; and the workers' 'refusal to return to work unless on the *hookum* (order) of their union'[35] similarly indicates the presence of 'outsiders'. However, this characterization of the strike situation as engineered by 'outsiders' is misleading. Given the economic stress the workers faced, it is hard to imagine how a strike of this type could result from 'outside interference' alone. Moreover, the fact that it started in some mills and within a short period affected other mills suggests, as B. C. Roy explained, 'the strike is not a preconceived action of mischief-mongers or communists but is the result of the appreciation by the labourers of the helpless conditions they are in.'[36] Jogesh Chandra Gupta, an MLC, thoroughly analysed the adverse impact of the system on the workers:

> In the single shift, a labourer works for 11 hours a day from 5.30 a.m. to 10.30 a.m., i.e. 5 hours, and again from 2 p.m. to 7 p.m., another 5 hours. The labourers in a single shift mill

worked before 1st of July for 11 hours for 4 days and 10 hours for another day in the week, i.e., 54 hours during one week. According to the double shift system, which varies in different mills, the mill runs for 13 hours, the full time allowed under the Factory Rules. In these mills, the labourers work for 9 hours a day for four days in one week and five days in another week, alternatively. Under the single shift system, 6 men are employed per loom on an average, while under the double shift system 9 men are employed per loom on an average. So, the average number of workers employed under the single shift system per thousand looms works up to 6000 and under the double shift system to 9000. Therefore, sir, when there is a conversion of a mill from a double shift system to a single shift system *one-third of the workers are sacked.*[37] [Emphasis added]

The immediate upshot of the reversion from the double shift to the single was, as the above account reveals, a sense of insecurity among the workers. In fact in 1929 130,000 jute workers lost their jobs.[38] Those still employed had lost one of their rest days because under the new arrangement they had to work for 11 hours per day during the first four days of the week and 10 hours on Friday,[39] and with its introduction disappeared the khoraki. By depriving the jute workers of khoraki and by discarding the appointment of daily labourers (who during the recess hours of the regular workers were employed to keep the machine running), the owners, *Ganavani* calculated, saved Rs4000 per week.[40] The mill owners, IJMA in particular, never considered the consequences from the workers' point of view and defended the introduction of the sixty hours schedule as one 'forced upon the mills in order to retain for India trade which would otherwise pass to Dundee and the [European] continent, to India's loss'.[41]

When the new system was introduced on 1 July 1929 in the jute industry, 'by far the most important and the largest employer in Bengal',[42] large numbers of jute workers responded to the strike call as the only way to recover or protect their jobs. What is interesting is that the strike spread so quickly from the Jagatdal group of mills and soon involved all Bengal and that the demands the strikers put forward included, not merely wage increases in a particular group of mills, but 'a general reconstitution of wages'. This was evident because, even after demands were granted at the Jagatdal group of mills,[43] they did not resume work. The strike was thus characterized by H. S. Suhawardy as 'not simply a small trade dispute which could be adjusted by negotiations between the employers and the employees, but a cataclysm of *an unprecedented nature*' (emphasis added).[44] From the debate in the Council it appears that both the government and the Congress politicians were keen to arrive at a solution. The IJMA, however, wanted the strike to continue. Edward Benthall welcomed the strike because 'without these strikes the funny market would have gone to pieces and the mills would have incurred heavy losses. So it is an ill-wind which blows us good.'[45] The IJMA chairman, R. B. Laird, was reported to have agreed with Benthall's idea.[46]

Although trade unionism in Bengal was weak compared to Bombay, the 1929 strike situation revealed that, even in the absence of an organized trade union, wage-cuts accompanied by contraction in employment could be a factor in working-class mobilization. As table 3.3 shows, the 1929 strike of the jute workers of Bengal was characteristically different from earlier ones. Strikes were widespread. In terms of the number of strikes, the 1926 situation was worse but the year 1929 was most alarming because it affected 92.2 per cent of the total jute workers and resulted in a loss of nearly three million working days, greater than the aggregate for the preceding three years. The strike was not peculiar to Bengal. The Bombay cotton mills, for instance, experienced the highest intensity of strikes, particularly in the period 1928–9, which resulted in a loss of 24 million working days and involved 326,196 workers.[47]

Table 3.3 Jute strikes in Bengal, 1926–9

Year	Number of strikes	Number of men involved	Total jute workers	Number of working days lost
1926	29	38,042	327,547*	794,384
1927	9	34,900	325,865*	218,000
1928	18	56,524	331,899*	1,508,708
1929	11	313,069	329,665*	3,345,067

Sources: for 1926 and 1927 see *Royal Commission on Labour in India*, evidence, vol. V, Part I (London, 1931), p. 126; for 1928 and 1929 see *The Census of India* (1931), vol. V, Part I, Appendix II, p. 311; asterisked information from A. Z. M Iftikhar-ul-Awwal, *The Industrial Development of Bengal, 1900–39* (unpublished PhD thesis, University of London, 1978), p. 348

The massive involvement of the jute workers in the 1929 strike revealed, according to the official report, a radical transformation of 'a docile work force into a self-conscious whole'.[48] Such a change did not occur spontaneously. The Committee on Industrial Unrest (1921), in its report, had classified labour leadership giving three categories:

1 The non-co-operators (those nationalists who accepted the Congress non-co-operation programme) who were active in the strikes of jute mills, printing presses, gas works, trams, engineering, taxi drivers, railways and inland steamers.
2 The liberals who were generally in favour of the status quo and active in the strikes of the printers, tram workers, taxi drivers and railway workers.
3 The nationalists who neither accepted the non-co-operation programme nor supported the liberals and were active in the jute mills and railways.[49]

While this classification may be useful in understanding the strike situation of the non-co-operation days of 1920–2, it was less relevant by 1928–9, by which time there had been a radical change. The communists who started working in the labour front had, for instance, established a well-knit organization by 1929. Moreover, the fact that a majority of the liberals actively involved with the Calcutta tram workers joined the communists in strengthening the 1929 strike, consolidated their organization further. Although the communists still had no separate organizational platform but were affiliated to the heterogeneous body known as the All-India Trade Union Congress (AITUC), regionally, however, they had a separate organizational existence. In the 1929 strike of the Bengal jute workers, the communist-run Bengal Jute Workers Association, for instance, not only maintained its separate identity but also played a decisive role in the strike.[50] The nationalists, Subhas Bose and Jawaharlal Nehru, had undergone a change too in the sense that they sought to enlist the working-class movement as a mass base for the nationalist ideology and programmes.

Bose's attitude to the jute workers' strike

As noted, the Bengal Congress decided to fight the cause of the jute workers, although until January 1929 its involvement with the strike was rather 'intermittent' and 'marginal' and a request for funds for the Bauria jute strikers had to be relayed to Subhas Bose via Jawaharlal Nehru.[51] The top leadership performed their duties in the Council by making long speeches favouring the demands of the strikers.

Like others, Subhas Bose in his legislative council speech on 9 August 1929 expressed his sympathy with the cause of the strike. He refuted the contention that the strike was the outcome of outside interference and attributed the 'cataclysm' to the introduction of the single-shift system. He was aware that the jute workers had to survive in tremendous hardship and thus he requested the employer to consider their modest demands for a subsistence wage, 'a modest demand in view of the fact that these mills for years and years have made huge profits'. Still a congressman of the C. R. Das type, Bose urged the government 'to intervene as soon as possible to bring about a satisfactory and honourable settlement of the dispute'. It is a speech which hints at a 'bhadralok' bias in Bose: he viewed labour militancy with trepidation. If this demand was not conceded, he warned, 'these workers will no longer be content with this modest demand but will put forward bigger claims for the ultimate ownership of capital'.[52] The moderate tone of the speech may appear to be inconsistent with the militant image Bose projected after the formation of the India Independence League at the Calcutta Congress of 1928, which, having rejected the 'Nehru Report', adopted resolutions supporting attainment of independence by any means. The speech is not a sufficient proof of 'Bose being scared of labour ascendancy' either, but as we proceed the theme hinted in the above extract will recur, and what appears to be a tactical move here will be shown to be an integral part of his political ideology.

The railway strike of 1928–9

Railway workers were also in ferment in this period. A secret official report states that between 1920–1 and 1930–1 there were forty-six strikes among the railwaymen.[53] Of these, the Bengal–Nagpur Railway strike (1928) and the East Indian Railway strike (1928) deserve mention. While the former was by far the largest involving 1000 labourers,[54] the latter, called to redress pay grievances, was unique in rousing the sympathy of other railway workers; and strikes occurred simultaneously at Howrah, Ondal and Asansol.[55] Moreover it attracted the attention of the Bengal Congress then under the control of Bose and the Big Five. It was this strike which provided Bose with an opportunity to open up a new dimension in his political career. It is true that Bose participated in some way or other in all the labour troubles of the period but, with the exceptions of Jamshedpur Iron and Steel, Tinplate and the Burma Oil company strikes,[56] he was not directly involved and confined his role to making public speeches espousing the cause of labour. He claimed that it was necessary for non-workers to take the leadership as he believed that the workers 'are incapable of assuming that responsibility'.[57] He therefore participated in the majority of the strikes not as a 'primary organizer' but as a 'leader' whose primary duty was to bring about a settlement by negotiation with the employers.

Bose's first involvement with the railway strike took place during the course of the East India Railway strike which lasted for about four months, from 7 March to 10 July 1928. The official report suggests that it was 'caused by the outsider agitators'.[58] The workers demanded a 25 per cent increase in wages, improved leave wages and free houses or housing allowances. Railway workers in Howrah, Ondal and Asansol struck in sympathy. The strike was resolved partly in favour of the workers and, as a result, wages increased and in some cases the employer agreed to consider the question of housing.

Bose arrived on the scene after the strike was called off,[59] although he tried to rouse sympathy for the cause of Liluah workers by making public speeches here and there.[60] His address to the 14,000 workers on 16 August is revealing. He said,

> the labour movement is very closely connected with the struggle for freedom movement and what is urgently needed is a co-ordination between the two; the swaraj movement loses much of its strength until and unless the gulf between the bourgeoisie and the proletariat is bridged over.

He was certain that 'once swaraj is won, all the grievances of labour will disappear.'[61]

This extract reveals quite a number of important dimensions of his political ideology: first, swaraj, political emancipation, is the most pressing objective. Though using Marxist terms, he did not conceive it as a stepping-stone in the achievement of 'human emancipation'. One can deduce from this reasons why he assigned a subordinate role to the working-class movement. His emphatic faith in the working-class struggle as an appendage of the freedom movement was indicated at the 1931 session of the All-India Trade Union Congress (AITUC), when the communists broke away and formed the 'Red Trade Union Congress' in order to assert that the working-class movement had an independent character.

The trouble started in the 1931 Calcutta session of the AITUC. The immediate cause was the decision of the Credentials Committee to disaffiliate S. V. Deshpande's group of the Girni Kamgar Union (GKU) of Bombay and affiliate instead G. L. Kandelkar's group.[62] Formed in 1927 by the communists, the GKU was a success not only in terms of enlisting a huge membership (54,000 by 1928, according to the Royal Commission on Labour),[63] but also in terms of replacing the jobbers – whom the earlier trade union leaders used as intermediaries with the elected mills committees.[64] The Meerut conspiracy case of 1929 caused serious damage by putting the top leadership of the GKU behind bars. It was evident, as the study of Richard Newman shows, that during the strike of 1928–9 in Bombay, the second rank leaders, B. T. Ranadive, S. V. Deshpande and G. L. Kandelkar, lacking in experience and status, not only failed completely but also 'destroyed the foundations of the GKU . . . by their involvement [in] fratricidal squabbling'.[65]

The personal difference between Deshpande and Kandelkar appeared unbridgeable at the Calcutta Congress. Neither of them was ready to accept the other as an ally. The first manifestation was over the question of who would represent the GKU on the Executive Council. Having been unable to decide, Subhas Bose, the President of the Congress, placed it before the Credentials Committee which allowed Kandelkar's group to represent the GKU on the Executive Council.[66] The matter was then put before the Executive Council on 5 July 1931. Before the discussion started, B. T. Ranadive of the Deshpande group moved a vote of censure on the chair. Subhas allowed discussion on that. What made the situation worse was Bose's decision to let Kandelkar (one of the Vice-Presidents of the AITUC) chair the meeting in his absence. Deshpande was reported to have challenged the appointment on the technical ground that the President had not formally proposed his name.[67] Both the groups endeavoured hard to prove their respective points. With the arrival of the outsiders who were reported to have been brought by the Deshpande group,[68] it was difficult for either Bose or Kandelkar to carry the meeting at all and it was adjourned. When the meeting restarted at 3 p.m. on the same day, the censure motion was put to the vote and the Deshpande group lost by two votes, 24 to 26.[69] In retaliation, the vanquished group broke away from the AITUC and formed the Red Trade Union Congress.[70] At a meeting of 6 July 1931 the followers of this new organization condemned the AITUC for its attempt to 'keep out the militant and class-conscious trade unionists from the Trade Union Congress'.[71]

What was the underlying reason? According to Bose's press statement,

> in the eyes of Mr Deshpande, the fault of our group is that we are opposed to the dictation of Moscow and many of us are members of the Indian National Congress and followers of the Mahatma Gandhi. We are not prepared to shout 'Down with the National Congress', 'Down with Gandhi'. We have no desire to sail under a false colour or to act on false preferences.[72]

Just after the breach, Bose made an abortive attempt to repair the damage by his appeal for the formation of a 'Federation of Jute Workers' Union in Bengal' under the BPC.[73] It was evident that Bose wished to see the AITUC subordinate to the Congress, a belief which also pervades his 1938 address as the Congress President.[74] Any attempt to challenge this position had at all costs to be defeated. The censure motion moved by the anti-M. N. Roy faction of the GKU was defeated,[75] and the two votes that decided the case were cast by Bose, first as an ordinary member and then as the President.[76] Though Bose saved his face by casting his vote twice in an unprecedented way, the split (resulting in the formation of the third group of trade unionists) weakened the trade union movement considerably because, as Nehru saw it, 'their mutual quarrels disgusted the rank-and-file workers'.[77]

The contacts that Bose had had with the communists since the 1929 Nagpur session of the AITUC[78] when, as a result of the first split, the Trade Union Federation emerged, and his support of the numerically strong pro-M. N. Roy–Kandelkar group in the 1931 split, illustrate his explicit desire to: (1) capture the labour movement for the Congress, so strengthening his claim to the national leadership; and (2) at the same time successfully project his image as a leftist leader. It has been claimed that 'the fund started for the defence of the accused in the Meerut Conspiracy Case by Bose was actuated by the hope of capturing the labour movement rather than by real sympathy for the arrested communists.'[79]

Bose's decision to cast his vote twice was determined not by his ideological affinity with the Kandelkar group but because the group decided to operate under the tutelage of the Congress. Bose would champion the cause of labour only if it sacrificed its independent existence, a theme which was evident during the Calcutta Congress of 1928 when Bose as the General Officer Commanding (GOC) ordered his Bengal Volunteers to resist the labour demonstration,[80] led by prominent communists including Bankim Mukherjee, Muzaffar Ahmad, Radharaman Mitra, Dharani Goswami, Sibnath Banerjee and Gopendra Chakrabarti,[81] which 'invaded the Congress pandal in spite of the opposition of the Congress Volunteers and of the refusal of the Congress authorities to allow the pandal to be used for a labour demonstration'.[82] This suggests that Bose, like any other national democrat fighting for political freedom, would never allow other forces to assert themselves at the cost of the Congress-led united platform.

The second important aspect of the Liluah speech is Bose's attitude towards the employers of labour. Though he believed that the strength of the swaraj movement depended on reducing the gulf between the bourgeoisie and proletariat, he was keen to protect the employers too. He thus urged the labourers not to insist on demands which would, in view of the depression, impair the interests of the employers.[83] Ideologically, Bose's position was similar to that of Gandhi, who was an advocate of 'humanitarian trade unionism', a preference derived from his concept of 'trusteeship' over wealth and property by the capitalist class whereby they would exercise a paternal care over labour. Thus it is not surprising that he requested the Jamshedpur steel workers in 1927 to co-operate with 'Mr Tata who', to him, 'appeared to be quite considerate and humane' and he believed that 'he would win his support by non-violence'.[84] By 1928–9, the native industrialists, Purushattamdas Thakurdas and G. D. Birla, had also felt the urgent need of maintaining an amicable relationship with the Congress[85] so as to contain the influence of communism in the industries. Birla, in a letter to Thakurdas, insisted on co-operating with 'those who through constitutional means want a change in the government for a national one'.[86] Though Subhas revolted against Gandhi by participating actively in the formation of the Independence League in the 1928 Calcutta Congress, he too conformed to Gandhian 'humanitarian trade unionism': when the Jamshedpur steel workers struck against the Tata's policy of repression, retrenchment and wage-cuts,[87] not only did he insist on non-violence as the only method but also, like Gandhi, he expressed his faith in 'the almighty God who', he believed, would 'render the good to the workers'.[88] It is thus evident that his militancy evaporated in this case. An explanation can be found in his concern for Indian-owned industries. One reason why he was willing to negotiate with the Tata management for a settlement of the 1929 TISCO strike was his belief that the earlier the decision, the better the future of the Indian industries. 'If as a result of a strike', Bose argued, 'the industry is forced into other than Indian hands, it would be highly detrimental to national progress.'[89]

On a superficial reading, Bose's concern for Indian industrialists may seem to have been derived from a Gandhian notion of 'trusteeship' designed to enable the owning class to undertake ameliorative measures for the workers. But once he argued against the strikes as ruinous for the future of Indian industries, Bose took a different ideological stance. His insistence on an early settlement of labour disputes, even at the cost of strikers in order to save Indian industries, indicates how committed he was to the national democratic logic of protecting the indigenous capitalists who were not only helping the nationalists financially but also posing a threat to foreign business. To Bose, the nascent Indian bourgeoisie was thus playing its historical role and it was the duty of the nationalist movement to strengthen them by curtailing the workers' demands or even controlling their movement if necessary.

The third important aspect in the Liluah speech was his attitude to the 1931 Royal Commission on Labour, or the Whitley Commission, which was appointed to inquire into labour conditions in India, a reflection of the government's anxiety about labour turmoil throughout the country. On the trade union front, the Commission caused a furore. The AITUC at its Nagpur session of 1929 adopted an Executive Council resolution advocating a complete boycott of the Commission by 53 to 41 votes.[90] This particular resolution contributed positively to the first split.[91] Nehru who presided over the 1929 session also castigated the 'right-wing leaders' for their reluctance to boycott the Whitley

Commission. He was in favour of complete rejection of the Commission because he felt that it was 'absurd to co-operate with the official commission when we are carrying on, or going to carry on, a direct action struggle'.[92] In his press statement on 20 September 1929, Nehru expanded the arguments for the boycott. According to him, in view of the recent legislative measures

> penalizing labour, like the Trade Dispute Act and the Public Safety Ordinance, the Meerut trial . . . use of police and military to break strikes and occasional firing on the strikers and peaceful workers, the Congress cannot consent to a commission . . . appointed to divert attention and to induce the workers to give up their militant attitude in the hope of getting some relief from the commission.[93]

Moreover, when Bhupendra Nath Datta, Vice-President of the AITUC, and Muzaffar Ahmad, a communist member of the Executive Council of the AITUC, issued a Manifesto urging all unions to boycott the Commission,[94] Nehru agreed to associate with it.[95]

Bose, too, expressed 'no confidence in the Whitley Commission' and characterized it 'as a ghastly mockery, a clumsy device to wean the labourers from the politically minded intelligentsia'.[96] He charged the right wingers in the AITUC, who seceded at the 1929 Nagpur session to form the All-India Trade Union Federation, with associating with the Commission. Cynically he explained their co-operation as natural because 'the boycott . . . would have entailed the resignation of [N. M.] Joshi and [Dewan] Chamanlal from that body.'[97]

Up to this point Bose's arguments are ideologically consistent; but his 1931 presidential address to the AITUC introduced a new element and the consistency in his argument vanished. The militant Bose who rejected the Royal Commission altogether now changed his stand:

> At the Nagpur session of the Congress, the boycott of the Whitley Commission had been decided upon. That Commission has just issued their report. If I were to act like a logician, I should ignore the report altogether but I shall not do that . . .
> The present report has laid considerable emphasis on the problem of welfare for labour, and though I voted for the boycott

of the Whitley Commission I have no hesitation in saying that, if the recommendations on this point are given effect to, there will be an improvement in the present position . . .

The industry of the country is today faced with a crisis owing to the application of the axe. I am not unmindful of the difficulties of the employers. It is something impossible for them to maintain their old staff and they are forced to resort to retrenchment.[98]

His arguments for accepting the Whitley Commission's recommendations indicate that he had a flexible view of political reality. He might be criticized for contradicting his earlier stand but it would be unfair to him if we did not evaluate his policy in the broader context. In a situation where the workers' sufferings were at their peak, any improvement should be welcome. Since the recommendations of the Royal Commission would marginally benefit the working class, Bose, concerned with the general amelioration of the working class, approved the suggested steps.

The Jamshedpur strike, 1928–9 (TISCO and Tinplate)

Unlike the jute and railway workers' strikes, where Bose's involvement was more or less indirect, the Jamshedpur situation provided him with an opportunity to participate actively in the struggle between labour and capital. His role deserves to be examined objectively in order to show how he failed to build a real organizational base in a situation favourable to him. An analysis of his way of handling labour grievances reveals to what extent the Congress policy of placating the indigenous industries was counterproductive in the 1928–9 Jamshedpur strikes. It exposed how fragile his position was, given the lack of a real organizational base on the Jamshedpur labour front. Clarification of these themes requires a contextual analysis and it is therefore useful to narrate the events that led to Bose's involvement.

The 1928 strike in the Jamshedpur Iron and Steel Company (TISCO) was preceded by two major strikes in 1920 and 1922. Both these earlier strikes were, an official report claims, 'due to causes other than labour dispute'.[99] It is difficult to agree since both the strikes were organized on the basis of certain specific economic demands which showed more than anything else the extent of TISCO workers' assertiveness.

The first significant strike of 1920 was called only after the management declined to concede the workers' demands which included a 50 per cent increase, improvement of the grain stores and a guarantee against abuse of Indian labour by European personnel.[100] The strike, lasting less than a month, from 24 February to 18 March,[101] was not resolved until after five Sikh workers had been killed in a police firing and thirty-nine wounded at a militant demonstration to prevent the strike breakers from entering the plant.[102] The Tata management did not accept the general demands but conceded a 25 per cent wage increase to those earning less than Rs50 per month and a 20 per cent increase to those earning more.[103] Though dissatisfied with the way the strike ended, the workers lost their morale as a result of police actions and the failure of their organization, the Labour Association (not recognized by the company), to put their demands as forcefully as they expected; and thus the Association had no role in the settlement.

The roots of the problem thus remained unresolved. As will be shown, the 1922 strike, of thirty-three days duration, had consolidated the workers on their economic grievances. By mid-1921 the Jamshedpur Labour Association (JLA) founded primarily on the initiative of the Swarajist politicians, Byyomkesh Chakrabarti and S. N. Halder, presented three demands: (1) a month's salary as bonus; (2) a 33 per cent wage increase; and (3) that the minimum wage for the weekly workers should not be less than eight anna per hour.[104] When R. D. Tata was presented with these, he refused on the grounds that the profits were inadequate to redress the strikers' grievances. The JLA itself accepted the explanation as satisfactory,[105] but insisted on the bonus demand as reasonable in view of the company's profit (Rs8.8 million).[106] Once this was refused, the TISCO workers struck on 10 September 1922.

The company threatened to dismiss those workers who refused to join the plant by 25 September.[107] The JLA was keen to resolve the dispute provided the Tata authority agreed to (1) no victimization and (2) recognition of the Association as the mouthpiece of the workers.[108] What is clear from the above demands is that the Association was as much interested in securing its position as a recognized trade union as in fighting the demands of the workers. This probably weakened the determination of the workers and the company's threat was effective because, by 25 September, a large number of clerical staff and workers went back to work. The Association had no role. Dewan Chamanlal, president of the AITUC, acted as a mediator and suggested the formation of a conciliation committee, comprising ten from each of the contending groups, the company and the workers, which would function as an arbiter in the future.[109] Although the TISCO management committed itself to the principle of 'no victimization', G. Sethi, secretary of the unrecognized JLA, was dismissed; but after the intervention of the Conciliation Committee composed of C. R. Das, Dewan Chamanlal, N. M. Joshi and C. F. Andrews,[110] Sethi was reinstated. The question of union recognition was put on one side, the company subsequently refusing it because of the presence of the 'outsiders' in the Conciliation Committee.[111]

Until August 1925, the issue remained unsettled. The JLA, as a formal organization of the TISCO workers, owed its birth to an intervention by Gandhi who, in a meeting with R. D. Tata, resolved this question and agreed to include TISCO officers within the C. F. Andrews-led Labour Association.[112] Though the Association was recognized, Tata himself received a guarantee from Gandhi that 'the concessions made will be appreciated by the employees and thus end all cause of friction between the company and the thousands who work in its employment.'[113] The agreement revealed the extent to which the Congress nationalists were keen to have the Association recognized even when it meant sacrifice, as the above guarantee shows, of the workers' immediate interests perhaps subsequently to fight better for the workers. Thus it is not surprising that the nationalist politicians, C. R. Das and Motilal Nehru, strongly supported Tata's fight for Tata's application for tariff protection in return for TISCO's recognition of the union.[114] Gandhi's conciliatory tone is understandable in view of his faith in the concept of 'trusteeship'. In his Jamshedpur speech he argued that labour and capital were not antagonistic and that capital had a duty of 'not only looking to the material welfare of the labourers, but their moral welfare also . . . capitalists being trustees for the welfare of the labouring classes under them'.[115]

Born out of the 'trusteeship' notion, the JLA's policies and programmes were derived from the Congress's concern for Indian industries. In order to weaken the union leadership, the company offered foreman and supervisory positions to those who led the earlier strikes[116] and in most cases the militant Bengali babus, the principal supporters, as the report of Singbhum Deputy Commissioner shows, acted as representatives of the company rather than championing the workers' cause.[117] The feeling was so widespread that a group developed within the JLA in opposition to the gradualist and passive methods of C. F. Andrews; and one of the workers, Nanigopal Mukherjee, emerged as the leader of that group.[118]

The development of the Jamshedpur strike

Neither of the earlier settlements satisfied the TISCO workers. The company, though accepting the idea of profit sharing with the workers, did not accept the demand of general wage increase. So the root cause remained. To this was added the question of redundancy. Taking advantage of the 1924 Tariff Board's recommendations which included, *inter alia*, the reduction of workers to avoid loss, the company reduced its work force. Though per head production increased remarkably the company had postponed the workers' demand for a wage increase.[119] Along with this general grievance, the TISCO workers were also aggrieved by the company's discrimination against Indian workers. In an anonymous letter to the editor of *Amrita Bazar Patrika*, it was emphasized that the company, in pursuit of the de-Indianization plan, preferred Europeans and Americans for the top positions and that they were treated differently though their 'service conditions' were just like any other covenanted company worker.[120] *Forward* was more categorical in characterizing the strike as nothing but a response to 'the racial bias that vitiates the management through and through'.[121] The Tata authority was also alleged to have maintained an association of the Parsis since 1924, the prime motivation behind which was to create a division among the workers should they try to become united.[122]

The groundwork for the TISCO strike was laid. The first of a series of sporadic strikes between October 1927 and May 1928 was primarily a protest against the abuse of a native worker by an American supervisor on 21 October 1927 in the Duplieix plant. However, under threat of dismissal the strike lasted only for the day.[123] In all the strikes of the period, as shown in the reent study of Vinay Behl, the question of a general wage increase was prominent but the JLA and its moderate leadership never insisted on it because according to them, 'increase of wage without corresponding profit rise was an irrational suggestion'.[124] This stand did not satisfy the radical section of the TISCO workers led by Nanigopal Mukherjee who, having already seceded from the Association, were in search of a new leader.

The schism within the JLA was evident in March when the rail-finishing department, having refused to tone down their demands, insisted on 100 per cent wage increase.[125] In order to put an end to labour militancy, the company discharged a few labour activists.[126] Since the JLA had not been consulted the strikers were refused any help. This was the situation when Manek Homi[127] appeared on the scene. A lawyer by profession, Homi (himself a Parsi), a former employee of TISCO, went to the United States for further training. When he came back, the company refused to offer him a top position, which he thought was unfair in view of his specialized training and he declined the job offered. In his evidence to the 1924 Tariff Board, though accepting the company's policy of reducing working hands to decrease production cost, he was not only critical of Jamshedpur management in general, but also argued against the company's application of 'bounty and protection' in particular.[128] Homi's stand was not liked by the company's senior officers and was perhaps the reason for the discharge of his father from the company's employment in 1924. When approached by Nanigopal Mukherjee and his associates he instantly agreed to assist the workers and expressed himself willing to lead the strike in a formally organized meeting of the dissident workers on 17 March.[129] Unlike the JLA whose association with the Congress explained its ideology, Homi had put forward no specific ideology. His speech of 17 March and demands laid down – an increase in wages, protection of the rights of low-ranking workers against the abuse of the higher ranks; creation of a permanent body to deal with the labour grievances[130] – show that his ideas were basically 'economist'. His personal bitterness towards the company also explained his favourable response to the requests of the TISCO workers because now he had a chance to hit back at the company. Even if personal opportunism brought Homi to the scene, he was nonetheless the only active leader of the strikers until Subhas arrived. The official union, the JLA, was non-existent, although there were abortive attempts at the beginning to challenge Homi: V. V. Giri of the AITUC, for instance, failed to persuade the workers to accept the JLA as their organization. Towards the end of May 1928, N. M. Joshi, president of the AITUC, came to Jamshedpur to settle the dispute between the two groups, but in vain.[131] The strikers declined to co-operate with Joshi because, as the Fortnightly Report explains, of the refusal of the AITUC to back Homi on the ground that it meant repudiation of the AITUC-affiliated JLA.[132]

Manek Homi invited leaders of different political persuasions to defend his cause. The top leaders of the AITUC refused, while the second-rank leaders, Mukundalal Sarkar, Singaravelu Chetty and W. V. R. Naidu, addressed the workers from Homi's platform.[133] By pointing out this, the government of India's report on the strike situation depicted the TISCO strike as one engineered by 'outside communists'.[134] The Deputy Commissioner of Singbhum, J. R. Dain, who was an eyewitness of the entire scene, refused to accept the interpretation because according to him, though they appeared on the scene at the outset, 'the communists exercised very little influence and soon fell into the background.' He argued further that 'until Bose intervened, the strike was in fact free from the influence of outsiders.'[135] Dain's account and the non-co-operation of the JLA suggest that the strike developed more or less spontaneously out of a sense of insecurity arising from the mass reduction of working hands.[136] This was more explicitly stated in the demands put forward to the Tata management which included, among others, the formation of a committee of fifteen workers for consultations before any man was suspended or discharged.[137] Thus even in the absence of an organized trade union, the 1928 TISCO strike involved 18,000 workers,[138] resulted in a loss of 2.5 million man days[139] and lasted over five months.[140]

The long duration was partly due to the fact that the workers had alternative sources of income,[141] and partly due to the company's reluctance to come to an agreement with the unrecognized Homi group. In fact, with the lock-out of TISCO on 1 June 1928,[142] there was pressure from within the Homi group against Homi. Nanigopal Mukherjee, for instance, requested Homi to give up the leadership, because as long as he was there negotiation with the company was impossible.[143] Homi himself realized this when his demand for the reinstatement of the dismissed workers and the payment of lock-out wages for the whole period were rejected outright by the company's directors when he met them in Bombay.[144] The company was adamant too and, in its zeal to destroy labour militancy, on 10 July 1928 it opened an 'Employment Bureau' for those willing to work.[145] Though the skilled workers did not join, a large number of unskilled workers enlisted their names and thus the plate and merchant mills started.[146] The reason why adequate numbers of unskilled workers joined their works may well have been due to their severe economic hardship as a result of the strike's long duration. In such a situation, the JLA's encouragement to resume work certainly helped the workers to break the strike. Disheartened by these new developments indicating lack of solidarity among the workers, Homi was desperate to open a dialogue with the JLA, but his discussion with G. Sethi, JLA's vice-president, was abortive.[147]

Not only was Homi keen to settle the dispute, the strikers, under severe financial strain, also strove to resolve it. Approached by the TISCO workers Bose, who was passing through Jamshedpur, expressed himself willing to assume leadership. Between 9 August when the workers first met him and 17 August when Homi saw him, Bose, still undecided, argued for Motilal Nehru to take the responsibility.[148] Since there was a sizeable Bengali work force in the steel plant, Motilal thought Bose was the right choice.[149] With the High Command's backing, and at Homi's personal request, Bose accepted the charge.

The High Command's decision to depute Bose showed its eagerness to revitalize the moribund JLA. Manek Homi's invitation was determined by three practical considerations:

1   He realized that the Tata management was not going to accept him as the leader of the workers.
2   The refusal of the Bengali supervisory, technical and clerical workers to join the strike weakened solidarity. 'The reason for their keeping aloof was, it seems,' Homi explained, 'not due to their being satisfied with the conditions of work and prospects of service – they had real grievances – but I regret to say, their extreme provincialism needed a Bengali leader whose call alone to duty they could respond.'[150]
3   In addition to the obvious advantage of unity, the JLA was an additional source of funding as it had a balance of Rs10,000. Thus as soon as Bose arrived Homi made an effort to secure the funds of the Association which it had 'perversely and purposely withheld from using in the present struggle'.[151]

To the TISCO management, the selection of Bose was apt. In fact, Lalubhai Samaldas, one of the TISCO directors, had requested Bose personally to intervene.[152] A deputy to Samaldas,

G. L. Mehta, explained the advantage of settling with a nationalist like Bose. In addition to weakening Homi, the agreement with Bose would ensure the future of TISCO as he 'recognizes that Tata Steel is a national industry and realizes that if it suffers heavily, American capital which is very anxious to get control over [steel] will step in'.[153]

Bose arrived in Jamshedpur on 18 August, four months after the commencement of the dispute, thereby conforming to the pattern of his earlier involvements; the only difference was that he was deputed by the Congress High Command and the strikers to act on their behalf and the management welcomed his intervention. Bose's presence enlisted the non-co-operating Bengali workers and vigorous picketing inaugurated by him reduced the men in work to its lowest level.[154] In his address to the TISCO workers, he praised their fighting zeal and expressed his sincere desire to lead the strike to a successful end because he believed that if the strike was defeated, the general trade union movement would be weakened to the detriment of the national movement.[155] On 20 August, Homi not only agreed to merge with the JLA but also accepted the vice-presidency of the Association of which Bose was already the president. The fact that Homi was offered a vice-presidency indicates that he had still some influence among the Jamshedpur workers.

At the beginning of September, Bose started negotiations with the company. Before he met N. B. Saklatvala, chairman of the TISCO board of directors, and Ibrahim Rahimtoola, also a director, he had discussions with Samaldas, another TISCO director. The company representatives did not allow Homi to participate in the negotiations. Since Homi was desperate to arrive at a solution, he reluctantly agreed.[156] After two days' discussion, Bose and the company directors arrived at a settlement which was published on 12 September. The terms of settlement[157] were as follows:

1   There will be no victimization.
2   All men of Boiler and Sheet Mill Department will be taken back and the strike period will be considered as continuity of service.
3   All men who have been reduced from 13 April 1928 onwards including any employee of the Traffic Department who may

have been reduced before the date will be taken back in the employment of the company and restored to continuity of service.

4   The cases of those who have been discharged for insubordination or neglect of duty etc. will be reviewed by the General Manager.

5   The company will take all men back with the exceptions of:
(a) those who have taken settlement;
(b) those who have gone away from Jamshedpur and will not return to work within three weeks from the date of resumption;
(c) Those who will leave voluntarily within three weeks by taking advantage of the following offer of the company: they will be given the amount of the Railway fares to their homes and also the full amount of their Provident Fund, including the whole of company's contribution. In addition they will get one month's pay for each completed year of service.

6   Reduction by not filling up the vacancies in the normal course of events will continue for twelve months from the date of resumption. If at the end of this period the necessary reduction is not effected, the company will be free to resort to immediate retrenchment.

7   All surplus men will be kept in a spare gang separate from the regular required staff and will be given the same or a higher rate of pay in their own or other departments, and an opportunity to fill vacancies where the work is such that they are qualified for it.

Three weeks will be given to the men who have gone home to enable them to return to work. All men who do not join within a period of three weeks from the date of resumption will have no lien on their jobs.

8   (a) The company will, in order to relieve the hardships of men, pay a loan of one month's wage to each man after he returns to work. After the end of the first month a further half month's wage will be given as loan to those who need it and apply for it. No repayment will be collected until January onwards; repayment will be collected in twenty instalments, of 5 per cent of the amount of loan.
(b) The company also agrees to allow the men to pay up their arrears in house rent in equal monthly instalments during the months of October, November and December 1928.

(c) *Strike pay according to the company*. The men agree to waive the lock-out wages according to the men as the company agrees to grant the above concession instead and to sanction a further sum of two lakhs of rupees for increment to the staff, making the total amount available for immediate increment seven lakhs instead of five as previously announced.

9   Alteration in the work Service Rules will not be put in force.

10   In the equitable distribution of bonus ten lakhs of rupees per annum, the Manager will give consideration to any representations that may be made by the Labour Association.

11   In the distribution of the increment sanctioned, the Management will give consideration to any representation that may be made by the Labour Association.

12   Those whom the company can do without and who intend to resign voluntarily within three weeks from the date of resumption will be offered the terms given in 5 (a), (b) and (c).

13   In the case of vacancies which cannot remain unfilled, preference will be given to the men of the Agricultural Implements Department in filling up those vacancies before any outsiders are taken in.

According to Bose, 'the agreement was extremely favourable to the workers.'[158] Contrary to what he thought, the settlement compromised on a substantial workers' issue: the reduction policy was to continue in the form in which it had begun before the strike, but immediate reduction was stopped; lock-out wages were refused but in their place recoverable loans were assured. From the workers' position, the most deplorable condition was the creation of a 'surplus labour force' (see above) which was kept as 'spare gangs'. This meant that the workers identified as 'surplus' were likely to face retrenchment if voluntary and regular retirement did not achieve the company target of 20 per cent reduction within twelve months.

Homi was critical of the settlement on two grounds: 'The first objection related to the workers giving up their claim to lock-out wages', and, he felt, 'two lakhs of additional increase was no compensation for twenty-two lakhs lost by labour during the course of the struggle'; secondly, 'a deliberate omission about the recognition of our association or of getting any undertaking in writing from the management that they would recognize the accredited representatives of the workers no matter who they are'.[159]

The JLA, however, defended the settlement as 'the maximum that could be got out of the company'. If the negotiations were broken off, the secretary of the JLA reported, 'there was a genuine apprehension in labour circles that men would begin going back to work.'[160] Homi's opposition to the policy of retrenchment was inconsistent because he himself, as his discussion with N. B. Saklatvala on 10 August 1928 shows, 'agreed to 18 per cent retrenchment'.[161] Subhas, while explaining the agreement, argued that the settlement as arrived at finally was the last possible resort. If the strike continued 'for a long period after 12 September, the strikers could have achieved what they wanted', but given the financial stress the workers were undergoing, without a settlement 'the strike would have ended ignominiously for labour'.[162] Moreover, as the future of India's steel industry lay with TISCO, Bose argued, it was his 'moral duty to save the company from bankruptcy . . . [which] the company was likely to face if the strike had continued'.[163]

Neither Bose's nor the JLA's justification pleased the TISCO strikers. After the terms of settlement were announced, the dissident group organized a meeting in which Bose was castigated. In order to counter his opposition, Bose and his associates decided to address the gathering. Though heckled and abused initially, Bose succeeded in his effort, though under the 'protection of a unit of Gurkha police', and managed to reduce tension[164] temporarily. This instance reveals that though the struggle with the company was over, the settlement provoked bitterness among the workers. The undercurrent of discontent was manifest on the day the plant restarted, when the Crane workers decided not to work because they were classed as 'spare labourers'.[165] Homi felt encouraged and saw a future for the Labour Federation which he founded on 11 September to include all Jamshedpur labourers.[166] By November 1928 the new Federation was reported to have 1400 members.[167] Encouraged by this, in order to test his strength, Homi threatened to call another strike if the earlier demands were not fulfilled. There were partial strikes in some departments in December.[168] But there was no attempt either by Homi or his federation to link them and organize comprehensive action in Bengal. This may have been because Homi's influence was declining and this was partly evident when the company filed a suit against him for compensation; he escaped to Patna and the strikes fell through.[169]

The agreement formula which brought the 1928 strike to an end was, like the earlier attempts, a compromise on the principal issues. By accepting the conditions of the agreement *in toto*, the workers exposed how weak they were in relation to the owner. Given the lack of necessary infrastructural backing from the AITUC, the TISCO workers had to depend on their own resources. Not only were the workers handicapped as regards funds, they were also organizationally weak because of their division. Subhas had initially succeeded in bridging the rift and thus with his arrival the non-co-operating Bengali section (a majority of whom were skilled workers) joined. In terms of attempting an organizational soliarity, this effort was remarkable, but within a short period Bose's sympathy for the young capitalist Tata and concern for indigenous industries frustrated the militant non-Bengali workers (skilled and unskilled alike). This lay – as P. K. Peterson, one of the Tata directors, explained – at the root of the schism which had manifestations in the formation of the Labour Federation.[170] Though the division had an ideological basis, Homi had neither adequate resources nor sufficient ideological clarity to lead the workers' struggle to a successful completion. The split labour camp provided the company with an opportunity to play the game according to their rules. In order to consolidate the division, the Labour Federation was recognized on 13 March 1929.[171] The consequence was the weakening of the trade union struggle itself because, after the formal recognition, the rival organizations, much to the satisfaction of the company, fought to prove their claim to be the genuine representatives of the workers. Neither Bose nor Homi realized that their rivalry for control of labour organization undermined the working solidarity in Jamshedpur and strengthened the company's hand. The divided working class and strong company appear to have enabled national democrat Bose to arrive at a settlement designed to protect the indigenous capitalist.

The Tinplate strike, 1929

The TISCO strike had a cumulative effect on the Tinplate company in the sense that since, as a result of the strike, the supply of tin-bar necessary for keeping the company running from TISCO was inadequate, the output of tin-bar had been reduced considerably and consumers had taken large stocks from other sources. This led to a fall in demand for Tinplate product and the company, in order not to incur loss, restricted the working days, which meant loss of wages to the workers.[172] What made the situation worse was the company's decision not to reduce the wage of the Europeans constituting a tiny minority of the workers even under restricted hours.[173] The union, recognized by the company on 28 October 1928,[174] began agitation against discrimination and demanded wage increases. An agreement was arrived at on 31 January 1929; the company instead of attending to the issue of discrimination conceded a general wage increase of Rs2. But the company was initially reluctant to comply with the agreement on the grounds of financial stringency. Later, however, a small section of the Hot Mill workers received an increment because, according to the company, they were underpaid compared to other workers.[175] In protest at this discrimination, two strikes of short duration were organized.[176] The demands presented to the company: (1) general increase of 25 per cent on the existing wages; (2) provision for sufficient number of quarters with moderate rents; (3) provision for service rules for security of service; (4) a provident fund; (5) a bonus; (6) maternity benefit; (7) leave rules; (8) provision for protecting equipment in required departments.[177]

However well-articulated the demands were, the union lacked sufficient organizational strength. Like TISCO, the union was split between the Labour Association and Labour Federation. At the outset, a compromise was arrived at and Md Daud, an alderman of the Calcutta Corporation, president of the Seaman's Union and vice-president of the AITUC, was accepted as the president of the Union by both the organizations. Daud's failure to reinstate six active union members disappointed the workers who urged Homi to take the leadership. What differentiated the Tinplate situation from that of TISCO was Homi's effort not only to establish a unity between the two organizations but also to ensure, as Nehru himself noted, 'co-operation between the different religious groups amongst the workers as well as between the low-paid and the better-paid staff'.[178] Though backed by a strong union which had 2700 members out of 3000 workers,[179] the 'militant' Homi preferred negotiation to strike action. Even after his interview with the Tinplate general manager failed to secure the jobs of six dismissed active union workers, he insisted on reconciliation through discussion. The workers resented this and he was thrown away (sic) on 8 April. The strike was declared on the same day under the presidency of J. N. Mitra, a nationalist with close ties with the left section of the AITUC.[180] According to an eyewitness account, the strike did not attract a majority of the workers at the outset, but within four months 83 per cent of the workers had joined.[181] This suggests the validity of Homi's caution. The demands of the workers were moderate too: (1) no further victimization; (2) appointment of an impartial committee consisting of representatives of workers and management to look into the grievances; and (3) withdrawal of cases pending in the courts against strikers for picketing.[182]

Against the consolidation of the workers, the management was equally strong. Unlike TISCO, the Tinplate was jointly owned by TISCO with a one-third and Burma Oil Company (BOC) with a two-third share.[183] The stubbornness of the management was evident from the beginning. This may well be due to the general weakness of the working class owing to their poverty. The management well knew that 'by remaining stiff and by starving the workers and making them helpless by prolonging the strike . . . [they] would break the solidarity of the workers soon.'[184] Moreover, as employers of labour, they had an advantage given the large pool of surplus labour which was especially marked after the jute and TISCO strikes.[185] The Tinplate company had no difficulty in obtaining 1500 workers from those thrown out of work within a month of the strike being declared.[186] And once it was apparent that resumption of work by old hands was unlikely, the company decided, as Dain's account confirms, to replace old hands by new as soon as possible.[187] By August 1929 the number of new recruits was more than twice the number previously working.[188]

The government helped the employer as it had done in other trade disputes. By declaring the gathering of more than five men within one hundred yards of the company illegal, the administration effectively checked picketing.[189] That the government was determined not to help the strikers was more explicit in its refusal to appoint 'a conciliation board' for the Golmuri strike on the ground that not only was it 'infractuous', but also under the present circumstances 'a court of inquiry under [the Trade Disputes Act (1929)] would equally serve no purpose'.[190]

While the organization of the management was solid, the rift among the leaders of the strike became clear by July. The replaced Homi caused serious damage to solidarity by his press statement that 'there was no strike in the Tinplate . . . and that it was only a question of unemployment of discharged hands'.[191] In terms of production rate and the men involved in the Tinplate, Homi's assessment was not unfounded. According to J. N. Mitra's figure, by July the company recruited 2000 new hands who, along with 300 old hands, kept the production at 50 per cent constantly; this low rate was, he explained, due to the 'lack of technical expertise of the new recruits'.[192] But unlike the TISCO strike, the AITUC and its president Nehru in particular backed the Tinplate Union as much as they could. Once Daud and Giri who were willing to negotiate with the management were refused an interview, Nehru was convinced of the 'obdurate mentality' of the company 'to starve the workers and break their solidarity' and thus urged the AITUC to take up the case.[193]

In terms of funds, the Tinplate Union was at first secure. At least until the end of May, J. N. Mitra reported, the union had the required funds to give strike pay to the 1500 strikers.[194] But from June onwards, the situation deteriorated. Mitra appealed to Nehru to arrange for funds, or at least a loan from the AITUC.[195] In order to help the Golmuri workers who, according to Nehru, were fighting against the 'sheer pigheadedness and obstinancy of the management', he requested R. R. Bakhale, secretary of the AITUC, to sanction a loan on behalf of the TUC.[196] His request fell through because Mitra reported to Nehru that Bakhale denied the money on the grounds that the AITUC fund 'was very small and was necessary for the purpose of the next session of the TUC'.[197]

Subhas appeared on the scene on 7 July 1929 when, in a closed-door meeting with Mitra, Md Daud and V. V. Giri, he suggested, as Mitra's letter to Nehru confirms, the extension of the strike to other industries, such as TISCO, Budge-budge and other Burma Oil concerns and also to organize an effective all-India boycott of Burma Oil products.[198] Having approved Bose's idea, Nehru also argued for utilizing the legislatures to make a strong case against the 'special tariff protection' the Tinplate was enjoying like other 'essential national industries'.[199] In view of the presence of an adequate number of workers and average production in the Tinplate, the arguments for withdrawal of tariff protection were, as Rajendra Prasad saw it, not as convincing as to draw the government's attention.[200] On the same ground, the decision to boycott Burma Oil products was, according to him, 'impractical'.[201]

In fact, what Prasad apprehended became true as Bose applied the strategy but achieved no success.

Bose attempted to organize sympathetic strikes in all the centres of the BOC, one of the two chief shareholders, to put pressure on the company, but there was no organizational backing. Mere declaration from a leader of stature was not enough. Only the Budge-budge section of BOC struck simultaneously, primarily because there were some genuine grievances; the strikers showed solidarity with the Tinplate in the sense that one of their demands was the resolution of the Tinplate strike.[202]

Bose's call for a sympathetic strike at TISCO also fell flat.[203] Having failed thus, he tried to put pressure on the Tinplate management by approaching its Tata counterpart, another principal shareholder, He argued unsuccessfully for intervention when he met P. K. Peterson, TISCO managing director.[204]

Bose's request to the members of Bengal Legislative Council to argue against the tariff protection the Tinplate enjoyed was unattended.[205] He urged them to fight for revocation of duty protection of any Burmah Oil products because it meant 'indirect taxation of the Indian people for a company which [was] not only foreign but its attitude towards Indian labour [was] inhuman'.[206] The Bengal Legislative Council was so engrossed with the strike of jute workers that Bose's call did not receive attention. His request for support to the provincial government of Bihar and Orissa was also refused. Both the governments declined to apply their discretion to intervene under the provisions of the Trade Dispute Act.[207]

Notwithstanding the efforts of the Congress leadership to help the Tinplate strikers, the strike had collapsed by the second half of November 1929 and production, the Governor of Bihar and Orissa reported to the Viceroy, 'continue[d] above the pre-strike level; the workers [were] no longer convoyed to work and the police from outside [were] returned gradually to their districts'.[208] Manek Homi was imprisoned on the charges of instigating a riot and assault,[209] and there were attempts by the Tinplate Company, as Bose alleged, 'to crush labour once and for all'. In his press statement of 23 September 1931 he defended the allegation by referring to the attack on him by an armed gang when he was addressing a meeting of Jamshedpur workers on 20 September.[210]

The Jamshedpur situation was remarkable for Bose's political career. On the one hand, his involvement with the TISCO and

Tinplate strikes projected his image as a trade union leader. On the other, the way he handled the strikes confirms his faith in the national democratic logic of maintaining an amicable balance between the workers and industrialists in a situation which, according to him, demanded co-operation between the apparently antagonistic classes for the achievement of freedom. One might argue that in so deciding Bose had damaged the burgeoning working-class movement. This is rather an extreme and ahistorical interpretation given the general weaknesses of the TISCO and Tinplate workers. By bringing about a settlement strongly biased in favour of the management, Bose seems to have upheld the historical role of the national bourgeoisie in the struggle against an alien rule.

Concluding comments

By his involvement with the strikes at an advanced stage, Bose projected a specific type of leadership: he was not a primary but a secondary organizer. Since labour was an additional constituency of the nationalist movement Bose, in response partly to the High Command's direction and partly to build a Congress support base among the workers, felt the urgent necessity of linking the working class with the broader nationalist movement. Apart from the above political purpose, Bose's intervention in the strikes enabled the strikers, he believed, to arrive at an amicable settlement.[211] He defended the presence of 'an outside leader' as essential because the 'irrational' and 'illogical workers cannot argue their case as strongly as he could'.[212] This reminds us of the role of a nineteenth-century philanthropist Sasipada Banerjee. In his recent study, Dipesh Chakrabarty has shown how Sasipada's concern for the 'ill-educated jute workers' led him to establish a school to produce 'not only orderly but also noiseless Bengalis . . . for the jute mills'.[213] Out of his concern for the poor workers, Sasipada took special care, as Chakrabarty has illustrated, to inject into them 'bhadralok values of . . . thrift, industry and money-lending' as ways of improving one's social position.[214] Subhas spoke, as his 1928 Legislative Council speech demonstrates,[215] in similar terms but in a different way. He was genuinely moved by the appalling hardship of the jute workers as a result of the strike; but his suggestion for an immediate government intervention to avert escalation of the worker demands to ownership of capital reveals the extent to which his arguments were conditioned by national democratic ideology. Sasipada strove to build 'an ideal working class imbued with bhadralok values'; Bose endeavouring to secure India's economic future did not differ much from Sasipada in his ideas.

Bose was in the same position as other Indian National Congress (INC) leaders *vis-à-vis* organized labour, the role of labour and the goal for which labour should struggle. A fact which Bose could not ignore was that the INC had to rely heavily on support from Indian businesses and capitalists[216] including Tatas and Birlas. The relationship between the Congress and the native capitalists was so remarkably tilted in favour of the latter that the Congress was accused of failing to protect 'the essential economic interests of the country' when the militant Girni Kamgar Union caused severe disruption in the Bombay textile industry.[217] By assuring help to TISCO during the 1928 strike,[218] Bose expressed his sincerity in strengthening the bond. In so doing, his primary concern was not to protect the interests of a group of indigenous capitalists but to ensure India's economic future because he felt that 'strikes in the cotton and steel industries are highly prejudicial to the economic interests of India and indirectly help the foreign manufacturers in enabling them to replace the quantity which India could not manufacture in consequence of such strikes'.[219] The nature of Bose's commitment to protect the native industrialists is indicated in G. D. Birla's letter to Purushottomdas Thakurdas where he says that 'Mr Bose could be relied on to help Tata Iron and Steel Works whenever necessary.'[220]

As regards the national industries, the concerns of the Congress leaders including Bose were substantially different from that of the workers. By according priority to the struggle for swaraj, Bose in his presidential address to the Maharastra Provincial Conference emphasized the co-operation between labour and capital in the Indian-owned industries.[221] The argument logically followed from his declared object to protect the native industries. The workers' experiences, however, demonstrated that national industry operated no differently from non-Indian industry in dealing with workers' demands or in its attitude toward trade unions. Thus the labourers, as *Amrita Bazar Patrika* commented, 'find nothing to discriminate between the Bombay mill owners who are Indians and the proprietors of Ludlow Jute Mill at Changail, for instance, who are foreign'.[222] In his determination to consolidate the alliance between the indigenous capitalists and Congress Bose eroded the possibility of a bond between the workers and the national movement in Bengal.

4 Bengal Provincial Congress: Operational Dilemma and Organizational Constraint

Contrary to the Cambridge historians' understanding of the pre-1947 Indian politics in terms of factional rivalry for spoils of institutional power, this chapter seeks to offer an alternative explanation by emphasizing that factional feuding within the Congress nonetheless corresponded to a not fully articulated ideological schism. By attributing 'political responses' exclusively to the British 'constitutional initiatives',[1] the Cambridge school seems to have ignored entirely the long history of confrontation with the alien state power in various forms at the 'unorganized' level. It is plausible to argue that the constitutional devices, the 1909 Morley–Minto reforms and 1919 Montague–Chelmsford reforms, increased the significance of the localities by linking them to the 'organized' world.

As a result of a more frequent flow of communication between the 'organized' and 'unorganized worlds, the provincial political scene underwent qualitative changes. Not only was there pressure from within the Congress to adopt radical plans and programmes to develop and consolidate its strength among the workers and peasants, but the Muslim political forces, backed by organizational ties with the localities, also posed a serious threat to Congress's continued dominance in provincial politics. There were also anti-Congress business communities which became politically more active in the late 1920s to protect their interests in a competitive situation. Under such complex circumstances, the Bengal Provincial Congress underwent a radical transformation to adapt to a qualitatively different socio-economic and political environment. By concentrating on the Congress organization and its operation, this chapter aims to analyse its 'decline' not merely by emphasizing factional rivalry but also by pulling together the whole range of factors likely to have contributed to the process.

We will focus primarily on the organization of the Bengal Provincial Congress as an institution of nationalist agitation and will try to explain why the institution never became as effective as it might have been in terms of factors ingrained within the organization. It should be kept in mind that our effort is directed exclusively to the understanding of the organization of the BPC in terms of in-built weaknesses and therefore in no way should it be seen as an attempt to understand the 'unorganized world' by the same criteria. Similarly, by the term *faction* is meant the disruptive subgroups within the BPC conforming more or less to patron–client networks. This implies that factionalism as a process refers to a structural arrangement linking the individuals both vertically and horizontally to a centre. The bond between the leader and the follower is mutually beneficial to both. Political actors at different levels joined factions to ensure gain for themselves or the groups to which they belonged. The basis of the patron–client network is mutual benefit. But from the archival sources it is evident that, in most cases, clients or followers supported one of the factions at the provincial level not for petty material gain but in response to the ideology of a particular leader.

The continual support Subhas had, for instance, from the Jugantor terrorist group, both inside and outside the Congress, cannot be explained solely by the fact that since they were employed in the Calcutta Corporation they were under obligation. Instead, in order to seek a plausible explanation, one must also highlight the militarism of Subhas as a determining factor. The official note, 'Terrorism in Bengal', ascribes Subhas's popularity among the terrorists to the fact that 'he is more outspoken than any other Congress leader of Bengal in praise of terrorists and in his demand for complete independence which is the avowed object of the terrorist campaign.'[2] Subhas agreed to absorb them so as to utilize their organization for the faction he was representing. Bose's support for the Jugantor as opposed to the Anushilan was influenced to a large extent by his preference for a pure 'terrorist' tactic. Anushilan had begun to deviate towards 'a mass movement involving the peasants and workers',[3] while Jugantor still clung to the 'terrorist' line. Similarly Bose thought of involving the actors of the 'unorganized world',[4] although he did not put real effort in that direction. In fact the very idea of fighting the war of independence by the INA formed out of the prisoners of war confirms that his strategy was conditioned to a significant extent by the prospect of immediate success.

From this one can deduce that the factional fight between Bose and Sengupta in the 1920s and early 1930s had an ideological content given that Bose was anti-Gandhi and Sengupta pro-Gandhi. The Bengal Gandhians had an advantage over the anti-Gandhians because of the organization they had built over the years in the rural areas. But the death of Sengupta, and the absence of a parallel leadership which could fill the vacuum and compete with the Bose-led anti-Gandhi Congress faction as effectively as Sengupta did, certainly gave Bose a fillip in efforts to become the undisputed leader of the BPC. Once this was assured, one might have expected that the importance of factionalism would have been reduced considerably. Although the factional fight seemed to have lost its significance once the question of provincial leadership was resolved, it continued in the rural areas where Gandhians with their well-organized network challenged the rival faction in its attempt to replace them on the local and district Congress committees. The controversy over leadership of the Bengal Provincial Congress was solved temporarily with the death of Sengupta in 1933 but surfaced again as his political heir consolidated his forces and displayed his strength by challenging Bose. Thus factionalism in some form or other continued until the last days of the Raj.

Why factionalism in Bengal?

A Bose versus Sengupta, 1923–33

Das's decision to take full advantage of council politics changed the nature of Congress as an organization. Now, Congress and the British administration were interlinked on the basis of an understanding mutually beneficial to both parties. As a result, the Congress, no longer purely a platform for agitation, was given the responsibility of local administration. This was the beginning of an era in which the Congress strove to combine the 'politics of establishment' with the 'politics of agitation'. Having dislodged the moderates from the BPCC, Das's main concern was to extend Congress control as much as possible over the institutions of

British administration at the provincial level. Crucial were the Calcutta Corporation and the Legislative Council. It was more or less well-established that the group controlling the BPCC would automatically determine the fate of these institutions. What was therefore vital was the control of the BPCC in order to get the best out of the government patronage.

On this reading factional rivalry could be attributed entirely to desires for personal aggrandizement. But this seems too simple, because, as we have seen earlier, underlying factional rivalry, in Bengal in particular, remained an ideological division. For instance, despite his professed adherence to the Gandhian ideology of non-violence, Subhas amply demonstrated his sympathy with 'terrorist methods too'.[5] It seemed, therefore, unlikely that Gandhians like Sasmol and Sengupta could get on well with Subhas. The division within the provincial leadership was buttressed by the composition of the BPCC. As mentioned earlier, Das was impressed by the organizing ability of the terrorists and hence incorporated them into the BPCC in order to strengthen the organization. In fact, as the official evidence shows, 'in 1924, twenty-eight ex-detenus or political ex-convicts were office bearers of the BPCC and twenty-one revolutionaries or sympathizers were elected to the AICC.'[6] Despite his professed adherence to Gandhism, Sengupta pursued the same policy and the revolutionaries had a majority of twenty-six in the BPCC in 1925. They received a set-back once Sasmol became the leader in 1926. While Sengupta appointed twelve of them to the Executive Committee, Sasmol reduced their number to four.[7] Subhas, with his professed inclination to militarism, responded favourably to the terrorists and brought them back to the Congress Executive Committee. Terrorist dominance continued as long as he was on the scene. Even after a gap of six years (1933–8), when he was away from the regional scene, he was quickly able to unite the terrorists under his leadership in order to reform the BPCC. Out of forty-nine members thirty-seven then were terrorist ex-convicts.[8] Not surprisingly, given the BPCC composition, 'the doctrine of violence as opposed to non-violent or constitutional action [was] daily being more widely advocated.'[9]

Factionalism in Bengal was thus not purely a fight between leaders and groups for petty gains. On the contrary, although the rivalry was factional in terms of modes of operation of the groups involved, it was not divorced from ideology in the sense that the formation of factions certainly followed a roughly defined (Gandhism and anti-Gandhism) ideological cleavage. Therefore the management and manipulation of elections to local, district and provincial Congress Committees seem to have had their roots in the ideological commitment of the groups. In other words, the driving force behind this alleged manipulation was not simply or largely personal equation but perhaps also the desire to prove the practicality of a particular ideology from the point of view of ensuring India's independence. But once electoral victory was achieved, patron–client networks were re-established, especially in the distribution of the spoils of victory.

Factionalism: its manifestation

Bose's incarceration until 1927 and Sasmol's removal in 1926 provided Sengupta with the opportunity to take over the leadership of the BPCC. But the task of retaining control was not as easy as Sengupta had anticipated. Once Bose came out of gaol he found in the Big Five support in his fight against Sengupta. Bose had no difficulty in capturing the top position of the BPCC, 'a position to which the Congress High Command had initially nominated Sengupta'.[10]

The alliance was helpful, but because of his surrender to this group he was also criticized. *Sanibarer Chhiti* (Saturday's letter), a weekly literary journal, commented sarcastically that 'Bose, in his effort to free Congress from the aristocratic influence of Gandhi, relied on peasants like Tulshi Goswami and Kiranchandra, workers like Nalini Ranjan and Nirmal Chandra and students like B. C. Roy and Sarat Bose.'[11] Having been backed by the Calcutta politicians and businessmen, Bose obtained what he had been striving for. This ready-made support undoubtedly eased his task, but underminded the possibility of exploring a support base of his own. As shown in chapter 3, Bose's efforts to organize the labourers in 1928 was constrained by his having been imposed from above. Even in the Jamshedpur labour strike (1928–9), where, as the chief of the PCC, he had an advantage over his counterpart, his endeavours proved futile because of the intrinsic limitations of his own ideology. Having thus failed, he concentrated primarily on the provincial Congress machinery in order to get his supporters elected to the PCC.

Das during his short period of office had established how

politically important the local organizations were for the consolidation of Congress. Calcutta, to him, was merely the headquarters.
Once he departed, the entire scene was reversed. Calcutta and the
PCC acquired so much importance that local organizations were
neglected and received attention only during Congress elections.[12]
Looking at the overwhelming importance of the centre, the political
nucleus of the periphery (local Congress Committees) realized the
importance of an alliance with the Calcutta-based political bosses
and their only function was, as *Amrita Bazar Patrika* commented, 'to
help the supporters and hinder the opposition of their masters in
Calcutta'.[13] The provincial leadership also felt the necessity of
winning as many local Congress Committees as possible in order to
increase the majority in the BPCC. So the relationship between the
local and provincial Congress organizations was transactional and
hence followed factional logic with specific emphasis on a
particular ideology. The numerical strength of the BPCC remained
unchanged until 1934 (see table 4.1). Bose's actions after becoming
President stemmed from his desire to ensure a majority in his
favour in the BPCC. In the following years, his efforts were
directed mainly at replacing pro-Sengupta elements as quickly as
possible. The consequence was disastrous, but Bose, being content
with immediate achievement and unaware of its long-term impact
on the organization, failed to perceive this.

Bose's first attempt in this direction was seen in 1929 when the
Sengupta group complained to the AICC that their supporters
were deliberately being replaced by Bose in order to secure his
position in the BPCC. At the 1929 Annual General Meeting of the

Table 4.1   Composition of the BPCC from 1923

Distribution	no. of seats
Elected by the DCC on proportion of population	268
Co-opted by these elected members, one for each DCC	32
Muslims	14
Women	110
Total	324

Source: J. Gallagher, 'Congress in decline', *Modern Asian Studies* 7.3 (1973), p. 594

BPCC objections were raised against the participation of the members from Chittagong, Sylhet and Darjeeling alleging that their elections were invalid.[14] Initially, Bose as the BPCC chairman refused to listen to the issue, but due to the insistence of the objectors, he agreed to put it to the BPCC session. Out of 250 members, 122 voted against the exclusion of the members and the objection to their participation was thus overruled.[15] Failing to prove their allegation, 118 members who were Gandhians and anti-Bose called for an AICC inquiry into the matter. Having attributed their defeat to the 'fictitious majority of four only', they spelt out their objections to the elections of the members to the BPCC from Sylhet, Chittagong and Darjeeling:

1 There was no election in Sylhet, yet twelve members were declared to have been elected.
2 Though there were no members from Darjeeling (as the Annual Report of the secretary showed), two members purporting to be returned were allowed to vote.
3 In the case of Chittagong, a constitutional question was involved for objections were pending before the AICC against the new Chittagong DCC which had voted to elect Chittagong representatives to the BPCC.[16]

Not everybody felt enthusiastic about the way the DCCs challenged the PCC. Nehru 'attributed this behaviour on the part of the DCC to the lack of discipline within the organization'.[17] In an anonymous letter addressed to the secretary of the BPCC, the very idea of 'wasting time and energy on a petty censure motion and internecine feuds', at a time when the whole energy, time and money available to Congress ought to be utilized for reorganizing the Congress,[18] was criticized strongly. Looking at the complaints sent from the area in question to the AICC directly, it is clear that in the case of Sylhet and Darjeeling procedural faults were emphasized. For instance, one of the major points of objection was the fact that 'no returning officer was appointed by the BPCC to conduct local elections.'[19] Objection was raised on grounds of insufficient time as well. The Sylhet DCC protested strongly that a mere two days' notice was too short to get ready for the election.[20] Requested by Jawaharlal Nehru, B. C. Roy, having inquired into the controversy, concluded that the arguments against the present DCC were too weak to deserve any serious notice. According to

Table 4.2 Chittagong DCC lists, 1929

List A	List B
1 J. M. Sengupta	1 J. M. Sengupta
2 Prasanna Kr. Sen	2 Hari Mohan Nath
3 Barada Prasad Nandi	3 Suryya Kr. Sen
4 Chandra Sekhar Dey	4 Mahim Ch. Dasgupta
5 Dwijendra Mohan Kundu	5 Lok Nath Baul
6 Charu Bikash Dutt	6 Ganesh Ghosh
7 Hakim Rafik Ahmad	7 Nirmal Sen
8 Moulvi Najir Ahmad	8 Ambika Chakrabarty

Source: AICC Papers, NMML, G–120 (1929), complaint from Chittagong to the secretary, Indian National Congress, 4 November 1929

him, the former president of the Sylhet DCC 'dissolved' the Executive Committee, but the Executive Committee 'refused' to accept the dissolution, censured the president and elected a new one. Thereupon certain members who belonged to the old president's party 'resigned'.[21] This lay at the root of two rival Congress organizations in the district. Roy, however, did not find any fault with the newly constituted DCC, as he felt that, according to the Congress constitution, 'the Executive Committee cannot be dissolved by the president and in view of shortness of time [the Lahore Congress was imminent], the Executive Committee by electing new members upheld the spirit of the constitution.'[22]

In their complaints to the AICC, the Chittagong DCC members raised objections on substantive grounds. They alleged that the election held on 21 September 1929 was 'invalid' and 'unconstitutional' because the majority of the members including the president and the vice-president left after the meeting was officially dissolved as it became rowdy and 'uncontrollable'.[23] On the same day, in the absence of the president and the vice-president, an election took place and a new DCC was formed. As the Lahore Congress was ensuing the new DCC was authorized by the BPCC 'under rule 17 of the Congress constitution, to elect representatives to the BPCC, and accordingly an election was held on 20 October 1929'.[24] It was in fact not so unusual to find two different lists from the same DCC, given the ideological cleavage among the congressmen in the district (see table 4.2).[25]

AICC decision

The complaints from the DCC were upheld by the AICC and accordingly President Motilal Nehru, who was authorized to deal with the matter by the Working Committee (WC), appointed Pattavi Sitaramiah to arbitrate in the dispute and in the meantime the BPCC was asked to postpone the AICC election pending arbitration.[26] The contending parties seem to have agreed to the idea of appointing 'an outsider'. Nehru, who at the outset did not encourage the idea of AICC intervention because it meant 'an attack on the PCC's autonomy',[27] also approved the idea because he thought that, 'given the present disturbed state of Bengal Congress politics, it may not be possible for the BPCC to give impartial consideration to each complaint'.[28]

There was controversy over the appointment of Pattavi as the arbiter. When Motilal, after having decided to confer the responsibility on Pattavi, wired to Sengupta and Bose, the latter 'expressed surprise at it',[29] though as Motilal mentioned, 'the decision was taken in his presence'.[30] Since the Lahore Congress was imminent, Motilal in his capacity as the president, 'allowed the old BPCC (1928) members to function in the AICC following the precedent of C. P. Marathi'.[31] The Subhas-led BPCC did not pay any heed to his order and elected a new body of Bengal representatives which included representatives from the controversial area too for the Lahore session. This led to an interesting situation. The representatives elected in 1929 had no right to participate in the Lahore Congress because the election took place without constitutional sanction from the Congress High Command. Motilal's acceptance of the 1928 List as genuine[32] raised strong criticisms.

In their letter to the secretary of the AICC, a group of congressmen elected as AICC members in 1929 questioned the decision. According to them,

> their election as members of the AICC cannot be affected by any dispute arising out of election of the members of the BPCC from any branch of Congress Committee. If the election of the members from a particular District Congress Committee is found to be irregular, the worst thing that may happen is that there should be re-election of the members of the same constituency, but that cannot invalidate the proceedings of any higher body,

viz. the PCC which duly exercised its rights and carried its functions under the constitution.[33]

This was not merely an attempt to deprive a group of genuinely elected congressmen of their elementary rights, conferred on them by the electors. Here, they felt, lay the root of authoritarianism, because 'the AICC did not let the BPCC inquire, instead it acted over its head and took the case up directly.' Moreover, 'if these purely local matters are thus interfered with by the WC, all Congress work in any district or branch Congress Committee may at any moment come to a standstill, pending any decision by the WC in any complaint laid before it by a number of persons.'[34] The AICC, however, did not budge an inch and the situation became worse in the Lahore session when 'the members elected from Bengal in defiance of Motilal's directions (six of them were present there) were barred.'[35] Bose walked out and tendered his resignation from the WC, claiming that 'the Working Committee by arriving at this decision has trampled upon the rights of the BPCC' and that 'the decision of the president was directly influenced by Mr Sengupta and his party who have openly opposed the present BPCC.'[36] But later, as a result of B. C. Roy's request, Motilal reversed his stand on the ground that this should not become a precedent.[37]

In the meantime, Pattavi came to Calcutta and the inquiry began on 7 December 1929.[38] The BPCC led by Bose, after having 'condemned the AICC decision to interfere into a matter exclusively within the jurisdiction of the local authority',[39] and identified Pattavi as someone 'absolutely incapable of being a judge owing to his partial prejudiced attitude',[40] withdrew from the inquiry. The other group led by Sengupta welcomed the decision and promised full co-operation with a view to reviving the 'purity' of the BPCC. To them, the attitude of Subhas 'is a reckless attempt to save himself and his group from ugly exposure'.[41] By 12 December the report was submitted to Motilal with whom rested the final decision.

Objections on substantive grounds were raised by the Bengal Gandhians who accused Pattavi of being partial to the Bose group. Pattavi's decision to form an opinion on the basis of evidence made available to him by the BPCC explains this to a large extent. In a letter to the Congress President, Prominent Gandhians like J. C. Gupta and S. K. Mitra expressed dissatisfaction with the way

Pattavi handled the inquiry. To them, the outcome of the inquiry was known long before Motilal arrived at a decision because 'Dr Pattavi did not insist on the BPCC producing all the papers before him regarding the three districts but rested content with the assurance that they would be produced as they proceeded with the BPCC case.'[42] But that was never done and 'when K. S. Roy, the secretary of the BPCC, was found to have been keeping back documents and telegrams which went against the BPCC case, representatives of the anti-Bose camp from Sylhet and Chittagong raised vehement objections and protests.'[43] Before Pattavi took any step to test the allegation the BPCC, without any prior intimation, decided to withdraw from the inquiry. This created a peculiar situation and put both Pattavi and the anti-Bose group in a dilemma. Pattavi wanted to go ahead but the petitioners 'thought it better to put the responsibility either on Motilal or Jawaharlal'[44] on the ground that Pattavi would not have access to evidences held only by the BPCC. Until this was done, they decided not to participate in any Congress activities 'because it would mean recognition of the new alleged BPCC'.[45] On the eve of the civil disobedience campaign of 1930, politicians' concern with an election dispute prepared the background for the deplorable happenings during the civil disobedience. Motilal who forsaw the damage appealed to the 'better senses of Bengal politicians' and requested them 'not to give up a better cause for petty gains'.[46]

With whatever evidence he had at his disposal, Pattavi prepared a report and submitted it to Motilal on 12 December 1929. Since Motilal was busy with the imminent Congress session, the Award was withheld; nonetheless he issued a statement expressing 'his profound annoyance for the bad treatment accorded to Dr Pattavi Sitaramiah'. He ordered the BPCC to offer 'an explanation to the Working Committee for its consideration'.[47] The Working Committee approved Motilal's action, but the person (K. S. Roy, secretary of the BPCC) supposed to offer an explanation on the BPCC's behalf, did not attend the Lahore session.[48]

With the completion of the Lahore Congress session (1929), Motilal came to Calcutta in order to investigate the case himself. Both the groups co-operated. His decision was announced on 22 January. According to his Award, 'there were no constitutional flaws with the elections of both Sylhet and Darjeeling; he found fault only with the Chittagong DCC election.'[49] In declaring particularly the Chittagong DCC elections – where the terrorists, as shown earlier, were dominant – null and void, Motilal seems to have been guided by his profound faith in non-violence. There were flaws as well in the conduct of the other elections. Viewed from the Congress Constitution Sylhet DCC elections had some major flaws but they escaped his notice. The Congress Working Committee, however, accepted Motilal's Award and resolved 'that in view of the circumstances, the Committee is of the opinion that fresh elections for the AICC should be held in Bengal'.[50] The AICC, by acting as a referee, arrived at a decision which did not satisfy either of the contending groups but helped consolidate factionalism by associating the congressmen more integrally with electoral politics.

Factional rivalry and the Calcutta Corporation

What Motilal saw as mild disorder in the Bengal body politic became chronic disease in the following years. To Sengupta, the Award was simply the product of Motilal's partisanship and hence he decided, so the BPCC secretary reported to the Congress President, 'to carry [out] a bitter propaganda campaign both on the platform and in the press through his paper *Advance* against the legally constituted BPCC'.[51] It was 'a sacred task', as his followers characterized it, because his effort was directed to keep the BPCC 'free from the dirty influence of Sj. Subhas Bose and Sj. Kiran Sankar Roy'.[52]

Though the controversy that led to the appointment of an arbiter in 1928–9 was confined to three districts only, it was symptomatic of the nature of the controversy that was to follow owing to the dissatisfaction of the Sengupta-led section of the Congress. The fact that Bose was the supreme commander of the BPCC certainly posed constraints on Sengupta and his group in their efforts to re-establish themselves in the BPCC. On the eve of the civil disobedience campaign of 1930–1, the fight within the BPC, whatever its basis, was undoubtedly an unhealthy sign. During 1930–3, factionalism reached its peak, weakening the BPC to such an extent that the organization of a united BPCC anti-British campaign was highly unlikely.

Rivalry between Sengupta and Bose again surfaced in 1931 over the control of the Calcutta Corporation, 'an urban honeycomb of power and pelf',[53] as Hardayal Nag of Tippera DCC defined it. The definition is an appropriate one because in reality the control of the Corporation meant access to the municipal budget of Rs300,000 per year.[54] While explaining the nature of factionalism in Bengal to Nehru, B. C. Roy, one of the Big Five, attributed 'factional rivalry among the Bengal congressmen to the control of Calcutta Corporation funds'.[55] Therefore, to both the contending parties, the control of city administration was of tremendous importance.

In his craving for 'purity of municipal administration',[56] Sengupta decided to fight the Bose-controlled BPCC in the municipal arena. His first opportunity came in 1930, on the eve of the elections to the Corporation. He challenged BPCC authority over the Corporation and formed a separate organization, known as the City Congress League, to fight the Corporation election.[57] In so doing, Sengupta argued, he was 'fighting the enemies of the country men who understand only Corporation and Councils and would not go beyond that, who don't understand civil disobedience'.[58] The Congress President, Jawaharlal Nehru, characterized Sengupta's action in setting up candidates in opposition to the BPCC nominee as 'utterly wrong'[59] because, according to the Congress constitution, 'DCCs are subordinate to the BPCC and the final authority rests with the BPCC itself.'[60] Even so, Sengupta won over four Calcutta DCCs which refused to co-operate with the BPCC.[61]

However, municipal rivalry, while it had an impact on the rift in the long term, did not immediately weaken Congress prospects. Out of a house of eighty-five councillors, Congress won forty-four seats.[62] Of these forty-four councillors, BPCC had no objection to forty-one members because 'thirty-nine of them were district nominees and the remaining two signed the BPCC election pledge.'[63] Direct conflict between the factions took place in only three constituencies, with the Bose faction winning in two and the Sengupta faction in one.[64] The outcome is understandable in view of the BPCC pledge to 'select as far as possible consistently with the interests of the city and of the Congress those candidates whose names found favour with the [Calcutta] DCCs'.[65] In order to establish that the City Congress League was independent of the BPCC, Sengupta 'refused to sign the BPCC pledge and stood, on behalf of the League, as candidate for aldermanship together with R. C. Deb and B. Kothari'.[66]

Both Deb and Kothari lost but Sengupta, along with four members of the Bose faction (Sarat Bose, B. C. Roy, Bepin

Sengupta, Dr B. C. Ghosh), was elected.[67] Though Sengupta himself had won, Sengupta and his League were defeated. Seeking to recover his position Sengupta decided to contest the BPCC candidate, Gokul Boral, in a Calcutta Municipal by-election in September 1931.[68] In defence of his latest act of rebellion against the BPCC, he said that he felt compelled 'to fight the coterie everywhere in order to ensure "purity" to the Congress organization in Bengal'.[69] Subhas in his telegram to the Congress President, Vallabhbhai Patel, expressed 'shock' at this decision because 'this act of revolt on the part of Sengupta, taking advantage of his position as member of the Working Committee, will certainly create anarchy in Bengal Congress.'[70] Roy, one of the aldermen, characterized 'this deliberate act on the part of a member of the Working Committee as an attempt to embarrass the BPCC and cause a split within the Congress organization'.[71] It would, he said, have been much better if Congress had not fought the Corporation election 'rather than have these pseudo-congressmen in the Corporation'.[72] Ordinary Congress workers were bewildered. According to Nandalal Roy, a Congress worker of Central Calcutta, 'we, the Congress workers, are at loss to understand for whom to vote. To our humble minds, it seems that the BPCC nominee should get preference, but [since] Mr Sengupta is a member of the Working Committee we are afraid to reject his candidature altogether.'[73]

To find a solution, Bose asked 'M. S. Aney, appointed to investigate the election dispute in Bengal',[74] to deal with the case as quickly as possible on the ground that 'delay in coming to a decision on the issue in question will mean the permanent breakup of the Congress Municipal Party and will further damage the cause of the Congress in the province.'[75] Aney however declined to intervene on the grounds that 'the matter was beyond the scope of the inquiry which was entrusted to him by the Working Committee.'[76] The Congress President, Vallabhbhai Patel, who disliked Congress's involvement in the Calcutta Corporation,[77] expressed annoyance and surprise at the behaviour of Sengupta who was himself a member of the Working Committee. In his letter of 11 September 1931 to Sengupta, Patel, who found it hard to reconcile Sengupta's actions with the dignity expected of a member of the Working Committee, held him responsible for putting the Committee in a very awkward situation. In his words, the Working Committee was extremely grieved to find that you suddenly thought fit to enter the Corporation in a manner which will create fresh cause for trouble and disputes at a time when the inquiry regarding the old dispute was pending. The Committee feels very strongly about the offensive language which you have used in your Manifesto and is of the opinion that you have grievously erred in restating a raging propaganda against the BPCC in spite of assurances to the contrary given by you at the time of the appointment of the arbiter.[78]

Strong in his stand, Sengupta did not withdraw, but fortunately for him and for the BPCC, there was no election 'as the nomination paper of the rival candidate was found invalid, and Sengupta returned unopposed'.[79]

In the meantime, by forming a separate party, 'out of the elected Congress councillors who seceded from the Congress Municipal Party',[80] Sengupta challenged the constitutional right of the BPCC to take disciplinary measures against those violating the Congress pledge. Not only did he cause a split within the Congress Municipal Party, he and his party, along with the Europeans, voted, as Subhas alleged, 'against the Congress at all Corporation meetings'.[81] Nonetheless, the BPCC supported his candidature for mayorship as a compromise, 'with a view to present a united front', and he was elected Mayor.[82] This was a calculated move on the part of the Big Five because his election as mayor for the year 1930 received BPCC backing on the condition that 'if on account of being in gaol, Sengupta was unable to fill the chair at the end of three months, B. C. Roy would take his place for the rest of the year',[83] and as Sengupta's prison sentence would exceed the stated three months, the BPCC knew well that B. C. Roy would automatically become mayor. On the expiry of three months, Roy was nominated for the mayoralty, but he withdrew in favour of Subhas. Sengupta decided to contest from prison. And 'The European and Muslim councillors decided to set up their own candidate against Subhas.'[84] Since the possibility of gaining their support was remote, Sengupta withdrew from the contest not in favour of Subhas but in favour of the European non-Congress councillors' nominee Prince Golam Mohammad Shah,[85] who lost to Subhas.

The story of factionalism within the Calcutta Municipal arena reveals how far Bengal Congress politicians were entangled in internecine rivalry at a time when Congress was supposed to be organizing the masses for the civil disobedience campaign. To Nehru, 'it has been an amazing sight: on the one side, the country ringing with preparation for civil disobedience; on the other, congressmen spending their time and energy and money in attacking each other for the purpose of gaining admittance to the Calcutta Corporation.'[86]

The factional rivalry in the municipal arena was a reflection of a deep-rooted organizational schism within the BPC. The 1929 Motilal Award and the way the Bose-led BPCC managed to retain control of the Calcutta Corporation made Sengupta realize the necessity of capturing the BPCC. The Congress High Command's strong dislike of Subhas and his group was a propitious point, but owing to his un-Congress activities in the Corporation, that was not much help to Sengupta. However, his persistently anti-Bose stand paid off later.

By June 1931 Sengupta had been able to persuade twenty-two out of thirty-two DCCs to challenge the BPCC's conduct of the PCC election,[87] and by July twenty-six had joined the anti-Bose faction.[88] The AICC was inundated with complaints and counter-complaints from Bengal. This new development gave the Congress High Command a chance to settle its accounts with the BPCC. Hence the Working Committee appointed Syt. Madhavrao. S. Aney of Berar to inquire rigorously into Bengal affairs.[89] Vallabhbhai Patel, the Congress President, did not like the idea of a referee from outside because 'this would instead of easing aggravate the situation', and he requested the politicians involved, 'to evolve with mutual goodwill a procedure which will satisfy the needs of the situation'.[90] But Nehru argued strongly in favour of the appointment of an outsider. He believed that 'there must be something seriously wrong in Bengal Congress politics to produce such a situation', in which 'the BPCC has alienated so many Congressmen in so many districts'.[91]

Factionalism and the BPCC election

Motilal's arbitration did not satisfy Sengupta who believed that the Award was the rationalization of coterie rule. By 1930 he had realized that, without the BPCC under his control, any talk of removing the coterie would be futile because, according to the

Congress constitution, at the head of each province was the PCC with powers to shape policy and supervise all subordinate activity. Hence whatever the BPCC did had constitutional sanction.

As a member of the All-India Congress Working Committee and an associate of those of the High Command who were opposed to Bose, Sengupta had however an advantage over his rival because he had established an ideological link with local Congress organizations by his efforts to implement the Gandhian constructive programme, whereas Bose was constrained by being confined to the city and mofussil towns. Bose was nevertheless far ahead of his contender because the entire Congress organization was linked by an indirect election (each unit acting as the electoral college for its immediate superior) and therefore his control of the DCCs gave a fair chance of capturing the BPCC. In fact, this electoral network explains to a large extent why Subhas and his group continued in uninterrupted control of the BPCC for three consecutive years.[92] The challenge they faced in 1929 did not affect their position as adversely as the other group had anticipated; therefore tension simmered and boiled over again on the eve of the civil disobedience campaign, when the Congress High Command was trying to 'enrol as large a number of members as possible for the civil disobedience campaign'.[93] It was decided that the Bengal Congress should fill the quota of 110,000 members before 1930.[94] The BPCC, as Subhas reported to Nehru, 'enrolled 95,000 primary members by 1930 and expected to fill the quota by June 1931'.[95]

Sengupta, who launched 'a revolt against fraud, corruption and coterie rule of the BPCC',[96] questioned the way primary members were enrolled. He complained that the BPCC continually pursued a policy of discrimination against Sengupta's followers in the distribution of membership forms. In his letter to Jawaharlal, Sengupta asserted that

> there is a determined attempt on behalf of a group of men with which the executive is in league to exclude people from membership of the Congress in the fear that the group would lose power and would not be able to run the Congress according to their group ideas. This is my deliberate conviction having watched the trend of events in Bengal for the last two years.[97]

In order to counter the allegation Bose told Nehru that 'so far 380,000 forms have been distributed for enrolment'.[98] Such a statement of fact does not of course disprove Sengupta's charges.

From the telegrams received from the DCCs,[99] it is fairly clear that the DCCs representatives had faced difficulties in getting membership forms and sometimes they were denied them. Jawaharlal was annoyed having heard that 'Mr Dhirendra Nath Mukherji of Howrah DCC', who was 'authorised by the Secretary of the DCC' to collect membership receipt on its behalf, was 'denied it without any explanation'.[100]

Further serious objections were raised regarding the appointment of the returning officers to conduct the BPCC election. In the earlier case of 1928–9, objections of this type were filed only against the Chittagong DCC. But this time complaints on the credibility of the returning officers came 'from a number of DCCs'.[101] In most cases, the returning officers were reported to have acted in a partisan way to help the Subhas faction capture the BPCC in 1931. The secretary of Jessore DCC, for instance, in his letter to the general secretary of the AICC, expressed utter disappointment at the way in which nomination papers were scrutinized by the BPCC-appointed returning officer, Mr Amaresh Kanjilal. He alleged that Mr Kanjilal, in his capacity as returning officer, 'illegally corrected' the nomination paper of Chandra Kumar Banerji, then president of the Chittagong DCC.[102]

Objections on similar grounds were raised from Mymensingh, Barisal, Chittagong, Comilla and Faridpur.[103] Kshitish Chandra Dasgupta, a rural Gandhian and a follower of Sengupta, described vividly how the BPCC in its Calcutta office manipulated the scrutiny of the AICC nomination papers from the DCCs. To his utter surprise, he found that envelopes containing ballot papers from the DCCs were not only open but had also lacked postal marks which led him to suspect that 'these covers were handed over to the office directly by the voters or other agents.'[104] While trying to ascertain how many covers without postage stamps there were, 'he was resisted by the returning officer' and, he reported, 'had to withdraw'.[105]

The overt anti-Bose stand of the DCCs strengthened Sengupta to such an extent as to enable him to 'run separate elections through other returning officers and to set up parallel district and provincial Congress Committees'.[106] The AICC did not concede this and Sengupta, disheartened by the AICC decision, decided 'to withdraw from active Congress politics and to resign his membership of the Working Committee'[107] in order to register his protest.

Meanwhile, the Congress Working Committee appointed

M. S. Aney as an arbiter to resolve the BPCC tangle. Unlike Pattavi, who was authorized to collect information for Motilal with whom lay the final authority in so far as 1929 arbitration was concerned, Aney was given 'full authority to supplement and amend the directions of the Working Committee and to decide finally every dispute relating to the elections'.[108] Bose was terribly upset because, according to him, 'the appointment of a supervisor with enormous powers in his hands was nothing short of a direct insult to the Provincial Congress Committee of a major and politically advanced province like Bengal', and such an arrangement was, he felt, 'calculated to encourage rather than prevent dispute'.[109] The Working Committee, though agreed in principle that 'indiscipline and anarchy in Bengal Congress ranks cannot be stopped effectively by outside authority but by a greater sense of responsibility and public spirit of Bengal congressmen',[110] concluded that it was impossible for an insider to deal with each and every complaint as impartially as was desirable.

Aney reached Calcutta on 16 July 1931,[111] but that was too late because factionalism by then had affected major political activities of the Bengal Congress.

Factionalism and civil disobedience, 1930–1

Congress in Bengal on the eve of the civil disobedience movement was highly faction-ridden with Subhas and Sengupta setting up rival organizations to conduct it. The BPCC set up a Civil Disobedience Committee (CDC) in March 1930[112] and Sengupta formed the Bengal Council for Civil Disobedience (BCCD) on the grounds that 'the BPCC did not give any indication that it was organizing the province for the ensuing fight.'[113] There was an attempt by the BPCC 'to arrive at a compromise with a view to take a concerted action in the matter of launching civil disobedience in Bengal',[114] but it yielded no results and hence two rival committees coexisted until the merger of the two groups in December 1930. The government was relieved because 'the Congress cleavage between J. M. Sengupta and S. Bose meant that the course of the civil disobedience movement in Bengal as a whole was not of quite the same intensity as in other provinces.'[115] It acted consciously in perpetuating factional squabbles. In an order issued to the Uttar Pradesh government, the Home Department, Government of India, specifically instructed it not to imprison

Subhas Bose who was coming to UP to address a meeting of the Naujawan Bharat Sabha because 'owing to Subhas' difference with Sengupta, the Bengal government might prefer him to be out of gaol'.[116] Stanley Jackson, governor of Bengal, was confident that the factious nature of Congress politics would certainly serve to weaken the civil disobedience campaign in Bengal and he too recognized the usefulness of Bose as a divisive force. Writing to Irwin on 9 January 1930, Jackson commented that the 'quarrel between Bose and Sengupta shows no sign of abatement. The result of the trial of Subhas Bose under section 124a and 120b will be known in the course of a day or two. I think it would be unfortunate if he is sentenced to imprisonment.'[117]

Within Congress circles in Bengal, the mutual rivalry even during the civil disobedience caused pessimism. For instance Roy, a member of the BPCC, in a letter to Motilal, expressed the view that 'if Subhas had been out of gaol, or if Sengupta had been working in conjunction with the BPCC, I would have been freer.'[118] A strong anti-faction attitude was evinced. In a letter to the *Amrita Bazar Patrika* editor, A. Chakravarty characterized factional fight as 'nothing but ugly dances of the so-called present-day leaders in Bengal'.[119] An appeal was addressed to the contending leaders, Bose and Sengupta, 'to put a stop to these ruinous activities and direct their energy for the good of the country and save Bengal'.[120] But there was no reduction in personal rivalry at the provincial level.

Though Bengal provided the 'largest contingent of 1930–1 arrests [15,000] as well as the highest incidence of violence',[121] the civil disobedience campaign never attained its full potential. In terms of actual performance, the Bengal CCD was more successful than its counterparts because Sengupta, its president, had a long-standing alliance with the rural Gandhians of Bengal, most of whom were the core of the no-changers, who having shunned legislative politics, had engaged in sustained constructive activities through national schools, khadi centres and ashrams in mofussil areas. These areas, Dacca, Khulna, Faridpur, Dinajpur, Sylhet, Comilla and Bankura, became decisive during the civil disobedience campaign.[122] In order to strengthen the bond, Sengupta appointed Prafulla Chandra Ghosh and Kshitish Dasgupta (two prominent Bengal Gandhians) as secretaries of the BCCD and following his arrest in April 1930, Satish Chandra Dasgupta, who resigned from the CDC, was designated to assume Sengupta's role.[123] Participation of the Bengal Gandhians provided the rare link between the Non-Co-operation and the civil disobedience movements.

Bose's Civil Disobedience Committee was predominantly urban 'with salt preparation centres in Ghatal (Midnapore) and Twenty-four Parganas and a few other centres (managed by the local Congress Committees but under the general supervision of the BPCC) in Barisal, Noakhali and Howrah'.[124] Of all the centres, Ghatal was most prominent because Congress activities there caused alarm to the district administration. In his letter to W. S. Hopkyns, Chief Secretary to the government of Bengal, J. Peddie, District Magistrate of Midnapore, corroborated official anxiety by saying that 'I see very little hope of any measure of peace in Ghatal before there are a few more shootings.'[125] The BPCC was extremely successful in mobilizing a large number of urban youths, students and women, but its role in rural Bengal was limited by the fact that the BPCC never realized the importance of espousing the no-tax cause, even when the anti-union board agitation was endemic in rural Bengal. The CCD, on the contrary, adopted the no-tax resolution in May 1930, long before the Congress mandate was obtained,[126] although the no-tax campaign was never pursued by the CCD volunteers as whole-heartedly as was necessary except in Mahisbathan of Twenty-four Parganas.[127]

Had it been widespread, the civil disobedience campaign could have drawn in the Muslim peasantry as well. Against a conscious policy of promoting 'division within the communities by the administration',[128] the involvement of the Muslim peasantry would certainly have contributed to communal harmony. Neither the BPCC nor the Bengal CCD, except for some vague unity calls, took any positive step in this direction. Where there were attempts at the elite level to enlist Muslim support the response was propitious: Moulavi Shamuddin Ahmed and Moulavi Ashrafuddin Ahmed Chowdhury, two MLCs, for instance, resigned from the Legislative Council and joined the civil disobedience.[129] Tanika Sarkar has established that the participation of the educated Muslim middle class in the civil disobedience was 'by no means negligible'.[130] Even so, because of the alienation of the vast majority of Bengal peasantry, the civil disobedience campaign never became as effective as the Non-Co-operation and Khilafat movements had been.

Factionalism and relief operation

Rivalry within the Congress leadership had its manifestation even in philanthropic activities such as flood relief. Here, too, the question as to whether the BPCC could legitimately carry forward the relief operation seemed to trouble the Bengal leadership more than the plight of the flood-stricken people. The High Command's support of the anti-BPCC group clearly indicated the future course of action likely to be pursued in relation to the Bengal.

The BPCC, in order to organize the flood relief operation, formed a Flood and Famine Relief Committee on 4 August; later, on 10 August, at a public meeting, P. C. Roy, the famous chemist, was elected president of the Committee.[131] Sengupta appeared on the scene not as a part of the above Committee but by forming a separate organization, Sankat Tran Samity, with a view to 'serving genuinely the flood-affected people'.[132]

Two committees operated simultaneously and initially there was, on the surface, no tension. Bose's statement in *Amrita Bazar Patrika* on the 1922 Relief Fund was the starting point of the controversy that followed. According to him, 'there was mismanagement of the Relief Fund of 1922 and two out of the three secretaries were in the dark about the way money was spent.'[133] This was a direct accusation of misappropriating funds by P. C. Roy, who along with Satish Chandra Dasgupta, Niren Duta and Dr Indranarayan Sengupta (as secretaries) happened to be managing the controversial fund of 1922. In a long statement in *Amrita Bazar Patrika*, Roy, who did not wish to defend himself against 'Bose's insinuation', expressed his inability to preside over a committee when his reliability was questioned.[134] Later, he joined Sengupta's Samity.

In terms of actual relief operations, this development was certainly damaging; but Subhas and his group showed more concern when Gandhi, before sailing for England to attend the first Round Table Conference, issued a message 'requesting the Bombay public to send money to P. C. Roy Sankat Tran Samity'.[135] This was a set-back to the BPCC because by then it was well established that whatever Gandhi, the supreme authority of the All-India Congress, said would undoubtedly have the backing of the Working Committee. Subhas, anticipating this (as his telegram to Gandhi who was on his way to London, asking for impartial support for both relief funds, shows),[136] wanted to arrive at a compromise with the other group. Sengupta however, declined on the ground that 'Gandhi's explicit support for the Samity' meant recognition of Sengupta and his group 'as real congressmen and therefore no agreement with the coterie whose only avowed object was to strengthen group rule in the name of Congress' was possible.[137] Patel, the Congress President, though approached by Bose 'to issue a statement supporting the BPCC Relief Committee',[138] refused 'to identify himself with either of the groups as the inquiry by the AICC-appointed arbiter was pending'.[139] Nehru too did not want to 'comment on Gandhi's decision'.[140]

Given this utter confusion, the district congress organizations were in a dilemma. Jnanendra Mohan Sarkar, president of the Murshidabad DCC, for instance, wondered 'which one of the Committees received Congress backing'.[141] The British administration, opposed to the militant BPCC from the outset, did not miss this opportunity to back the less dangerous Congress group led by Sengupta. In a public meeting, the District Magistrate of Mymensingh urged the people not to assist the BPCC Relief Committee in raising funds as it belonged to Congress but to send help through the rival Committee.[142] The District Magistrate was also alleged to have 'insulted' the chairman of the Municipality and vice-president of the District Board and other Congress leaders when they went to discuss relief operation in the district.[143]

Aney Award

In order to inquire into the factionalism which permeated political activity in the province, Aney had been appointed as the supreme arbiter by the Congress High Command. The purpose of the appointment was ostensibly to save the Congress organization from internecine feud. In reality, as the inquiry proceeded and the Award showed, it was an attempt by the Congress High Command to remove the militant Congress leadership and to install the Gandhians in its place.

Though Aney was appointed in early June, the actual inquiry did not begin until September 1931. Both groups filed complaints against each other: the BPCC lodged eleven and the rival group as many as forty-two.[144] Once the inquiry started, Subhas Bose tendered his resignation and on 19 September, at an emergency meeting of the BPCC executive, a resolution withdrawing all complaints against Sengupta was adopted.[145] Sengupta responded to this gesture and expressed 'a desire to try for an amicable settlement of the points of dispute between the two parties'.[146] The BPCC decision to withdraw all charges, together with Bose's resignation from the presidency in particular, seems surprising especially in view of Bose's long-sustained effort to defeat Sengupta. On the basis of the AICC's role in relation to the factional fight in Bengal it is possible to hypothesize that Subhas, having anticipated the result of Aney's inquiry, decided to relinquish the BPCC presidency in the hope of convincing the people that he was indifferent to the positions of power, a sentiment that could be used for later election.

As a result of a mutual understanding between the contending groups on the surface, a committee consisting of K. S. Roy and Sarat Chandra Bose as representatives of the BPCC, and Nishit Sen and J. M. Sengupta as representatives of the other group, was formed, with T. C. Goswami, one of the Big Five, as the mediator, in order to resolve the rivalry.[147] The terms and conditions of these deliberations found expression in Aney's Award, which was 'accepted by the Congress Working Committee *in toto*'.[148] The Award dismissed the present BPCC executive on the ground that 'the way it was formed was unconstitutional' and stipulated specifically that

> all presidents of the DCCs, ex-presidents of the Indian National Congress and ex-presidents of the BPCC should be the ex-officio members of the BPCC. And there should be seven Mohamadan and seven women members among those who will be co-opted as members of the BPCC. The total of the ex officio and co-opted members should not exceed fifty-six.[149]

With regard to the returning officers who were charged by Sengupta as pro-Subhas and therefore guilty of manipulating the DCC elections, the Award clearly laid down that 'the president of the DCCs shall be ex-officio returning officer and, in case he is unable to work personally, can delegate his powers to the senior vice-president of the DCC. As regards appointment of the polling officers, the returning officer's decision is final.'[150]

The present BPCC was completely denied any role in the coming election of 1932 and accordingly an Election Board consisting of Santosh Kumar Bose, Sushil Kumar Raichaudhuri, Kiran Sankar Roy (from Bose's group), Nishit Sen, Sures Mazumdar, Jnan Mazumdar (from Sengupta's group), with M. S.

Aney as president, was formed to conduct and directly deal with the matters connected with the election, and to hear and adjudicate disputes and all appeals.[151]

As an immediate replacement to the present executive, Aney formed 'a Joint Committee under the presidency of Nirmal Chandra Chunder with an equal number of representatives from each side to continue till the new BPCC was duly formed'.[152] The Committee included names from the 1930 BPCC executive and, among the rest, some had been in the 1928 executive,[153] but the majority were 'new and Calcutta-based congressmen'.[154] In principle, Aney accepted that the members of the BPCC elected in 1929 would continue as members until the next election. This seems puzzling in view of his firm belief that the 1929 elections were fought by unconstitutional means. However, the Congress High Command was not at all confident but, once Bose surrendered, the task was easy and it acted as firmly as possible to thwart the young militant group led by Bose.

In fact, the Award was an attempt to establish in Bengal those in league with the High Command. Though Aney was congratulated by the Congress President,[155] he pushed the factional struggle to a bitter conclusion. There was enough indication of that in the letters the AICC received once the decision was made public.[156] The major charge was that 'the Award is one-sided in as much as it conceded all demands made by Sj. Sengupta's party, and, by forming the Joint Committee, the AICC has precipitated factional rivalry more than anything else.'[157] So on the surface, though there appeared to be a reunion of Subhas and Sengupta,[158] the Aney Award left sufficient grounds for factionalism to raise its head in the near future.

The restoration of the Sengupta group by the High Command did not last. Once the Round Table Conference failed, the Subhas group, 'bade goodbye to the Gandhi–Irwin Pact and engaged in organizing anti-government agitation in the province'.[159] A concrete step was taken at the Berhampore Political Conference, held in December 1931, by adopting 'a resolution to that effect'.[160] It was a shock to the Joint Committee which did not wish to sanction such an extreme resolution. The adoption of the resolution, in spite of the Joint Committee's disapproval, raised the question of discipline; Nirmal Chandra Chunder felt insulted and resigned.[161] So what emerged as a hopeful prospect for the Sengupta followers as a result of the AICC backing soon evaporated.

B   Bose versus Sengupta's men, 1936–40

The death of J. M. Sengupta in 1933 and the exile of Subhas Bose
(1933–6) deprived Bengal of its able if competitive leadership. Yet,
factionalism continued unabated. After Sengupta's death, J. C.
Gupta assumed the leadership of the Sengupta group and B. C.
Roy led the other group. A brief re-entry into the provincial
Congress was made by B. N. Sasmol through the Municipal
Association in 1933[162] not as a leader but as one of the pro-
Sengupta men.

As seen earlier, Aney, in order to get Gandhians back into the
provincial leadership, established an Election Board; but with the
resignation of Nirmal Chunder, its president, and the official ban
on Congress activity in the wake of the civil disobedience, the
Board was prevented from operating. Once the ban was lifted, the
Election Board was reconstituted with Aney himself as president,
N. C. Sen and Kiran Sankar Roy as joint secretaries and an equal
number of members from each side.

In June 1934, elections to the DCC and BPCC were held. A total
of 316 members were elected with 191 members from the K. S.
Roy–B. C. Roy group (pro-Bose) and 125 from the J. C. Gupta-led
pro-Sengupta group.[163] The majority group, having elected B. C.
Roy as the president, constituted the executive of the BPCC which
was alleged to have been composed of 'Bidhan Babu's men'.[164]
Meanwhile, the Congress constitution was amended at the 1934
Bombay session, and according to the new regulation, the Bengal
Congress, which had been shown to have 49,040 primary members,
was allowed a PCC with 100 members only (500 primary members
= 1 member).

Despite the reduction of members to 100, the proportional
strength of the two groups (60:40) remained the same.[165] Some of
the congressmen felt however that both groups should be equally
represented, otherwise the majority group taking advantage of the
numerical strength could do whatever they decided at the cost of
the minority.[166] The AICC did not consider it feasible; therefore
the earlier arrangement prevailed. In order to approve the change,
a meeting of the BPCC was held in December 1934 when B. C.
Roy's refusal to continue as president led to the unanimous election
of Subhas Bose who was then in exile.[167] True to the spirit of the
Aney Award, Bose, in his letter to the secretary of the BPCC,
'insisted that the Executive Council of the BPCC should be

reconstituted with an equal number of members from each group'.[168] He justified his suggestion as the only way of ensuring a balance between the contending groups.[169] In so directing, Bose – as K. S. Roy alleged – had the purpose of removing Roy's followers who constituted the majority in the Executive Council.[170] Roy had by then indicated that in the near future he was not going to sail with Bose who was too left wing for him. It was, therefore, certain that the order of Bose – by then the BPCC president – would not receive an easy acceptance.

Characterizing Bose's direction as 'an effort to undermine the democratic basis of the selection of members of the Executive Council', the entire executive resigned.[171] With a view to reconstituting the executive council of the BPCC for 1935, a general meeting of the BPCC was held in November 1935 but only 34 out of the 100 members attended. Resolutions were passed requesting the Congress President to empower Sj. Sarat Chandra Bose to (a) form the executive council of the BPCC for 1935, and (b) nominate the general body and the executive council for 1936.[172] Roy who was drifting away from the Bose group raised the question of the 'constitutional validity of Sarat Bose's nominating the BPCC for the year 1936, because he [Sarat] was nominated by minority votes [only 19 out 100 voted for Sarat]'.[173] The AICC was inundated with complaints from Bengal 'alleging that a great part of membership reported to the AICC was bogus, that there had been no enrolment nor any payment of fees but that names had been copied out from some voters' list, such as that of District Boards or Municipal Boards'.[174] The AICC was therefore aware of the situation and the objection of K. S. Roy provided it with a solid ground to intervene in the provincial Congress's affairs. The Working Committee, in 'a resolution, adopted in January, 1935',[175] authorized its president Rajendra Prasad to inquire into the affairs of the Bengal Congress.

Rajendra Prasad Award

Aney's task had been made easier by a temporary agreement at the provincial level. In the case of Rajendra Prasad, this was highly improbable because by then the polarization of the ideological forces was more complete and therefore K. S. Roy's objection to Sarat Bose, though involving a constitutional question, was based on an emphatic ideological commitment to oppose any kind of leftist politics, which gained ascendancy in the post-1939 Bengal.

Rajendra Prasad had two tasks before him: (1) to select delegates for the Lucknow session of 1936 from those districts where no elections were held; and (2) to ascertain how genuine the electoral rolls were. Having looked at the documents relating to the first, he found that out of 100 delegates allotted to the BPC, 'there was no election in respect of districts which would be entitled 19 delegates and, among the supposedly elected 81 delegates, objections were raised against 20 members.'[176] With regard to the second task, Prasad was in a dilemma. The complex nature of the complaints and counter-complaints reminded him of 'his past experience of courts with all their tricks and hoodwinking',[177] and thus it was impossible for him to prepare the list within such a short period. Subhas, convalescing in Europe, admitted too that there had been a competition on the part of the DCCs to include 'bogus membership'. He requested Prasad to consider 'whether after the roll is finally passed by the AICC, the BPCC can cancel it in whole or in part, as a result of further inquiry'.[178] In order to check the reliability of the list of primary members, Prasad appointed Surendra Mohan Maitra and Birendra Nath Mazumdar as scrutineers.[179] There was objection, too, on the ground that 'both the scrutineers were pro-Sarat Bose and therefore the outcome of the scrutiny was likely to be biased.'[180]

On the basis of the inquiry, Prasad announced his Award on 31 May 1936.[181] With regard to the election of delegates for the Lucknow session, the president instructed the BPCC to conduct the election in those districts, undisputed from the point of view of the way the election was fought or the electoral roll; accordingly the date of the election (4 April 1936) was announced.[182] The BPCC raised the question of the 'constitutional validity of the piecemeal election'.[183] Prasad characterized this as an unreasonable interpretation of the terms of the constitution because if it was followed the area would have to go unrepresented through no fault of its members.[184]

As regards the electoral roll, Prasad failed to arrive at a specific conclusion as the scrutineers were unable to provide the report. In order to enable the delegates of those 'disputed' districts to attend the Congress session, he evolved a formula allowing the controversial districts to prepare 'an agreed list of delegates who would be returned without contest'.[185] In conformity with the president's direction, the BPCC adopted a resolution authorizing those districts to arrange for elections provided that '(a) scrutineers finish their scrutiny and dispose of the disputes, or (b) disputes are withdrawn and (c) the Congress President fixes the quota of delegates and elections are finished within the time allowed by the Working Committee'.[186] The scrutiny was not complete by the specified date and therefore the Working Committee authorized the president to nominate delegates from those districts as soon as scrutiny was complete.[187] With the completion of the scrutiny, six districts, namely Bogra, Rangpur, Howrah, Mymensingh, Tippera and Rajshahi, were found to have included 'bogus membership' in their primary membership roll.[188] The elections in these districts were stopped and, according to an earlier decision, Prasad was given authority to select delegates for the coming Congress session (1936). Roy, who disagreed with the outcome of the scrutiny, insisted that 'the information on which the decision was taken must be publicly shown.'[189] The AICC could afford to ignore the demand because the disunited BPCC provided it with an opportunity to play the game according to its own rules.

Similarly with regard to the seats allotted to the 'undisputed districts' (see table 4.3) there was dissatisfaction too. Both the groups sent complaints as 'the principle followed in fixing the quota of members to be elected from the undisputed districts was

Table 4.3 Seats allotted to districts, 1931

Name of district	Total membership	Seats allotted
Svlhet	2831	5
Barra Bazar	1565	2
24 Parganas	1798[a]	2
Dacca	798	2
Burdwan	792	2
Khulna	1296	3
Cacher	516	Nil

[a] This figure does not conform to that of a later table relating to Congress membership

Sources: NAI, Rajendra Prasad Papers, F.N. IX/36/31, Report of Rajendra Prasad on Bengal election dispute; AICC, P6/Part II/1936, AICC Report, Bengal Congress Affairs

not clear.'[190] Rajendra Prasad reiterated the earlier decision of the AICC that 'there would be one delegate per 500 primary members.'[191] It seems unintelligible because had he followed the above principle, the number of delegates would have been different and Cacher would have had at least one delegate. The AICC did not budge and elections were held on 4 July 1936, within two weeks of the final decision. On 15 March at a meeting of the Working Committee it was decided that 'the undisputed districts should not be allowed to go unrepresented in the Lucknow session.'[192]

Though both the groups had been fighting to outbid each other, they seemed equally to have disliked the 'big brother' attitude of the AICC. In their correspondence, both voiced strong opposition to the idea of disregarding altogether the views of the provincial politicians. In fact, Rajendra Prasad – unlike the earlier arbiters who resolved the feud by providing AICC sanction in favour of one group against the other – required the PCC's complete submission to the AICC. The BPCC, devoid of able leadership, failed to make its case as strongly as it would have done under the leadership of Bose or Sengupta and accepted the arrangement as a temporary measure and agreed to hold new elections to constitute the BPCC for 1937.[193]

Prasad's attempt to bring about an amicable settlement between the contending groups did not last long. Group rivalry reappeared in its most ugly form in the post-1939 period and the erstwhile supporters of Bose (B. C. Roy and K. S. Roy, for instance) conspired not to fight for their mentor but to let him down. Though Sarat Bose was brought to power by the Award, he was not as strong a leader as his brother Subhas. Moreover, the dissension within the Big Five and the dissociation of Sarat from the group on the 'question of joining hands with the government-cum-European non-Congress group in the Corporation election of 1935',[194] weakened Sarat to a large extent. Those like K. S. Roy, B. C. Roy and Nalinkshya Sanyal who fought hand in hand with Subhas in order to ensure that the Congress Municipal Association was the sole authority for nominating candidates to the Calcutta Corporation, opposed the BPCC once they were 'denied the right to select candidates according to their choice'.[195] Not only did they carry on anti-BPCC propaganda in the press, but also at public meetings they 'condemned the official Congress candidates'.[196] Even after the conclusion of the 1935 Municipal election which ensured the defeat of the Congress, Kumud Sankar Roy (cousin of K. S. Roy) joined hands with the Coalition group (government-cum-European Non-Congress group) to be elected as an alderman.[197]

Rajendra Prasad's main concern was to resolve the election dispute of the provincial Congress hierarchy and the terms and conditions of the Award suggest that he was ignorant of the ugly manifestation of group rivalry within the municipal arena. Though he confirmed Sarat Bose and his faction in power, he did not dispute the appointment of B. C. Roy as the chairman of the Provincial Parliamentary Committee and K. S. Roy as the secretary of the BPCC. This caused bewilderment among some primary Congress members who explained Rajendra Prasad's stance (even after K. S. Roy and B. C. Roy violated the Congress pledge by opposing the official Congress candidate in the muncipal election) as 'submission to the betrayers of the Congress'.[198] Similarly, by declaring Tippera DCC null and void, Prasad was reported to have acted in accordance with the direction of Sarat Bose, 'who, having failed to capture the DCC, had resorted to a clever device of having a complaint filed by Swarna Kamal Roy, the junior secretary to the DCC, against many Congress workers and sufferers of the district for disciplinary action on false accusation'.[199] The arrangement suggested by Prasad, however fragile, continued until 1939.

Factionalism revived

By 1936 the Bengal Congress had had three Arbitration Committees, appointed by the High Command, attempting to resolve its problems. In each case, the arbiters had examined the rival statements and sought swift solutions to a conflict that was more fundamental than electoral malpractice: the ideological battle between those who accepted the creed of non-violence and those who did not. Though the former had a strong base in certain areas of west Bengal, the latter had an appeal to the people of Bengal because of their inclination to militancy. And given the strong tradition of terrorist agitation, the militant leader had no difficulty in getting a ready-made group of dedicated cadres around him.

Similarly, the terrorist groups who valued 'freedom of the country' more than their lives, co-operated with the militant leader, though under the Congress banner, primarily because he was not Gandhian *per se*. The bond that emerged as a result of an ideological affinity (though not well defined) was established by C. R. Das and consolidated by Subhas Bose. The sudden death of Das and the factional fight between Bose and Sengupta failed to gear the alliance between the revolutionary terrorists and Congress to the broader aim of independence. The alliance was used more often by both the successors of Das – Bose and Sengupta – to attack the opponents either in the DCC or BPCC or Calcutta Corporation.

With the departure of Sengupta in 1933, Bose faced politically less powerful opponents like B. C. Roy and K. S. Roy (Bose's erstwhile lieutenants). At first sight, the High Command seemed willing – witness the Prasad Award – to come to terms with the militant leadership of Bengal. There was no alternative because the High Command-sponsored K. S. Roy and his group had no substantial support base in the localities. The rural Gandhians, who had given solid organizational support to Sengupta through- out, faded from the provincial political scene disgusted with the factionalism of the leaders. So the High Command found it difficult to counter the militant Congress leadership of Bengal within the province. The arrangement Prasad provided was thus a response to the exigency of the situation rather than an attempt to incorporate the Bengal militant leadership within the vortex of Congress nationalism. Similarly, the choice of Bose as the Congress President for the year 1938 was illustrative of the extent to which the Congress High Command was willing to concede to the left. The new President by his strong dislike of the Congress ministries, opposition to federation and, more specifically, open disagreement with Gandhi on some fundamental political issues[200] proved that the dissension between the High Command and the militant group had its root in their respective ideological preferences. Neither was prepared to give way. On the rivalry the Bengal Governor commented that the 'Tripuri [Congress] has been given a taste of the hysterical temper and the politics at the national level that we in Bengal have had to endure for so long from a large section of the non-violent Bengal Congress.'[201]

Though Subhas had succeeded in organizing a solid block of supporters in the 1939 presidential election, the strong opposition of the High Command backed by solid organizational strength, and aided by a split within the left group, had forced him to resign in April 1939. Organization prevailed over ideology. Bose looked at

Bengal, still controlled by his men, hoping to 'reassert himself at the national level by showing', the Bengal Chief Secretary commented, 'he still carries with him the whole of Bengal'.[202] Given the composition of the BPCC, consisting of 'terrorists and persons with left inclination',[203] it seemed likely as the Bengal government anticipated that 'the BPCC may strike out a line of its own with Mr Bose as leader distinct from and opposed to that of Congress as a whole.'[204] Though Bose formed Forward Bloc (in May 1939) – continuing Das's tradition of forming pressure groups within the parental body – he never dissociated openly from the National Congress. But the relationship was hardly amicable, as each tried to outmanoeuvre the other.

Serious conflict developed between the AICC and the pro-Bose Bengal Congress that continued till the provincial unit was suspended in February 1940. In the following few pages we will concentrate on how the battle was fought, who were the participants and what were the issues involved.

Exhibition of strength

The re-election of Subhas Bose as the BPCC president (21 April 1939), on the eve of the AICC session in Calcutta (29 April 1939) and the BPCC decision to vest absolute powers in him to nominate the Executive Council according to his choice, meant that he still carried with him a majority at least within the BPCC. Although the decision did not go unchallenged, there was hardly any organized resistance to it. Apart from Bose's own followers, the BPCC, according to *The Statesman*, had three distinct groups:

1　The pro-AICC group led by K. S. Roy though a compact group with considerable power and resources had no substantial following in the ranks of Congress workers.
2　The Khadi group, with P. C. Ghosh as its leader; a disciplined group oriented to orthodox Gandhism, and probably the most well-knit party possessing the courage of conviction.
3　The group of M. N. Roy, though critical of Bose's 'leftism without any concrete programme', preferred Bose to the right-wing Congress and hoped to reduce Bose's left inclination in concrete programmes.[205]

Bose formed the Executive Council, reducing the right-wing

congressmen to 'a minority of 37' out of a total of 175 members.[206] The right wing anticipated a further blow. On 19 July 1939, the BPCC published a notice 'convening a general meeting of the BPCC on 26 July 1939, in pursuance of a requisition signed by the majority of the BPCC members for removal of the Executive Council (including the office bearers) and for the formation of a fresh Executive Council (including office bearers)'.[207] An immediate purpose of the meeting was to remove those in league with the High Command and to ensure a three-fourths majority in the Executive Council in favour of Bose to enable him to form a provincial Election Tribunal (according to the 1939 amendment to the Congress Constitution) within the province of his own choice.

Once this was achieved, the opposition group apprehended that Bose and his group 'would block their entry to the provincial Congress hierarchy permanently'.[208] In his letter to Patel, B. C. Roy of the opposition group suspected that the Election Tribunal, likely to be formed by the majority group, was likely to be partisan. 'The fear', as he explained, 'lies in the fact that a party man if put on the Tribunal will cancel all elections which are in favour of Kiran Babu and our group.'[209] The AICC did not react immediately: it was preparing to fight the disloyal BPCC to the finish.

The decision to hold a requisition meeting less than two months after a new Executive Council was formed reveals how desperate Bose was to establish that the entire Bengal Congress was solidly behind him. He was confident especially after being re-elected as the Congress President for the second time in the face of the High Command's strong opposition, believing that whatever he did would receive whole-hearted support from those opposed to the right wing of the Congress. This proved to be a miscalculation as his faith in 'the end justifies the means' was not shared by other constituent left forces, despite their general ideological affinity with Bose. Though he had played a decisive role in consolidating the left forces behind Bose in 1939, M. N. Roy disapproved of the move for requisitioning the BPCC with the object of replacing the present executive by another 'which will be completely composed of Subhas Babu's followers'. For him, 'the fight against Gandhi or even the Congress High Command cannot justify activities harmful to the Congress as a whole and therefore he was reluctant to support him any longer.'[210]

The opposition group led by B. C. Roy, K. S. Roy and Prafulla

Ghosh decided not to participate in the proposed requisition meeting because 'the present meeting by Bose's followers aims at the complete elimination of the minority group within the BPCC.' '[I]t is strange', they argued, 'that the protagonist of a composite cabinet in the AICC cannot tolerate the presence of less than 40 members in the provincial Executive Council of 149 members.'[211]

After the requisition meeting was over, Bose nominated the executive of the BPCC. The office bearers of the newly formed Executive Council remained the same as in the outgoing body;[212] but the numerical strength of the opposition group underwent a major change. In the old Executive Council, K. S. Roy and the Khadi group had a total strength of thirty-seven, while in the new one their strength was reduced drastically to only thirteen.[213]

What happened in the post-requisition meeting period was a repetition of what we have seen earlier. The opposition group heckled at the provincial level, and issued press statements challenging the validity of the meeting 'on the ground of gross violation of the Congress Constitution and request the AICC's intervention to save the Bengal Congress'.[214]

From July onwards tension grew within the Bengal Congress. While the Bose group was trying to consolidate its position in the Congress committees at the provincial as well as local levels, the minority groups were busy making a case against the BPCC before the High Command. The Bose group had an advantage because, at least in terms of numerical strength within the BPCC, it constituted the majority; the minority groups were weak on that account and therefore there was no way in which they could influence BPCC decisions. The only recourse left was to mark their protest by resigning from the BPCC. At the first meeting of the new Executive Council (30 July 1939) the leaders of the minority group, B. C. Roy, K. S. Roy and Prafulla Ghosh, resigned from the BPCC on the ground that the new BPCC was unconstitutional because the meeting in which it was formed was not convened according to the prescribed constitutional procedure.[215] The Subhas group felt confident. Resignation to them meant that the minority group had lacked sufficient organizational backing within the BPCC to make their case. A provincial Election Tribunal was formed consisting of Muzzafar Ahmad (a communist worker), Charu Chandra Roy (a Forward Bloc member from Mymensingh) and Charu Chandra Banerji (a member of the Congress Socialist Party).[216] Though the members of the Tribunal, as their party affiliation shows, had strong political views, they were selected, Ashrafuddin Chowdhury the secretary of the BPCC claimed, 'because [the] personal integrity of these gentlemen is above question'.[217] The appointment of committed political workers gave the opponents of the BPCC, who had already raised the constitutional validity of the Requisition Meeting, another solid point for their case to the AICC. In a memorandum to the Congress President, they appealed to him to cancel the Requisition Meeting because 'the technical procedure of the Constitution was not followed', to set aside all subsequent steps taken by the illegally constituted Executive Council, and to form an impartial Election Tribunal.[218] There were complaints from several districts relating to the composition of the Tribunal.[219]

The High Command, having waited so long, had at last a chance to discipline the BPCC. It sensed danger when the new BPCC executive flouted the AICC decision regarding the 'ban on satyagraha and criticism of ministries': first, 'at its executive meeting'[220] by adopting a resolution to the contrary; and secondly by organizing an 'All-India protest day on 9 July, against the above resolution of the AICC',[221] 'in spite of the warnings given by the President, Rajendra Prasad'.[222] The High Command was infuriated and Rajendra Prasad expressed the feeling by saying that 'it is impossible to allow such flouting by any provincial executive of the Working Committee's resolution'.[223] In order to discipline the disloyal BPCC, the Working Committee, 'having disqualified Bose from presidentship of the BPCC and from being a member of any elective Congress Committee for three years from August 1939, empowered the President to take disciplinary action against others who persisted in indiscipline'.[224]

Subhas seemed to have been prepared for this. According to him, 'the decision is [a] logical consequence of the process of right consolidation which has been going on for the last few years and which has been accentuated by the acceptance of ministerial office in the provinces.' He was confident that 'by exposing the limitations of constitutionalism and reformism of the right-wing congressmen . . . we [Forward Bloc] shall be able to rejuvinate the Congress and restore to it its revolutionary character and role and resume the struggle for independence in the name of the Indian National Congress.'[225]

The High Command was now on the war-path and was to spare no effort to crush the militant leadership of Bengal completely. On

17 August 1939, Rajendra Prasad declared 'the meeting of the BPCC held on 26 July – the Requisition Meeting – null and void'.[226] The Executive Council of the BPCC reacted instantly and at its special meeting on 25 August adopted resolutions 'reaffirming its full confidence in Sj. Subhas Chandra Bose' and deploring the AICC decision as 'an attempt to strengthen the hands of the supporters of the Congress Working Committee in the BPCC'.[227] It also raised the constitutional validity of the AICC authority because 'the infliction of punishment on the ground of indiscipline ought to be the function of the judiciary'.[228] There was no trouble at all in getting these anti-AICC resolutions accepted. As the Executive Council consisted of predominantly pro-Bose members, the resolutions got through; but they were opposed tooth and nail by the anti-Bose group when they were put before the general meeting of the BPCC on 30 August 1939. 'Out of 541 members of the BPCC, 353 members attended the meeting.'[229] The resolutions were ratified by '213 to 138 votes'.[230] The absence of more than one-third of the members may well have been due to their reluctance to get involved in this tangle.

Votes were counted four times,[231] indicating the frenetic atmosphere; but B. C. Roy, K. S. Roy and Prafulla Ghosh had to concede to the Bose-led Bengal Congress.[232] The meeting was an example of left unity in the sense that, except for the M. N. Roy group, the left – the Communist Party, CSP, and Kishan Sabha – actively participated in order to show, according to the *Amrita Bazar Patrika*, 'the consolidation of the left forces under the leadership of Subhas Bose'.[233]

The victory was however marred by violence: K. S. Roy and Prafulla Ghosh were allegedly assaulted by Bose's supporters 'to silence the voice of those who happened to differ from Sj. Bose'[234] – they did not deny the charge but disclaimed his responsibility.[235] This provided the AICC with further grounds for asserting that 'in Bengal politics, lathi is taking the place of logic.'[236] The central leadership now formed an Election Tribunal, consisting of Satish Chandra Dasgupta, Kshitish Prasad Chattapadhyay and Priya Ranjan Sen.[237] According to the Bombay decision (1939), an election tribunal should consist of men with no party affiliation. In this case, each of them was a well-known Gandhian and opposed to Bose. In his letter to the Congress President, Sarat Bose outlined the known affiliations of the members of the Tribunal: 'Satish Chandra Dasgupta and Priya Ranjan Sen belong to the Khadi

Table 4.4   Congress membership in 1939

District	No. of primary members		Muslim members	% of Muslims	Women members	% of women
	1936	1939				
Hindu-majority districts[a]						
24 Parganas	(1,716)	31,855	1,215	3.81	1,553	4.87
South Calcutta	(1,018)	7,673	106	1.38	89	1.15
Central Calcutta	(1,087)	NA	259		167	
Jalpaiguri	(1,915)	NA	56		186	
Howrah	(4,790)	19,336	283	1.46	127	0.65
Burdwan	(792)	9,262	198	2.13	540	5.83
North Calcutta	(1,844)	9,008	95	1.05	421	4.67
Bankura	(1,545)	8,394	38	0.45	314	3.74
Midnapore	NA[b]	31,223	154	0.49	1,286	4.11
Bara Bazar	(1,563)	3,397	67	1.97	24	0.70
Hooghly	(797)	26,945	316	1.17	1,049	3.89
Birbhum	(606)	11,366	329	2.89	258	2.26
Cacher	(516)	3,268	126	3.85	217	6.64
Darjeeling	NA	2,539	15	0.59	27	1.06
Muslim-majority districts						
Jessore	(1,539)	18,445	1,055	5.71	1,486	7.78
Rajshahi	(1,913)	8,723	739	8.47	1,120	12.83
Murshidabad	(819)	18,922	2,087	10.52	594	2.99
Dinajpur	(2,932)	NA	330		617	
Nadia	(1,350)	11,336	1,518	13.39	800	7.05
Sylhet	(2,831)	19,305	1,046	5.41	1,772	9.17
Dacca	(798)	24,517	721	2.94	3,141	12.81
Noakhali	(1,436)	8,057	994	12.33	708	8.78
Khulna	(1,296)	9,737	431	4.42	1,805	18.53
Rangpur	(1,161)	14,944	3,264	21.84	845	5.65
Malda	(1,014)	9,898	612	6.18	569	5.74
Bogura	(1,154)	5,628	812	14.42	361	6.41
Pabna		11,133	314	2.82	1,915	17.20
Mymensingh	(1,314)	53,255	5,552	10.42	1,238	2.32
Faridpur	(2,737)	19,629	2,244	11.43	3,047	15.52
Barisal	(661)	NA	2,606		5,427	
Chittagong	(71)	18,237	1,262	6.91	1,148	6.29
Tippera	(8,958)	21,332	4,343	20.35	2,417	11.57
TOTAL	(49,040)	464,167[c]	33,187	7.14	34,468	7.42

NA = not available

[a] By Hindu majority is meant a district where Hindus constituted more than 50% of the population. The case is similar with regard to the Muslim majority districts
[b] Congress was banned in Midnapore
[c] This figure includes members from the districts not shown in the table

group and Kshitish Chattapadhyay is an active member of the pro-K. S. Roy group.[238]

Not surprisingly, the first decision related to Rajshahi District Congress affairs. The AICC-appointed Election Tribunal ordered 'the old secretary and office bearers of the Rajshahi DCC to function pending a final decision of the dispute by the Tribunal'.[239] The BPCC condemned it and 'reconstituted the DCC'[240] by members 'alleged to have been pro-Bose'.[241] Different DCCs protested against the 'interference of the Executive Council of the BPCC in the working of the Tribunal'.[242] The leader of the anti-Bose group, K. S. Roy, demanded that all powers 'should be vested in the Election Tribunal to ensure free election of delegates'.[243] Prasad, who condemned the idea of a provincial Executive Committee flouting Working Committee decisions gave his verdict in favour of the AICC-appointed Tribunal.[244] As expected, the BPCC executive expressed 'its complete lack of confidence in the Election Tribunal set up by the Working Committee and specifically its interference in a democratically constituted Rajshahi District Congress Committee'.[245]

Despite (and because of) the internal feuds and the tussle with the AICC, the BPCC seems to have achieved remarkable success in enrolling a large number of primary members. Within the period of three years (between 1936 and 1939), the increase was about 90 per cent. Given the sudden jump, one might attribute this exclusively to the inclusion of 'bogus members'. It is difficult either to substantiate or to refute the contention because we do not have information to cross-check the numerical strength of the Bengal Congress (as shown in the AICC files). Even so, table 4.4 is interesting in the sense that, apart from indicating the numerical strength of the Bengal Congress, it gives a rough idea of its nature in terms of religion and sex.

The table is not exhaustive, but clearly the Bengal Congress failed to enrol large numbers of Muslim members in a province where more than half of the population were Muslim. Out of a

---

Sources: AICC, P5/1939, Defiance and Insubordination of the Executive Council of the BPCC (list of primary members was enclosed in this file). The list was published in the *Hindustan Standard*, 14 October 1939. For Congress membership in 1936, see NAI, RPP, IV/1936, Prasad to the BPCC secretary, 8 March 1936, and NMML, AICC P6/1936, Bengal Election Disputes. For Muslim and women members see *Hindustan Standard*, 24 November 1939

total membership of about half a million, less than 8 per cent were Muslims; the numerical strength was even less than that of women. It is also evident that even in the Muslim majority districts, Muslim representation in the Congress was remarkably meagre. Muslim share in those districts, for instance, was about 11 per cent, while in the Hindu-majority areas their share was negligible (3.8 per cent). This shows that Das's theory of 'composite patriotism', however appealing it was to the elite, had an insignificant impact on the masses. Neither Sengupta nor Sasmol, who fought hard to keep the Bengal Pact alive, succeeded in making the Congress a platform for all. The very fact that they wanted to incorporate the 'educated Muslims' into the world of bhadralok was evident in their fight for the retention of the Pact. Subhas too, as shown in chapter 2, preferred pact-type concessional arrangements to build Muslim support (the Bose–League Pact of 1940). Concentrating very much on city politics, none of the leaders adopted concrete agrarian programmes in order to bring the vast majority of (Muslim) peasantry into the Congress fold, and as a result the Congress never became a mass organization in the real sense of the term.

Audit controversy

Bose was no longer a Congress member but a majority of the BPCC members had backed him. The new president of the BPCC, Rajendra Chandra Dev, after his election deferentially declared that 'he can do not better than be guided by his [Sj. Bose] advice as long as he has to discharge the duties of the president.'[246] At its executive meeting on 30 October the BPCC placed Rs5000 at Bose's disposal 'for keeping trim and ready the Congress organization for all eventualities'.[247] This decision was a clear defiance of the Working Committee's resolution that the 'AICC fund in Bengal, created from the contributions of the Congress members of the legislature lying in deposit with the leader of the Congress Legislative Party, be transferred to Maulana Abul Kalam Azad who may hold it on behalf of the AICC'.[248] Rajendra Prasad, the Congress President, took exception and requested Sarat Bose, the leader of the Bengal Legislative Party, to 'act in accordance with the above resolution'.[249] The money thus transferred, Azad assured, was meant for 'the parliamentary activities of Bengal and under all circumstances would be utilized for Bengal only'.[250]

In view of the clear defiance of the Working Committee resolution, the AICC appointed an auditor to examine the accounts of the Bengal Congress fund[251] in the face of strong opposition from the BPCC; it was not the first time that the AICC had appointed an auditor to check the accounts. During 1931 the AICC Audit Inspector, in his audit report of the Bengal Congress Fund, mentioned that 'the account books of the DCCs and the PCC were not satisfactory.'[252] In defence the BPCC submitted that '(a) it was never the practice to get a statement of accounts from the DCCs, and (b) all the office records, account books and even the office furniture taken away by the police even after the truce [Gandhi–Irwin Pact of 1931] were not returned.'[253] Nehru, having looked at the first reason, expressed 'shock at the deplorable state of the Bengal Congress fund'[254] and requested the BPCC secretary to 'insist on regular reports of the accounts from the DCCs'.[255] However, faced with the second argument, the AICC withdrew its decision to have the accounts audited again by another auditor.

In 1940 it was highly unlikely that the AICC would abandon its plan. Accordingly, a resolution was adopted with a view to appoint 'an auditor to audit the accounts of the funds raised out of contributions by the members of legislatures'. Sarat Bose, the leader of the Assembly Party, was 'requested to place all accounts, vouchers and other papers before the auditor for audit and to furnish explanation and such other assistance in the audit as may be required'.[256] This decision seems to have aggravated the situation further although Sarat Bose did not express dissatisfaction when he was asked to transfer the money to Maulana Azad. A cheque for 'Rs5000 and a receipt for Rs10,075 fixed deposit payable in February 1940'[257] were handed over to Azad. He did not agree with the High Command that Rs5000 was given to Subhas.[258] What he denied however does not correspond to what he did. In sending the money to Azad, he upheld that 'the BPCC has every right to suggest the ways the money should be spent.'[259] He referred to Nehru's letter which stated clearly that 'this money was to be used for provincial purposes on the advice of the Provincial CC and the Congress Legislative Party in the Assembly in that province.'[260] On this basis he transferred, as his letter of 21 January 1940 shows, 'Rs5000 to Subhas Bose for the Congress work in the province'.[261] Technically he was right in saying that there was no transfer of money because the BPCC had no bank account until 31 October 1939[262] and the Executive Council directed Sarat Bose to hand over the money on the 30th.

Sarat Bose took particular exception to the appointment of the auditor when 'all disbursements shown in the statement of accounts were made after reference to the proper authorities and during the last three months no exception has been taken to any item therein'.[263] He felt that the appointment was 'an expression of lack of confidence in him and of a desire to humiliate him'.[264] The AICC stuck to its decision and accordingly S. R. Batliboi and Company were appointed. Sarat Bose questioned the efficiency of the company as an auditing firm in view of the fact that 'their audit of the Bengal Immunity was declared null and void by the Calcutta High Court'.[265] Since the appointment was made against the will of the BPCC, a clash was certain over the question of audit. Annoyed by the pressing demand for accounts of the Assembly Party fund, Sarat expressed utter dissatisfaction in his letter to Rajendra Prasad[266] who thought it legitimate given his order that the audit report should be completed before the next meeting of the Working Committee, to be held on 30 December 1939.[267] Sarat therefore 'declined to co-operate with the AICC-sponsored audit operation'.[268] The AICC 'regretted the decision'[269] and finally instructed Batliboi and Company not to deal with the fund at Sarat Bose's disposal.[270]

The withdrawal of the audit operation did not prevent the events which followed. The Congress President, Prasad, who was already informed of the 'shady state of the Congress Fund in Bengal',[271] expressed 'dissatisfaction with the way the Congress fund in Bengal was handled by the BPCC'.[272] Since the appointment of the auditor was made in November, it is possible to assume that the report came from that source; and the decision of forming an *ad hoc* committee, consisting of Maulana Azad as chairman, and B. C. Roy, P. C. Ghosh, Suresh Banerjee, K. S. Roy, J. C. Gupta, Ananda Prasad Chowdhury and Benoyendra Nath Palit as members, to run the provincial Congress in the absence of a duly elected BPCC[273] on 21 December 1939, even when the outcome of the exercise was unknown, certainly shows that the AICC anticipated what the audit report was likely to be.

The audit report

The offshoot of the controversial audit exercise, in spite of the non-co-operation of the BPCC, corroborated the AICC's contention. In their reports, Batliboi and Company concentrated on three points to prove how unsatisfactory the Bengal Congress Fund was:

(1) The cash books, produced before the auditors, were not maintained properly, and sometimes money received by the BPCC was not shown in the cash book. (2) Though the Secretary certified that the BPCC had Rs18,598, the money remained unbanked until 31 October; but according to BPCC Constitution, whatever amount the BPCC received should be kept in the bank. (3) There was no proper account of the money spent by the BPCC.[274]

Ashrafuddin Ahmad Chowdhury, the BPCC secretary, conceded the first and third points but rejected the second on the ground that 'for the greater part of the year under survey, the BPCC had no surplus cash to deposit in a bank.'[275] This is hard to believe because even when the BPCC had at its disposal Rs18,598, there was no bank account; only after the instruction of the auditors was an account opened 'with a deposit of Rs500 with the Pioneer Bank Ltd, Calcutta'.[276] This confirms the fact that 'whatever funds the Provincial Congress organization had were transferred to the private accounts of Subhas Bose before the new committee came into existence.'[277] The BPCC secretary 'deposited the money in instalments'[278] and 'the entire cash due by him was not put into the bank'.[279] As much as Rs10,000 was transferred to Subhas Bose out of the BPCC account 'in view of the critical situation in the country'.[280]

The infuriated Working Committee now 'directed that the admitted cash balances should be handed over to the Treasurer, Mr J. C. Gupta (of the Ad hoc Committee) and be deposited by him in a bank without the least further delay'.[281] In reply the BPCC, at its executive meeting of 5 January 1940, adopted resolutions condemning the manner in which the Congress Working Committee appointed an auditor over the head of the BPCC and characterized the Working Committee resolution on the auditor's report as a 'calculated move to retard Congress work and undermine Congress prestige in Bengal'.[282] To prove this more convincing, a subcommittee was appointed to examine the auditor's report. The members – Rajen Chandra Dev (chairman, Maulvi Abul Hayat, Jnan Majumdar, Satya Ranjan Bakshi, Niharendu Dutta Majumdar and Harendra Nath Ghosh[283] – were drawn exclusively from the pro-BPCC group. Its report concluded that 'the cash statement up to December 1939 has been correctly made and the entire cash balance has been deposited with the Pioneer Bank Ltd.'[284]

The Ad hoc Committee and after

The appointment of the Ad hoc Committee, over the head of the BPCC, led to an unprecedented crisis within the Congress organization as a whole. Neither the High Command nor the provincial leadership fully appreciated the adverse effects of internal feud on the organization as a fighting platform. Congress was engaged in an ugly internecine conflict at a time when it might have been utilizing the war crisis to strengthen its position and support.

When the Ad hoc Committee was appointed, the BPCC reacted immediately. At its Executive Council meeting, held on 30 December 1939, the Ad hoc Committee was rejected since 'the acceptance of this Committee would reduce the BPCC to a non-entity and would mean its virtual death or abdication. Since the present executive of the BPCC enjoys the full confidence of the public, it does not feel called upon to abdicate.'[285]

To confirm this, a general meeting was convened for 6 January 1940. The minority group, led by K. S. Roy and B. C. Roy, comprising 140 members out of a total of 325 members, decided to abstain from the meeting[286] to vindicate their loyalty to the Working Committee. In their press statement, it was made clear that 'the opposition to the BPCC, a champion of caucus rule, meant fighting for democracy within the organization.'[287] A minority still sought accommodation. For example J. C. Gupta, an active member of the anti-Bose campaign group who had resigned from the Treasureship of the BPCC in 1938, neither accepted the membership of the Ad hoc Committee nor approved the fighting gesture of his colleagues. In his view the 'Working Committee needed to be persuaded to make up with Mr Subhas Bose in order to ensure a strong united front in the present crisis'.[288]

The 6 January meeting of the BPCC was not totally unyielding. The BPCC condemned the Working Committee resolution appointing the Ad hoc Committee over its head; but there were signs that negotiations were still possible. It authorized Sarat Bose to place the case before the Working Committee for further consideration.[289]

The Working Committee, however, was determined to oust the Bose group once and for all. It is evident from the available archival sources that, had the Working Committee withdrawn the Ad hoc Committee, the Bose group would have had constitutional sanction for their past activities. The handling of funds by the BPCC, as assessed in the audit report, damaged its image. Further, its 5 January resolution postponing elections within its jurisdiction[290] increased alarm both locally and nationally. Nehru, who had so far taken no public stand on BPCC affairs, now told the Congress President that the 'disloyal Bengal Congress' should be disaffiliated and that the anti-Bose group be assisted to secure control of the Congress in Bengal.[291]

The aforesaid resolution postponing all Congress elections was viewed with apprehension among the left as well. A CSP member, J. P. Narayan, for instance, was certain that 'this resolution would consolidate the split between the Bose group and the minority. Since there were 140 members opposing the BPCC, the strength of the anti-Bose group cannot be overruled.'[292] Jibanlal Chattapadhyay, a member of the League of Radical Congressmen (founded by M. N. Roy), also foresaw in the resolution Bose's attempt to maintain a majority within the BPCC. In his letter to M. N. Roy, Chattapadhyay corroborated J. P. Narayan's assessment. 'With the support of 140 members and strong backing of the Working Committee', he calculated, 'the creation of two BPCCs is almost certain.'[293] Under these circumstances, what should be their stand, Jibanlal asked Roy. Having condemned Subhas's move against the Working Committee as 'disruptive' and identified the minority group as 'full-blooded right-wing reactionaries', there was only one course left to him – neutrality. Accordingly he suggested that his colleagues in Bengal maintain 'equidistance from both the groups'.[294] Suresh Banerjee, a member of the Ad hoc Committee and the President of the All-India Trade Union Congress Committee, for instance, condemned Bose's move to put the Executive Council's rejection of the Working Committee's decision before the BPCC as it meant 'flouting by the subordinate body of a decision of a higher body'. He urged the BPCC members 'to make up the differences in order to preserve organizational unity, an urgent necessity in view of the imminent struggle'.[295] The CPI and the CSP accepted that the substance of the audit report was convincing and sustained a whispering campaign 'against Bose'.[296] Both the CPI and CSP agreed not 'to give an ultimatum to the

Working Committee' and unsuccessfully sought an appropriate amendment to the resolution. Defeated, they decided to maintain neutrality.[297]

It is evident that the BPCC lost ground on two points: the audit report was persuasive; and in view of the war, internal squabbles impaired the organizational unity of the Congress. The BPCC with the support of the old Jugantor members, Sri Sangha and the Bengal Volunteers, was confident of its victory over the Working Committee.

While asked to comment on the BPCC resolution on 6 January, Rajendra Prasad made it clear that the Working Committee was not going to tolerate 'an undemocratic and partisan BPCC involved with muddling of public funds and flouting of the Working Committee any longer'.[298] Flagrantly defying the Working Committee decision, the BPCC secretary issued a circular (on 31 January 1940) to the DCCs 'not to co-operate with the Ad hoc Committee', arguing (unconstitutionally) that 'since the BPCC had majority support, it is empowered to do whatever it thinks suitable for the province'.[299] Sarat Bose, anxious to prove that the majority of congressmen were with the BPCC, 'sought permission from the High Command for a referendum in Bengal against the Working Committee decision' and requested the President 'to tour Bengal, address public meetings to justify his decision'.[300] Prasad declined to accept the idea to hold a referendum because 'the constitution does not provide for appeal against the Working Committee to referendum.'[301] Abandoning decorum Sarat characterized the Working Committee 'as a packed majority to support the President's decision irrespective of merit',[302] to which Prasad replied that 'it was an insult not only to the members of the Working Committee but also to the electorate which returned them.'[303] '[T]he Congress constitution gives power to the Working Committee', he noted, 'to superintend, direct and control all Congress committees and to take disciplinary action against a committee or individual for misconduct, wilful neglect or default.'[304]

Deadlock had now been reached; and no elections for the delegates to the Ramgarh Congress of 1940 were held and so Bengal was unrepresented in the Congress presidential election held on 15 February 1940.

District Congress Committees (DCCs) and the Ad hoc Committee

Of the DCCs, if the report of the BPCC assistant secretary is to be
believed, out of thirty-three units, eighteen decided not to co-
operate with the Ad hoc Committee, eight accepted the central
order and eight remained neutral (see table 4.5). The BPCC
almost certainly had the support of the majority of the DCCs. On
the other hand, the AICC was authorized constitutionally to
demand unquestionable loyalty from the PCCs. When, taking
advantage of its majority, the BPCC 'disaffiliated three DCCs
[Mymensingh, Hooghly and Jessore] for their continued disobedience of the BPCC mandate',[305] the High Command, using the
power under article XIII of the Congress constitution, 'suspended

Table 4.5 DCCs' responses to the Ad hoc Committee

Division	DCCs not to co-operate	DCCs still undecided	DCCs to co-operate
Presidency	(1) Murshidabad (2) Nadia (3) Khulna (4) North Calcutta (5) South Calcutta (6) Central Calcutta	(1) Barisal (2) 24 Parganas	(1) Jessore (2) Chittagong Hill Tracts (3) Bara Bazar
Rajshahi	(7) Jalpaiguri (8) Rangpur (10) Bogura (11) Pabna (12) Maldah	(3) Rajshahi (4) Darjeeling	(4) Dinajpur
Chittagong	(13) Noakhali	(5) Tippera (6) Chittagong	
Burdwan	(14) Howrah (15) Birbhum	(7) Bankura (8) Burdwan	(5) Hooghly (6) Midnapore
Dacca	(16) Dacca (17) Faridpur		(7) Mymensingh
Surma Valley	(18) Sylhet		(8) Cacher

Source: *Hindustan Standard*, 23 February 1940, quoting BPCC Assistant Secretary,
Kalipada Bagchi

the BPCC, vested all powers in the Ad hoc Committee and declared null and void the disciplinary actions against three DCCs by the BPCC'.[306]

The warnings of the AICC – as manifested in the sacking of the president, depriving the BPCC of its right to form an Election Tribunal and imposition of an Ad hoc Committee – had not been heeded. The AICC had therefore taken the ultimate step.

The constituents of the BPCC naturally 'condemned the high-handedness of the Working Committee'[307] and resolved to 'continue to work under the name of the BPCC and in consultation with Subhas Bose'.[308] Those on the fringe – the CSP and the League of Radical Congressmen – were nonetheless opposed to the idea of establishing a parallel congress on the basis of the old logic, namely, it would weaken the anti-British front. The CPI, following the people's war logic, resolved to dissociate itself from any anti-British campaign. Apart from the Kishan Sabha leader, Swami Sahajanand, who remained with the Forward Bloc all through,[309] none of the left forces (CPI, CSP and Roy group) was ready actively to support Bose. They were in a dilemma because if they supported Bose they would contradict their past judgement regarding him. If they did not condemn the Working Committee's action, they would be shown to have acquiesced to the undemocratic step of the higher body. The CPI and CSP remained within the BPCC not 'to support Bose but to consolidate the anti-left forces'.[310] A middle course was evolved by M. N. Roy 'as a temporary expedient, viz., opposing the move of the Working Committee and maintaining a working alliance with the opposition'.[311]

The BPCC, as mentioned earlier, had eighteen DCCs under its control. When the official Congress (Ad hoc Committee) decided to turn every District Congress Committee into a Satyagraha Committee according to Gandhi's direction, there was opposition. In his letter to the general secretary, Arun Chandra Guha, secretary of the official Bengal Congress, corroborated this by mentioning that 'since some of the DCCs are yet in a mood of revolt, it is impossible to act according to the High Command's decision'.[312] The official Congress, according to the official BPCC President Surendra Mohan Ghosh, faced 'difficulty in enrolling primary members'.[313] Subhas, as the BPCC leader, on the other hand did not put forward a concrete programme to mobilize the DCCs in his support. He thought of starting 'a country-wide

Satyagraha campaign'.[314] That nothing came of it can probably be explained by the fact that, as early as the beginning of 1940, a secret (official) report believed that Subhas had started exploring the possibility of fighting the British with the help of its enemies.[315] The idea rooted in his faith in revolutionary terrorism was shaped concretely by his life-long association with the revolutionary terrorist groups who had remained within the Congress since the days of C. R. Das and were his most loyal followers.

Factional rivalry and student politics

Factional rivalry for the control of the Congress organization had also permeated provincial student politics. In spite of general political differences among themselves, the students continued to maintain a single organization until 1929 when the militant section broke away from the parental body. Although the division was based on ideological preferences, the split weakened the student organization. In this section, an attempt will be made to trace the roots of factionalism in student politics and its consequences.

From the beginning of this century, the Bengal Congress had organized students and youths. Though there was no formal organization of their own, young people actively supported the Non-Co-operation movement by coming out of British schools. According to an official estimate, '6,306 out of 23,887 college students (26.4%) and 45,006 out of 196,548 high-school students (22.9%) came out of the British education system during the Non-Co-operation days of 1920–2'.[316] The increase of students in the national schools during the period, from '13,468 to 15,000',[317] illustrates the political make up of the Bengali student community. Edward Shils, explaining this early involvement of the students in the nationalist movement, has argued that 'students in Bengal were moved primarily by the sacrifice of the nationalist leaders and they thought that by leaving schools they were contributing to the nationalist cause too.'[318] The argument seems convincing in view of the fact that with the arrest of C. R. Das and Subhas Bose 'thousands of students began to enlist as volunteers'.[319] During the civil disobedience movement, the number of students participating was far less. The official estimate shows that 'only 2,360 out of 23,280 college students (10.2%) and 10,700 out of 285,479 high school students (4%) struck for a month.'[320] The national schools, so popular during the Non-Co-operation days, also saw a sudden decrease in their student rolls. During the peak of the civil disobedience, there were 'only 19 schools with 1,647 students'.[321]

To explain the decline of national schools, B. R. Khan has emphasized the in-built infrastructural weakness of the system itself. According to him,

> staffed by unqualified and inexperienced teachers recruited from among the local Congress workers, and filled with wayward deserters from the official system, these schools were no substitute for those under the government. Financially handicapped, the national schools depended solely on occasional windfalls from the individual Non-Co-operators given more as a means of maintaining their credibility than from serious concern for education.[322]

Not only did the number of national schools decrease over time, but students' participation in Congress activity in general also registered a sharp decline. An explanation can be provided when it is recognized that until 1928 Congress never thought seriously in terms of organizing the students permanently for the national cause. Those who joined the Non-Co-operation movement and became Congress volunteers did so less as a result of serious thinking on their part about the cause of independence and more in response to an emotional attachment to the cause. In fact, this can be substantiated by mentioning that one very interesting feature of student participation in the Congress agitation was 'the comparative non-involvement of maturer postgraduate students; the career-minded engineering and medical students with their fairly secure future remained completely aloof'.[323] It was the younger and the non-vocational students who constituted the core of student agitation during the Non-Co-operation days.

Congress had itself contributed indirectly to the relative passivity of students in general by neglecting the hidden potential of the student community in Bengal. In fact, apart from some isolated attempts at mobilization, there was no effort on the part of the Congress politicians to organize them formally until 1924, when the Calcutta Students Association was founded under Congress patronage.[324] In May 1928, this association became the All-Bengal Students Association (ABSA). An immediate impetus to its formation certainly came from the anti-Simon Commission agitation of 1928. Students of Calcutta organized a hartal on 3 February

1928, the day the Commission arrived in Calcutta. 'The students of Presidency College of Calcutta took an active role and the military was called in to the vicinity of the college to avoid further trouble.'[325] Once the strike was over, the college authority 'expelled some students and closed the college and the attached Eden Hindu Hostel *sine die*'.[326] Subhas arranged accommodation for those driven out of the Hindu Hostel. These temporary hostels seem to have provided the rendezvous for all the student activists. Subhas, as Suren Ghosh – one of Bose's followers who became an active worker in the factional feud that followed soon – mentioned, used to come regularly and urged the students to form a broad-based political organization in place of the narrowly confined Calcutta Students Association.[327] This had a direct bearing on the formation of the All-Bengal Students Association which was formally inaugurated by Jawaharlal at the All-Bengal Students Conference, held at Calcutta in September 1928.[328] Although formed ostensibly for the purpose of social welfare work, 'a revolutionary tone pervades the proceedings of all the meetings of the ABSA.'[329]

What appeared to be a real possibility with the formation of a student organization at the behest of the Bengal Congress received a set-back with the outbreak of factional feuding at the provincial level. Here too, the preference for a specific ideology lay at the root of the schism. Those who were less militant preferred Sengupta to Bose, who by then had established himself more as a 'revolutionary than a typical Gandhian'.[330] The first sign of a separation of pro-Bose students from the other group became evident at the Annual Students Conference at Mymensingh in 1929. The feud came to the surface on the question of who would be the president of the conference. The Bose followers, dominating the Reception Committee, suggested the name of Subhas Bose, but he was rejected by the pro-Sengupta ABSA executive on the ground that a prominent Gandhian should preside. Accordingly Dr Muhammad Alam (a Gandhian from Lahore) was proposed. The recommendation of Bose's name by the Reception Committee was, as the Annual Report of the ABSA shows, the handiwork of Sj. Surendra Mohan Ghosh – a BPCC member – who was alleged to have adopted 'dishonest means' to get Bose elected. The name of Dr Alam was then proposed by the district ABSA branches.[331] The choice of the Sengupta followers prevailed, but the conference, because of the determined opposition of the opposite group, 'ended on the second day with no achievement whatsoever'.[332]

Division within the student community was consolidated with the formation of a separate organization by the Bose-followers in December 1929; the Bengal Presidency Students Association (BPSA) was born.

From now on, the factional fighting between two student organizations became an integral part of Bengali student politics. The BPSA attempted several times to take over the control of the ABSA executive, a body elected directly by the members of ABSA. Having realized its inadequate support among the students, it proposed to reserve the office of the president and one of the joint secretaries for the BPSA.[333] The ABSA declined to accept but was willing to take the BPSA members back to the parent body provided they agreed to abide by the ABSA constitution.[334] It was possible for ABSA to dictate to BPSA because, by the late 1920s, it had a widespread organizational network all over the province, while the other group, because of its late arrival on the scene, lacked sufficient organizational support. Even then, there had been attempts by the BPSA members to wrest control by any means. The Mymensingh incident of 1931 amply illustrates this. The roots of the problem lay in the selection of president and the venue of a student conference. The Mymensingh ABSA wanted Sengupta to preside over the conference to be held there on 24 April; while the BPSA, with strong backing of the local DCC and dominated by pro-Bose congressmen, chose Purna Chandra Das (a Jugantor member) for the presidency and decided also to hold the conference at the subdivisional town of Netrokona at the same time as the Political Sufferers' Conference.[335] Both groups were determined to go to any length to implement their decisions. Sengupta when about to preside 'was picketed by the adherents of the opposition party so that he had to give up his project'.[336] The ABSA followers retaliated equally strongly. 'Purna Chandra Das was lured out of the train in which he was proceeding to a rival students' conference at Netrokona and was detained on the platform until the train had left.'[337]

The way the entire situation unfolded might be explained in terms of the desire of the contending groups to dominate the power nucleus of student organization – such a conclusion looks plausible if one looks at the events as they appeared on the surface. But the explanation is revealed to be superficial if one goes below the surface. As mentioned earlier, factional squabbles in Bengal corresponded to an existing ideological division in Bengal. In this case, it is evident that the BPSA members were attracted to Bose because of his militancy. In fact, the pro-Sengupta congressmen were 'scared' by the BPCC resolution achieved at Netrokona that swaraj would be adopted by the use of any means.[338] The ABSA, with full faith in non-violence, attacked Bose who was alleged to have maintained a double standard: 'a Gandhian in public, but in terms of faith and actions ... certainly otherwise'.[339] To the government, the BPSA posed a serious threat by its explicit revolutionary tone and 'could go beyond control because of its leader who was not quite reconciled to Gandhi's politics'.[340]

Apart from this general apprehension, the BPSA's activity at the grass-root level caused alarm to the administration in some districts. The report of the District Magistrate of Mymensingh is illustrative here. The District Magistrate was worried by the rapid progress of the BPSA activity among the common people and astonished to find that 'everywhere the volunteers were and are fed free, [and] request[ed] extra police to suppress the revolutionary work of the BPSA'.[341] There were indications that the BPSA was undergoing a radical transformation during the late 1920s. Proscribed literature, available to the Intelligence Bureau of the Bengal government, revealed that youth in general and those in the BPSA in particular (at Mymensingh), having understood the inadequacy of the theory of spasmodic political risings along terrorist lines, realized that 'the real revolutionary armies are in the villages and factories: the peasantry and labour.' Emphasizing that the youth should strive for 'socialist revolution', the pamphlet specified that socialist revolution aimed

> not at the transfer of power from the British to Indian hands, but at the total transformation of the system, because what difference does it make to them [peasantry and factory workers] whether Lord Reading is the head of the government or Sir Purshotamdas Thakordas? What difference for a peasant if Sir Tej Bahadur Sapru replaces Lord Irwin?[342]

That the ideological debate within the BPSA had its impact on the ABSA too, which decided to toe the Congress line with the outbreak of the civil disobedience, was evident in the emergence of a third group among the student political activists. The process certainly contributed to the formation of the All-India Student

Federation (AISF) in August 1936.[343] Though it was a united political platform for the students, the left wingers were prominent and the rift between the left and right took place in 1938 at the AISF session in Madras.[344] The arrival of the AISF further weakened the already crippled BPSA and ABSA (no longer under the patronage of the Congress leaders) to such an extent that they became skeletal organizations.

Though the BPSA had a left orientation and the ABSA had no anti-Muslim bias, neither of the groups succeeded in incorporating a substantial number of Muslim students into anti-government political activity. The general social and political cleavage between the two communities had a bearing on this. While explaining how social distance between the Hindus and Muslims in day-to-day life had its impact in schools, Abul Mansur Ahmad, a non-co-operator himself, refers to a situation when he was a victim of it. 'At Mrittunjoy School of Mymensingh', as he recollects, 'there were separate benches for the Hindus and Muslims in each class. On his first day at the school, since he sat on a bench specified for the Hindus, he was heckled by the students as well as by the teachers.' Not only that, he used to be called 'Mian Sahib', a derogatory expression to abuse Muslims, 'by the students and the teachers'.[345]

Muslims were reported to have had a general apathy to English education and therefore there were fewer Muslim students, most of whom in any case could not afford to go to the high schools and colleges in towns (the centres of student political activity). Those who came to the urban areas for education were more career-minded and thus psychologically may have been apolitical and sometimes anti-political too. Moreover the close association of both the organizations with the Hindu-dominated Congress aggravated the situation further. Muslim politicians' pro-government stand and success in ensuring 'gains' for the Muslims encouraged Muslim students to dissociate themselves from nationalist politics.

With the formation of ABSA, the Muslim politicians also considered creating a Muslim student organization. Though formed in 1932,[346] the All-Bengal Muslim Students Association (ABMSA) had an informal existence earlier through its pro-government activities in different forms. During the civil disobedience, when ABSA decided to boycott English educational institutions, the Muslims, under the patronage of their politicians, adopted a resolution urging the students 'not to boycott the institutions as it was detrimental to the national interests and that of the Muslim community in particular'.[347] With its formal inauguration, the organization became more integrally connected with the administration, and on occasions, the representatives of the administration were invited too.[348] The pro-government stance of the ABMSA precluded the possibility of any united Hindu–Muslim organization.

Assessment

The analysis of the period between 1928 and 1940 strongly suggests that internecine conflicts between the groups over the control of the Congress organization had its root in an ideological schism. It has been shown that the majority of the Bengal congressmen, because of their antipathy to Gandhism, lacked ideological solidarity with either the High Command or High Command-sponsored congressmen in Bengal. Worried by the rise and growing consolidation of the left forces at the national level under Subhas, the right wingers, such as Azad, Prasad and Patel, lost no opportunity to thwart the threat. In the face of strong hurdles (the opposition of the Indian business community, the consolidation of Muslim forces and the operation of imperial interests) Subhas maintained his support at least in terms of controlling the majority of the DCCs. His alliance with Gandhi whom he did not oppose openly until 1939 reflects his tactical sense. However, even though Bose had built a strong anti-right-wing forum at the regional level and created its possibility on a national level, he failed to evolve sufficiently concrete policies. Here is the limitation of an urban leader who failed in building an organization to back his ideology of action. He conceived of a mass uprising involving the peasants and workers but his ideology emphasizing terrorist means was not adequately suited to it.

Successful Bengal provincial leaders thought of involving the actors of the 'unorganized world' in the anti-British struggle; but they never endeavoured to draw them by way of evolving concrete plans and programmes espousing their cause. In the case of industrial labour, as shown in chapter 3, the Congress because of the national democratic line not only failed to attract workers but also alienated them to a large extent.

Concluding comments

The phenomenon of the decline of Congress in Bengal was so complex that it deserves to be studied with reference to the entire socio-economic and political matrix of the region. Attributing it primarily to factionalism, as J. Gallagher has, is to leave out other important dimensions of political reality. Factionalism, based on vaguely defined but real ideological differences, partly accounts for the failure of the Congress; and this factor contributed to a process which began, in fact, from the beginning of the century with the Congress's lukewarm attitude towards the actors of the 'unorganized world'. The advantage was reaped by the KPP with its ostensibly pro-peasant stance.

Concentration on urban politics also contributed to the decline. The KPP leadership emerged from below in the sense that it had its roots in the rural society, while the Congress leadership consisted primarily of the 'middle class' with a residual rural link; it is therefore not surprising that their political idioms made little noticeable impact on the masses. The small impact it did make was the result of the successful effort of the local Congress workers in making the Congress message intelligible to them. Congress's success in Arambag, Bankura and Midnapore exemplifies this. On the other hand, Congress faced serious threats to its representative character in east Bengal. The economic grievances of the predominantly Muslim pesantry against their upper-caste Hindu landlords, the gradual emergence of a powerful Muslim intermediary tenurial class, and the Congress's intimate ties with the upper-caste Hindu intermediary tenure holders, created a milieu that was easily susceptible to communalist propaganda. Under these circumstances, conflicts at the grass roots, which were agrarian in nature, became communal. The persistent failure of the Congress, as a result of ideological limitation, to adopt concrete steps to change popular impressions, prepared the ground for the communal elements to operate politically, putting the Bengal Congress in a suffocating situation, from which it could not escape.

Conclusion

Not only did the period between 1928 and 1940 witness a radical transformation in the Bengal agrarian economy, it was also marked by significant changes in the prevailing ideological orientation of both the Hindu and Muslim political leadership. A consequence of these changes was the drive to extend the 'organized' politics into the hitherto neglected 'unorganized' world. What it meant was the adoption of concrete programmes, designed not only to mobilize but also to incorporate the new constituents as integral parts of both socio-economic and national movements.

To the provincial Congress leadership, it was not an easy task because of the historically deep-rooted Hindu–Muslim cleavage, the emergence of Muslim political organizations with communal aims, and the weakness of the BPC as a result of factional schism based in significant degrees on a not fully articulated ideological division. Given these features of the provincial political arithmetic, Bengal was radically different from the rest of India; and, therefore, political movements within the province, both against the state and against local vested interests, never quite fit into the all-India pattern. In this concluding chapter, an attempt will be made to seek an explanation on the basis of the diverse facts which have emerged in the foregoing analysis.

Bengal was characteristically different from the rest of India. The fact that it was more thoroughly 'colonized' than any other part of India marks it off from the rest. Thus it should be emphasized that Bengal's socio-economic development was influenced significantly by the conditions imposed under colonialism. The British system of land tenure, the lack of industrial development and the destruction of indigenous manufacturing contributed directly to the formation of a 'middle class' who became 'rent-receivers', virtually divorced from land except in some cases as suppliers of credit. With a gradual decrease of rental income, this social category responded energetically to English education which provided them with an alternative source to supplement or increase their earnings. The fact that this group, comprising principally the Hindu upper castes, continued to depend on English education not only maintained but also extended the distance of this group from the agricultural production process. The entire socio-economic and cultural context thus created a new social category, identified neither with the class owning the means of production nor with those selling labour for survival.

Similarly, the heterogeneous demographic composition of Bengal and the disproportionate economic development of Hindus and Muslims created unique political tensions. The combination of religious appeals with economic grievances of the Muslim peasant led to a situation in which conflicts which were primarily agrarian in character assumed communal dimensions. The problem was aggravated by the growing desire of the educated Muslims for a share in government jobs and learned professions, hitherto monopolized by the upper-caste Hindus. As a result of a temporary successful accommodation of the newly emerged Muslim middle class by agreement at the elite level, C. R. Das built a united anti-British platform involving both Hindus and Muslims following on the Non-Co-operation–Khilafat movement. Likewise, by championing the working-class cause against the employer, he introduced a new constituent to nationalist politics. The unity forged between Hindus and Muslims and the linking of sporadic working-class agitations to the broader political struggle were indicative of a new phase in provincial politics. In fact, as our analysis has shown, Das's political ideology and strategic calculations set the general tone of Congress politics in Bengal even after his death.

What was hinted at in Das's politics was more fully developed by Subhas Chandra Bose, one of his principal lieutenants who endeavoured to build a strong Congress support base following his mentor in a changed socio-economic and political environment which saw the emergence and consolidation of anti-Congress political forces. The formation of the Praja Samiti, and later of the KPP which had a declared objective of protecting one community against the other, drew a large number of Muslims from Congress. By highlighting the uneven development of the two religious groups, the newly emerged Muslim leadership developed its support base quickly among the Muslims irrespective of socio-economic differences. The Congress's intimate ties with upper-caste intermediary landed interests, and its explicit policy of protecting them through institutional means, consolidated the division further. Constrained by its communal aims, the KPP was however unable to link the agrarian question with the broader anti-imperialist struggle and thus was confined to the east-Bengal Muslims. Because the KPP leadership saw the explanation of Muslim economic backwardness in the disproportionate Hindu dominance in all spheres of life, it failed to perceive the nature of contradictions in a colonial society; and therefore the possibility of a movement involving the underprivileged, regardless of religion, was unrealized.

Moreover, the inherent political differences between the KPP and the BPC provided the colonial state with an autonomous character. By enacting agrarian legislations, the state strove to demonstrate its willingness to ensure the economic interests of a relatively underprivileged section of the agricultural population. The Congress's opposition to the 1928 Bengal Tenancy (Amendment) Act and neutrality on the 1938 Amendment not only alienated the peasant masses from the Congress but also projected the image of the state as an arbiter of justice in view of the ameliorating stance of the above legislations.

So the situation facing the BPC leadership, including Subhas Chandra Bose, was more complex than in Das's time. In order to expand the boundaries of national political struggle, the Bengal Congress strove to incorporate peasants and workers into its organization. The peasantry as a constituent was less probable because of the BPC's pronounced bias toward intermediary landed interests – a bias utilized by Muslim political groups to consolidate the anti-Congress platform especially in east Bengal where a significant proportion of mahajan and talukdar were Hindu. Among the workers, the Bengal Congress had an initial success. But its national democratic ideology, insisting on an amicable relationship between the workers and the industrialists, divided the working class. Although the Congress never succeeded in bringing a large number of workers to its platform, its ideological position is nonetheless defensible. As a national democratic organization fighting for political freedom, the motive force of the Congress was nationalism and thus its leaders intervened in labour struggles on behalf of the nation to control/oppose working-class movements perceived as contrary to the national interest. In other words, to the Congress, since the 'national bourgeoisie' were playing a historical role in strengthening the anti-imperialist struggle, they were to be protected against working-class efforts to undermine their economic strength. In so consistently defending indigenous capitalists, Congress also ignored the inherent contradiction between labour and capital. Subhas Chandra Bose's role in the 1928 TISCO strike exemplifies Congress's concern in guarding the native capitalist.

Congress's involvement with the labour movement indicates another dimension of its ideology: trade unionism was not independent of the nationalist struggle which brought together antagonistic socio-political forces with anti-imperialist sentiments. Bose's insistence on this at the 1931 Calcutta session of the AITUC caused a split within the working-class organization. Although the split had a significant impact on the Indian labour movement, it nonetheless illustrated an ideological consistency of Bose who, as a national democrat, never allowed other socio-political forces to undermine Congress and its goal.

Bose's way of forging a link between the 'organized' and 'unorganized' worlds of politics marks him off from other contemporary Congress leaders. His nationalism was primarily one from the top. He was opposed to the alien power but strove at the same time to utilize the state machinery to the advantage of the nationalist cause. His faith in a strong state was so deep-rooted that he, in the public speeches and private correspondence, always argued in its favour as the only means to solve India's multifarious problems. This is what differentiates Bose from Gandhi who insisted on decentralization of government and providing the masses with the power for self-rule. By simultaneously defending a strong authoritarian state and accepting 'leftism', Bose indicated another interesting part of middle-class ideology. Although his leftism was exasperatingly vague and corresponded with anti-Gandhism, his elaboration of the theme clearly indicates that he upheld parliamentary left tradition. In consistently following this line, Bose posed serious threats to the Gandhi-led Congress High Command. The 1939 Tripuri crisis exemplified the battle between two ideological forces; Bose's resignation from the Congress presidency and later suspension from the Congress showed the weakness of the Bose-led militant leadership *vis-à-vis* the High Command.

What is evident in Bose-type middle-class leadership is the tendency to operate from the top. The provincial political structure and the excessive importance of Calcutta helped strengthen it further. For instance, the fact that the vast Bengali rural masses had no role in the Calcutta-based formal representative institutions clearly indicates the distance between the seats of power and the majority of people. By the continued dominance of the middle classes in these forums, they became, without any link to the grass roots, the representatives of the nation. With the advent of mass politics in the 1920s, there were effective challenges to the provincial Congress leadership from those local Congress leaders with a mass base. The Congress survived the attack by adapting its policies and programmes to the changed environment. But what eclipsed Congress power was the emergence and consolidation of Muslim political groups under the KPP–League alliance on the basis of communal sentiments. Not only were the urban Muslims organized, the vast majority of east-Bengal Muslim peasants were brought under its banner to end Hindu-dominated Congress hegemony in the province.

The drive to organize the underprivileged against vested interests had potential for a qualitatively different political movement; but because of the utilization of communal socio-economic grievances to mobilize the masses, the movement never became an all-Bengal phenomenon. Likewise, the hinted possibility of a rich-peasant movement – as was manifested in the KPP's stated objective of protecting the Muslim intermediary landed interests – was never realized because of the overarching dominance of the Muslim middle class in its leadership. By acting as representatives of specific socio-economic and cultural interests, the Muslim leadership, like its Hindu counterpart, failed not only to rise above narrow sectional interests but also to adopt a purposeful programme for leadership over economy and society.

It can be argued that, because of the peculiar social development of Bengal under colonial rule, there emerged a unique middle class which, unlike its European counterpart, lacked a clear vision of its 'class goals' and therefore never succeeded in building a provincial alliance of all anti-imperialist classes. The political implications of these distortions had a far-reaching impact on Bengal's political economy: the middle-class political activists were nationalists and therefore their aim was to replace the British with Indians. While their sacrifice for the nationalist cause deserves much appreciation, their failure to build a broad anti-British political platform needs to be critically analysed. By insisting on agreement between the Hindus and Muslims at the elite level, the Hindu middle-class-dominated Bengal Congress ignored the agrarian dimension of the problem. Similarly, in its zeal to protect the native capitalists, the Hindu leadership overlooked the inevitable contradictions between labour and capital. Also, by developing and consolidating the organization on communal sentiments, the Muslim leadership equally failed to understand the complexity of the Hindu–Muslim question which deserved to be evaluated within the broader socio-economic, political and cultural nexus of a colonial society. Thus to attribute Muslim backwardness to Hindu economic dominance evades the adverse effects of imperialism and also demonstates the failure of the leadership to view the phenomenon in its proper perspective. Although there were movements in some localities indicating the contrary, the dominating influence of the middle class, backed by a strong organizational network, determined the political future of the province. Thus, notwithstanding the opposition of a number of leading Bengali politicians, the 1947 partition plan appeared to be the only plausible political solution to the Hindu–Muslim question.

Even after the 1947 division of Bengal, the middle-class tradition continued to influence the political arithmetic of the respective states. Although the flow of communication between the 'organized' and 'unorganized' worlds of politics was more frequent, there was a definite continuity between the pre- and post-colonial Bengali political leaderships: it was an urban professional group with virtually no link with the production economy. It is difficult to discern a pattern among the east-Bengal leaders because of the imposition of military rule practically from its inception. There have been indications of a different type of leadership (e.g. Maulana Bhasani), but given the restriction on normal political activities and the maintenance of junta rule, the possibility has not been realized.

In west Bengal, the parliamentary tradition continued more firmly. What is remarkable is the similarity between the pre- and post-1947 west-Bengal leadership. Until 1967, the Bengal Congress, dominated by middle-class professional people, maintained its hegemony in the provincial institutional political authority. There were several ameliorating legislations designed to benefit the working class and the agrarian masses; but they were devices from the 'top' to temporarily dampen the tension which had its root in the antagonism between 'haves' and 'have nots'. Since 1967, left political forces have continuously ruled the province except for a five-year gap between 1971 and 1976. In its composition, the leadership is qualitatively different in the sense that it is broad based, incorporating new elements which decisively influence policy decisions. What distinguishes the present leadership from its past counterparts is that policy formulation is not always the result of initiatives from the top but is also a response to demands from the grass roots. But the acceptance of parliamentary left tradition provides a continuity in the nature of leadership: the state is still regarded as the instrument to gain maximum advantage for the oppressed classes. By adopting legislative measures aiming to benefit the landless/agricultural labourers, the left forces have been striving to expand their support base. Since there is no landed magnate *per se*, the nature of contradiction between the 'haves' and 'have nots' in rural west Bengal has changed.

In the challenge – backed by the left-front government as a matter of principle – of the agricultural labourers to the petty landowners, a new contradiction has arisen. It is too early to predict the outcome. Likewise, on the labour front, the left state power adopted an ideology aimed at reconciliation between labour and capital by striving to bargain a maximum for the labour. The insistence on a peaceful settlement within a democratic set-up reminds us of the pre-1947 middle-class leadership. But there exists a qualitative difference between the two: unlike its pre-independence counterpart, the present leadership is perfectly aware of the inherent antagonistic contradiction between labour and capital, and the defence of the peaceful settlement indicates its strategic sense. Notwithstanding these noticeable changes, there is still a striking continuity between the pre- and post-1947 Bengali political leadership.

Appendix I
Biographical Sketches of Leading Political Activists

Ahmad, Abul Mansur (1897–?) A journalist-cum-politician and a leading member of the KPP, Mansur joined the Muslim League in 1944 and held a responsible position. See Abul Mansur Ahmad, *Atmakatha* (Dacca, 1878).

Ahmad, Mazzaffar (1889–1973) Belonged to a poor lower-middle-class Bengali family; matriculated in 1913 but could not succeed in the Inter-Arts examination; drawn to politics in 1916; became assistant secretary (1918–20) of the Bangiya Mussalman Sahitya Samiti, and ran its monthly journal *Bangiya Mussalman Sahitya Patrika* almost single handed; with Nazrul Islam, he edited *Navayug*; was deeply influenced by Marxist ideas and the 1917 Bolshevik Revolution; implicated by the government in several conspiracy cases, first in the 1917–24 Peshwar Conspiracy Case and detained in 1923, but released in 1925 on medical grounds; attended the 1925 Kanpur Communist Conference. Along with Nazrul Islam, Muzaffar Ahmad organized the Workers and Peasants Party in 1926. He edited its weekly mouthpiece *Langal*, which in 1926 became *Ganavani*. Became the vice-president of the AITUC, 1928–9; played a prominent role in the 1928–9 strike of jute workers. Detained in the 1929 Meerut conspiracy case. After his release in 1936 he organized the All-India Kishan Sabha. A BPCC member, 1927–8 and 1937, and an AICC members in 1929 and 1937. Imprisoned in 1942, went underground after release in December 1942; became elected to the CPI central committee; imprisoned between 1948 and 1951, again held after the 1962 Chinese attack; founder member of the CPI(M). See Naresh Kumar Jain ed., *Muslims in India: a Biographical Dictionary* (New Delhi, 1983), vol. II, p. 78.

Ahmad, Shamsuddin (1889–1969) Belonged to Nadia, graduated from Presidency College, Calcutta; took a Law degree and joined

Calcutta High Court in 1917. He participated in the Non-Co-operation movement; became secretary of the provincial Khilafat Committee; he was also the secretary of the BPCC between 1921 and 1925. Elected to the Bengal Legislative Council in 1927 as a nominee of the Congress. He was an elected Calcutta Corporation commissioner from 1933 to 1936. A founder member of the KPP, Shamsuddin was elected its secretary in 1935. He was elected to the 1937 Bengal Legislative Assembly. He was the leader of the KPP when Haq joined the Muslim League. He was a minister in the first provincial cabinet, between 1941 and 1943, and also between January 1946 and August 1947. He joined the League in 1944. After the creation of Pakistan, he was appointed Pakistan's Ambassador to Burma. See Humaira Momen, *Muslim Politics in Bengal: a Study of the Krishak Praja Party and the elections of 1937* (hereafter *Muslims in Bengal*) (Dacca, 1972), pp. 89–90.

Ali, Nausher (1890–1972)   Born to a poor but respectable family of Jessore, he had a struggling academic career. A law graduate of the Calcutta University, Nausher Ali began his legal practice in 1915. In 1927 he was elected chairman of Jessore District Board, a position he held for a decade. In 1929, he was elected to the Bengal Legislative Council. He was associated with the Praja Samiti since its inception in 1929. He was elected to the Bengal Legislative Assembly in 1937 as a KPP member. He joined the Haq ministry. In 1938, he resigned from the cabinet owing to his differences with Haq over the question of the release of poitical prisoners. In 1941 he joined Congress and was imprisoned in 1942. He was speaker of the Legislative Assembly 1943–5. He opposed the 1947 partition plan. He was a member of the Indian Provisional Parliament from 1950 to 1952 and of the Rajya Sabha 1952–6 and 1962–8. He was also a member of the West Bengal Legislative Assembly between 1957 and 1962. See H. Momen, *Muslim Politics in Bengal*, p. 92.

Aney, M. S. (1880–1968)   Educated at Morris College, Nagpur, Aney was appointed a teacher of Cashibai Private High School, Amraoti, 1904–7; he joined the bar in 1908 at Yeotmal, MP; became vice-president of the Home Rule League, president of the Berar PCC, 1921–30, and acting president of the AICC, 1933; member, Berar Legislative Council, 1924–6, 1927–30; member Congress Working Committee, 1924–5, 1931–4; general secretary, Congress Nationalist Party, 1934; general secretary of the anti-Communal Award Conference, 1935; vice-chancellor,

Tilak Vidyapith, Poona in 1939. See *Whos Who in India, Burma and Ceylon (illustrated), 1940–41* (Bombay, 1940), pp. 100–1.

Ansari, M. A. (1880–1936) Sunni Muslim, joined Edinburgh University in 1901 and took MB, LRCP and MRCP in 1903 and MD and MS in 1905. Led an all-India medical mission to Turkey in 1912–13, to provide medical aid to Turkish army in the Balkan War; joined All-India Muslim League in 1915 and had a prominent role in the 1916 Lucknow Pact; member of the 1920 Muslim deputation to the Viceroy regarding Khilafat issue; member of the 1921 Khilafat deputation to Europe; in 1926, he joined Congress and was Congress general secretary in 1929, 1931 and 1932. He opposed council entry. He was elected president of the All-Parties Conference, Calcutta, 1928. Took a leading part in the Home Rule League Movement, 1917–18; had a prominent part in the eighteen days hartal against Rowlatt Bills, 1919; played an active role in the boycott of the Simon Commission and was imprisoned in 1930 for six months; one of the founders of the Jamia Millia University, Delhi and Kashi Vidyapith, Benaras. See Jain, *Muslims in India*, pp. 94–5.

Azad, Maulana (1888–1958) Real name Muhiyuddin Ahmad; was born in Mecca of Arab descent on his mother's side; had no formal education at any *madrassah* (school of Islamic learning); he had received a strict religious education at home, yet he was reputed as a scholar through his writings on literature and religion. In his early youth, he became involved with 'revolutionary terrorism'. A stalwart of the Congress, he became Education Minister of independent India. See *DNB*, vol. I, pp. 92–3.

Bahar, Habibullah (1906–?) Born in Noakhali of east Bengal, graduated from the Calcutta Islamia College in 1928; took active part in the Non-Co-operation movement and later joined the KPP and became its joint secretary; joined the Muslim League and became member of its working committee, 1937–47; secretary of the Bengal Provincial Muslim League, 1940–3; member of the Bengal Legislative Assembly, 1944. See Jain, *Muslims in India*, pp. 116–17.

Baqui, Abdullahel (1890–1952) Born in Dinajpur and educated in different madrassahas. He actively participated in the Khilafat–Non-Co-operation movement of 1919–21. As Fazlul HHaq assumed the presidency of the Bengal Provincial Muslim League in 1937, he became President of the KPP in 1938. See

Abul Mansur Ahmad, *Amar Dekha Rajnitir Panchhas Bachhar* (Dacca, 1968), pp. 180, 183.

Bose, Sarat (1889–1950)   A renowned Calcutta lawyer, joined active politics under C. R. Das. He represented the Calcutta University constituency in the provincial legislature from 1926 to 1929 when the Congress members withdrew from the council in pursuance of the AICC directive. He became the leader of the Congress Parliamentary Party in Bengal under the 1935 Act. He was also a member of the 1946 interim Indian government. See *DNB*, vol. I, pp. 223–4.

Chamanlal, Dewan (1892–?)   Founder member of the AITUC; member, Central Legislative Assembly 1923–31; member, Royal Commission of Labour 1928–31; represented India at the International Labour Conference in Geneva in 1928, 1932 and 1946; member, Punjab Legislative Assembly 1936–45; member, Constituent Assembly 1946–8; Ambassador of India in Turkey 1948–9; member, Rajya Sabha 1952–67. *JNSW*, vol. III, p. 128.

Chatterjee, Amarendranath (?–1957)   A Brahman, came from Hooghly and was actively associated with the revolutionary movement from 1907; imprisoned several times; in 1929 he was elected to the central legislature; a member of the Bengal Legislative Assembly 1937–45; in 1935, he joined Madan Mohan Malaviya's *Jatiya Dal* which he left in 1945 and joined M. N. Roy's Radical Democratic Party. See *DNB*, vol. I, pp. 267–9.

Chatterjee, Jibanlal (1889–1970)   A Brahman, hailed from Faridpur and joined revolutionary terrorist campaign at its early stage; imprisoned 1916–20. On his release, he temporarily worked with Mazaffar Ahmad of the Communist Party, At this stage he had contact with M. N. Roy; became BPCC secretary in 1930; joined M. N. Roy and remained there until 1943 when he formed his own party, the Democratic Vanguard Party, which later became the Workers' Party of India. See *DNB*, vol. I, pp. 274–5.

Chaudhuri, Ashrafuddin Ahmed (?–?)   Born to a Bengali middle-class family with some connection in land; associated with various local movements in Comilla; drawn to the provincial Congress politics as a recognition of his active part in the Non-Co-operation–Khilafat movement; became the BPCC secretary in 1928; organized civil disobedience in east Bengal; a lieutenant of Subhas Bose; elected the BPCC secretary again in 1938 and continued until 1940; joned the Forward Bloc in 1939.

See Abul Kalam Shamsuddin, *Atit Diner Smriti* (Dacca, 1968), p. 138. WBSA, W/498/1940, Ban on Forward Bloc.

Chunder, Nirmal (1885–1953)   One of the Big Five, Chunder came of a wealthy and influential Kayastha family. He, a solicitor, representing the family law firm founded by his great grandfather, entered public life as a commissioner of the Calcutta Corporation in 1915, ending it with the mayoralty in 1953. He was elected to the BLC in 1923 and the India Legislative Council in 1926 on the ticket of the Swaraj Party. He held the BPCC presidency in 1931 (for a short period). In 1935 he became an AICC member and left the position in protest against the Congress's ambivalent attitude to the Communal Award. He then joined the Congress Nationalist Party. He was elected to the Bengal Assembly on its ticket. See *DNB*, vol. I, p. 319.

Dasgupta, Satis (1881–1979)   A Baidya, who was a favourite student of the renowned nationalist-chemist P. C. Ray, became a staunch Gandhian in the 1920s. Founder of the Kahdi Pratisthan, a handloom industry at Sodepur of 24 Parganas. After independence, he remained associated with the Village Industrial Board, Bharat Sevak Samaj and Khadi Commission. Author of several books on cottage industries, he was also the editor of the Bengali edition of the *Harijan* and translated a number of Gandhi's works in Bengali. See *DNB*, vol. I, pp. 371–2.

Ghosh, S. M. (1893–?)   A Kayastha, the leader of the Mymensingh group of the Jugantor Party. He simultaneously held the presidency of the Mymensingh DCC in 1928. In 1938, he became the BPCC president. He was elected to the Constituent Assembly in 1946. He was a member of the 1957 Lokshaba and was elected to the Rajya Sabha in 1962 when he also became the deputy leader of the Parliamentary Congress Party. See *DNB*, vol. II, pp. 63–4.

Ghuznavi, A. H. (1876–1953)   Beginning his political career in the 1905–8 Swadeshi agitation, he joined the Muslim League in 1916. He represented the Bengali Muslims on the 1931 Round Table Conference and was a member of the Joint Committee on Indian Constitutional Reform in which he argued strongly for a 'separate electorate'. On the eve of the 1947 partition, he joined Sarat Bose in strengthening the 'Greater Bengal Movement'. See Jain, *Muslims in India*, vol. I, p. 180.

Goswami, T. C. (1898–1957)   A Brahman and a member of the Big Five, Goswami gave up his legal practice and joined the 1921 Non-Co-operation movement. A financier of the Swaraj Party he also edited, for some time, its English language mouthpiece, *Forward.* He represented Bengal in the Indian Legislative Assembly in 1923. He was elected to the Bengal Legislative Assembly in 1937 and became the Finance Minister in the Nazimuddin ministry in 1943. He left the Congress in protest against the 1947 partition plan. He retired from politics following his defeat in the 1952 Indian parliamentary elections. An Oxford graduate, he was well versed in contemporary mathematical philosophy, a fluent speaker in French and German and a brilliant parliamentarian in English. See *DNB*, vol. II, pp. 87–8.

Haq, A. K. Fazlul (1873–1962)   Born in the Kazi family of Chakkar in Bakerganj of east Bengal, Fazlul Haq had a brilliant academic career. He joined the government service as a Deputy Magistrate and Collector in 1906 and became Assistant Registrar of Rural Co-operative Societies in eastern Bengal and Assam. He was a member of the Bengal Legislative Council from 1913 to 1936. He took a leading part in the formulation of the 1916 Lucknow Pact and was both the general secretary of the All-India Congress and the president of the All-India Muslim League in 1918. In 1924 he became the Education Minister of Bengal for a short period. Haq was the founder member of the Nikhia Banga Praja Samiti which became the KPP in 1936. In 1930–1 he participated in the Round Table Conference and advocated a 'separate electorate' for the Muslims. In the 1937 provincial elections, he was elected with an overwhelming majority from two constituencies. He then led the first coalition ministry which lasted till 1940. Meanwhile Haq joined the Muslim League. In March 1940, he moved the Lahore Resolution (known as Pakistan resolution). At the end of 1941, he was expelled from the League as he differed with Jinnah on the question of his resignation from the Viceroy's War Council. He then led a KPP–Congress coalition ministry until 1943. After the creation of Pakistan, he became the Advocate-General of East Pakistan. In 1955 he joined the central cabinet of Pakistan as the Minister of Interior. He was the East Pakistan Governor between 1956 and 1958. See H. Momen, *Muslim Politics in Bengal*, pp. 81–2.

Haque, Azizul (1890–1947) Born at Shantipur of Nadia, Azizul Haque graduated from Presidency College, Calcutta, and after obtaining a law degree he started legal practice at Krishnanagar in 1915. He became chairman of the Municipal Board of Shantipur. He was appointed Public Prosecutor for Nadia district in 1926. He was elected to the Bengal Legislative Council in 1929. He was education Minister of Bengal from 1934 to 1937. Joined the Muslim League in 1937 and was elected speaker to the 1937 Bengal Legislative Assembly. He became Vice-Chancellor of Calcutta University in 1938. In 1941 he became High Commissioner for India in London, and in 1943 member in charge of commerce and food, Government of India. He continued to be a member of the Governor's general executive council till 1945. He was elected to the Bengal Legislative Assembly in 1946. He was knighted in 1937 and was bestowed a CIE in 1942. See H. Momen, *Muslims in Bengal*, pp. 83–4.

Homi, Manek (?–?) Born to a Bombay-based Parsi family, Manek started his professional career as a petty officer of TISCO; went to the USA for training in steel-making; he was refused employment in TISCO when he came back; he criticized the Tariff Commission for approving TISCO's application for 'trade protection'; his father lost his TISCO job; never a trade unionist, but a good orator and had a good sense of tactics; involved in the 1928 TISCO strike from the outset but never succeeded in uniting the workers; had participated in the 1929 Tinplate strike but without much success; left Jamshedpur in 1931. See IOR, V/26/670/1931, memorandum on labour dispute in Jamshedpur, 1920–30 by J. R. Dain, Singhbhum District Commissioner; and also L/PJ/12/1926, Fortnight Report for the first half of June, 1931.

Islamabadi, Maniruzzaman (?–?) Born to a lower-middle-class Bengali Muslim family of Chittagong; started his career as a journalist and was actively involved in *Dainik Soltan*; drawn to provincial Congress politics during the Non-Co-operation–Khilafat movement, 1919–21; supported Subhas Bose after J. M. Sengupta's death in 1933; joined the Forward Bloc in 1940; imprisoned in 1942 for his alleged link with the INA. See Abul Kalam Shamsuddin, *Atit Diner Smriti* (Dacca, 1968), pp. 137–8.

Isphani, A. H. (1902–?) Belonged to Punjab, son of Mirza Isphani, a leading industrialist; joined family business in 1925; elected a councillor to the Calcutta Corporation in 1933, but resigned in 1935 and worked for the introduction of separate electorate in the Corporation; re-elected in 1940, became deputy mayor, 1941–2; elected to the Bengal Legislative Assembly in 1937 as a Muslim League member; re-elected in 1946; secretary of the Bengal Provincial Muslim League, 1936–47, member of All-Indian Muslim League Working Committee till 1947; member of the 1941 Muslim League committee to draw up a five-year plan and for the educational, economic, social and political advancement of Muslims; active in Pakistan politics after 1947. See Jain, *Muslims in India*, vol. I, p. 221.

Kasem, Abul (?–1936) Belonged to Burdwan, west Bengal; participated in the anti-partition agitation and Swadeshi movement in Bengal; perhaps the only Bengali Muslim to attain any kind of prominence in Congress affairs or organization prior to 1905; was elected member of the 1904 Congress Constitutional Committee; secretary, Bengal Muhammadan Association, founded in 1906 to counter the Muslim League; was the editor of the English weekly *Mussalman*; took active part in the 1913 Muslim League annual session; moved a resolution urging the repeal of the Press Act; wanted Muslims to be given effective (but not separate) representation in the legislature; member of the 1916 Reforms Commission; favoured the implementation of the 1916 Lucknow Pact; member of the committee to frame a scheme for organizing public activities among Muslims in consultation with the Working Committee of the Central Khilafat Committee, 1924; chairman of the Aziz group Muslim League – in his welcome speech, he defended the Communal Award. Jain, *Muslims in India*, vol. I, p. 46.

Khan, Aga III (1877–1957) Belonged to an illustrious Shi'a family of Persia; led the 1909 Muslim deputation to Lord Minto to demand separate Muslim electorate; was perhaps the only top Muslim leader to welcome the undoing of the partition of Bengal, 'as it had deeply wounded and not unnaturally the sentiments of the great Bengali speaking millions of India; wanted the Muslims to voluntarily abandon the public slaughter of cows to win the goodwill of Hindus; resigned from the Muslim League in 1913; presided over All-Parties Muslim Conference in Delhi, 1929, and All-India Muslim Conference, 1936, which accepted 'dominion status'; was loyal to the British (Davidson's diary); was sent as an emissary to various countries to remove misunderstanding between them and the British; a leading delegate to the 1931-2 Round Table Conference, where he pressed for the claims of Muslims and other minorities; led Indian delegation to the League of Nations, 1932, 1934-6; first elected (Indian) president of the League of Nations in 1937; represented India at the World Disarmament Conference, 1934; was a privy councillor, 1937; decorated with British galore; granted rank and status of first-class chief with a salute of 11 guns; KCIE, 1898; GCIE, 1902; GCSI, 1911; GCNO, 1923; founder member of the Aligarh University, its pro-Vice-Chancellor, 1920-30, Vice-Chancellor, 1921. See Jain, *Muslims in India*, pp. 54-6. Also see Robert Rhodes James, *Memoirs of a Conservative: J. C. C. Davidson's Memoirs and Papers, 1910-17* (London, 1969), p. 394.

Khan, Akram (1868?-1968) Born at Hakimpur of Twenty-four Parganas, he came of a family that traces its descent from the 'Pirali Brahmans', a collateral branch of Rabindranath Tagore's family of Joransanko. He was educated at his village school and at Alia Madrassah, Calcutta. He acquired a mastery of both the Bengali language and literature and Arabic and Islamic lore and came to be known as *maulana* (Islamic teacher). He founded several Bengali journals and newspapers which contributed a great deal to the regeneration of Muslims of Bengal. These are: *Weekly Mohammadi* (1910), *Daily Sevak* (1922), *Monthly Mohammadi* (1927) and *Daily Azad* (1936). He wrote *Mustafa Charit*, a monumental work in Bengali on the life of the prophet of Islam. See H. Momen, *Muslims in Bengal*, pp. 88-9.

Khan, Tamijuddin (1889-1963) Graduating from Presidency College, Calcutta, Khan obtained MA and BL degrees from the Calcutta University and started legal practice in 1915. Joined the Non-Co-operation–Khilafat movement and became involved in the National College in 1921. He was imprisoned for his association with the Congress. After his release in 1922, he resumed his legal practice and became vice-chairman of Faridpur Municipality and chairman of Faridpur District Board. He was elected to the Bengal Legislative Council in 1926 as a Swaraj Party member; elected to the 1937 Bengal Legislative Assembly as a Muslim League member. A member of the Bengal cabinet between 1937 and 1941, and again from 1943 to 1946, he was also elected to the Indian Legislative Assembly in 1946, to the Pakistan Constituent Assembly in 1947 and to the National Assembly in 1962. He was elected President of the Constituent

Assembly of Pakistan in 1948 and held the position until 1954 when the Assembly itself was dissolved by Goalm Mohammad, the Governor-General of Pakistan. See H. Momen, *Muslims in Bengal*, pp. 93–4.

Majumdar, Bhupati (1890–1973)   A Baidya, came from Hooghly of west Bengal and was an influential member of the Jugantor group; incarcerated in 1930 and released in the early 1940s; became a minister in the west-Bengal cabinet in 1950. See *DNB*, vol. III, pp. 19–20.

Malaviya, Madan Mohan (1861–1946)   President of the Indian National Congress, 1909 and 1918; member of the Imperial Legislative Council, 1910–19 and of the Indian Legislative Assembly, 1924–30; President of the Hindu Mahasabha, 1916–17, 1923–4, 1926 and 1935; founder of the Benaras Hindu University and its Vice-Chancellor, 1919–31; was well known for his devout orthodoxy. See *JNSW*, vol. I, p. 127.

Mukherjee, Jadugopal (1886–?)   A Brahman, was the son of a lawyer of Tamluk, Midnapore; joined the Calcutta Anushilan Samity in 1905; an active member in the Indo-German conspiracy to land arms in Bengal for the revolutionary terrorists; joined the Congress in the early 1920s; he went into semi-retirement from revolutionary activity in 1929 after a projected amalgamation scheme of the Jugantor and Anushilan groups had failed; he severed connections with the Congress party in protest against its acceptance of the 1947 partition plan. See *DNB*, vol. III, pp. 159–60.

Mukherjee, Shyama Prasad (1901–1951)   A Brahman, educated at Presidency College and in London; started his career as a lawyer in the Calcutta High Court; member of the Bengal Legislative Council from 1929 onwards. In 1938 he was Vice-Chancellor of the Calcutta University; elected to the Bengal Legislative Assembly in 1937. See Balraj Madhok, *Portrait of a Martyr: Biography of Shyama Prasad Mukherjee* (Bombay, 1969).

Nariman, K. F. (1885–1948)   A lawyer of Bombay; president of the Bombay Youth League 1928–9; president of the Bombay PCC 1929; mayor of Bombay 1935; left Congress in 1937 and helped Subhas Bose in forming All-India Forward Bloc; rejoined Congress after 1947. See *JNSW*, vol. III, p. 320.

Nazimuddin, Khwaja (1894–1964)   Born in the well-known Nawab family of Dacca, Nazimuddin was educated at Aligarh, London and Cambridge; elected chairman of the Dacca

Municipality, an office he held until 1929; became Minister of Education in 1929 and continued till 1934; member of the Bengal Executive Council from 1934 to 1937; appointed Home Minister in 1937 and held this office until he resigned in 1941; leader of the opposition and Muslim League in the Bengal Legislative Assembly between January 1942 and March 1943; member of the Muslim League Working Committee, 1937–47; in 1943 he formed the Muslim League ministry and became Chief Minister and continued to hold the office till 1945; elected to the Central Legislative Assembly in 1946 and to the Pakistan Constituent Assembly in 1947; became the first Chief Minister of east Pakistan in 1947 and succeeded Jinnah as Governor-General in 1948; in 1951 he succeeded Liaquat Ali Khan as Prime Minister of Pakistan; in 1953 he was removed from the office on grounds of inefficiency by Goalm Mohammad, the then Governor-General of Pakistan. See H. Momen, *Muslims in Bengal*, pp. 86–7.

Pant, Govind Ballabh (1887–1961) Educated at Almora and Allahabad; advocate of the Allahabad High Court; leader of the Swaraj Party in the UP Legislative Council, 1923–30; severely beaten along with Jawaharlal Nehru at Lucknow in the Simon Commission demonstration 1928 and received injuries from which he never fully recovered; suffered many terms of imprisonment; Premier, UP, 1937–9 and Chief Minister, 1946–55; Home Minister, Government of India, 1955–61. See *JNSW*, vol. III, p. 106.

Patel, V. J. (1870–1933) Elder brother of Vallabhbhai Patel; a barrister of the Bombay High Court; member of the Bombay Legislative Council, 1914; member of the Legislative Assembly, 1923; President of the Legislative Assembly, 1925–30. See *JNSW*, vol. III, p. 322.

Prasad, Rajendra (1884–1944) Set up legal practice in Patna; joined Gandhi in the 1917 Champaran Satyagraha; joined Non-Co-operation movement in 1920; President, Indian National Congress 1934, 1939 and 1947–8; served several terms of imprisonment; in charge of Food and Agriculture portfolio 1946–8; President of the Indian Constituent Assembly 1946–50; President of India 1950–62. See *JNSW*, vol. III, p. 4.

Roy, Anil Baran (1890–?) Born in the district of Burdwan; graduated in 1910; an MA in Philosophy and English, he also passed BL; worked as a lecturer in Philosophy in Hetampur

College at Birbhum and later at Bankura Wesleyan College; joined the Non-Co-operation movement in 1921; he joined the Swaraj Party in 1923; elected to the Bengal Legislative Council; arrested in 1924; after his release in 1926, he went to Pondicherry. See *DNB*, vol. III, pp. 530–1.

Roy, B. C. (1882–1962)   A Brahman, an MRCP and FRCS from Britain, joined politics while still teaching at the Carmichael College by defeating Surndranath Banerjee in the 1923 provincial elections; a member of the Big Five, he held various important positions in both provincial and national Congress hierarchy; became Mayor of Calcutta in 1931 and 1932; became the BPCC President; Calcutta University Vice-Chancellor between 1942 and 1944; in 1948 he became the west-Bengal Chief Minister and continued till his death in 1962. See *DNB*.

Roy, K. S. (?–1949)   Member of the Anushilan Samity who later joined C. R. Das's Swaraj Party in Bengal; leader of the Bengal Congress in 1939; leader of opposition in Bengal Assembly 1946; Deputy Chief Minister, west Bengal 1949. See *JNSW*, vol. III, p. 74.

Roy, M. N. (1893–1954)   His real name was Narendra Nath Bhattacharyya; founder member of the Jugantor Party in 1914; left India in 1916 and participated in revolutionary movements in Mexico and in European countries; in 1919 founded the Mexican Communist Party; one of the founder members of the Communist International; in 1927 he went to China as the representative of the Comintern; differed from the Comintern in 1928; returned to India in 1931, was arrested and sentenced to six months imprisonment; joined Congress for a short period; later founded the Radical Democratic Party and the Indian Federation of Labour; supported the government during the Second World War; after his break with communism became one of the principal exponents of radical humanism. See *JNSW*, vol. III, p. 250.

Sarkar, Nalini Ranjan (1885–1953)   From a middle-class Kayastha family of Mymensingh, east Bengal. Unlike the other Big Five leaders who were well educated, his formal education did not go beyond passing the Entrance examination; he entered the service of Hindustan Co-operative Insurance Society Ltd in a humble position from where he rose to the position of general manager and president. He had successfully sponsored several other groups of industrial and business concerns, like general insurance, a building society, glass works and heavy chemicals. His success in business had, in turn, opened his career in politics. In 1923 he was elected to the Bengal Legislative Council as a Swaraj member. He was also appointed the chief whip of the parliamentary Swaraj Party. In 1935, he became Mayor of Calcutta. Having served as a minister in the Bengal government under the 1935 Government of India Act, Sarkar became the Finance Minister in the west-Bengal government in 1948 and acting Chief Minister for a few months in 1949. See *DNB*, vol. II, pp. 71–2; and also *The Statesman*, 27 January 1953.

Sasmol, B. N. (1881–1934)   A Mahisya, an accredited leader of the agriculturally rich mahisya caste, Sasmol, a bar at law of Middle Temple, was a leading lawyer of Midnapore district court and Calcutta High Court. As a public figure he was more notable as the leader of the successful anti-Union Board agitation in Midnapore during the Non-Co-operation movement, he held the BPCC secretaryship in 1921, 1926 and briefly in 1927. He was the whip of the parliamentary Swaraj Party under C. R. Das. His relationship with the Swaraj Party became strained and he severed connection with it after 1927. See *DNB*, vol. IV, 1974, pp. 80–1.

Sengupta, J. M. (1885–1933)   A Baidya, educated at Presidency College, Calcutta, and Cambridge; started legal practice in Calcutta but abandoned it in 1921 and joined the Non-Co-operation movement; succeeded C. R. Das as the BPCC president; held 'triple crown' (BPCC, Swaraj Party leader and Mayor of Calcutta), between 1925 and 1926; acting President of the All-India Congress, 1930. See *JNSW*, vol. III, p. 174.

Siddiqi, A. R. (1887–?)   Sunni Muslim, born in Bombay; educated at Aligarh; went to Wadham College, Oxford, was called to the bar in 1922; started business in England; returned to Calcutta in 1923; visited west Asia several times and led the Muslim delegation to the Palestine Conference at Cairo, 1938; Mayor of Calcutta 1940; editor of the *Morning News*, Calcutta; attended the All-India Muslim League session and actively participated in its deliberations; was liberal in his views and wanted Hindus and Muslims to live in amity; Muslim League member to the Bengal Legislative Assembly between 1937 and 1946; member of the Indian legislature, 1946. See Jain, *Muslims in India*, vol. II, p. 159.

Sitaramayya, Pattabhi (1880–1959)   Physician at Machilipatnam in Andhra; AICC member, 1916–52; member Congress Working Committee, 1929–31, 1934–6, 1938–46, 1948; official candidate for the Congress presidentship but defeated by Subhas Bose in 1939; president All-India States People's Conference at Karachi, 1936, and Navasari Convention 1938–9 and working President 1946–8; President of the Congress 1948; Governor of Madhya Pradesh 1952–7. See *JNSW*, vol. III, p. 285.

Suhrawardy, Hussain Shaheed (1892–1963)   Born into a highly cultured and distinguished family of Midnapore, Suhrawardy was educated at St Xavier's College, Calcutta; went to Oxford for his BCL and was called to the Bar from Gray's Inn; started his political career as a labour leader, he became deputy mayor of Calcutta in 1923; elected to the Bengal legislature between 1921 and 1936; secretary of the Bengal Provincial Muslim League, 1937–45; elected to the 1937 Bengal Legislative Assembly; served as minister in the Haq cabinet between 1937 and 1941 and in the Muslim League cabinet between 1943 and 1945; in 1946, he became Chief Minister; he was an active supporter of the 1947 sovereign Bengal plan; founded Awami League in 1949; joined the Pakistan cabinet in 1954; became the Premier in 1956 and held the office until martial law was imposed in 1958. See H. Momen, *Muslims in Bengal*, pp. 84–5.

Yaznik, Indulal (1892–1972)   A Brahman, Yaznik stood first in the BA examination from St Xaviers' College, Bombay in 1912; worked with the Bombay newspaper *Bombay Samachar*; started a Gujrati monthly *Nawijiban Ane Satya* in 1915; in 1917 he joined the Home Rule League movement in Gujrat; in 1921 he became the secretary of the Gujrat PCC; in 1922 he started another Gujrati monthly, *Yugadhram*; in 1923 he was arrested for his involvement with the Non-Co-operation movement and was released in March 1924; between 1930 and 1935 he was in Europe; organized an India–Ireland Friendship Association; from 1936 he was actively associated with the Kisan movement; formed Gujrat Kisan Parishad in 1939; imprisoned for his anti-war propaganda in 1940; presided over the annual session of the Akhil Hind Kisan Sabha in 1942; started *Nutun Gujrat* in 1943; in 1956 he took the lead in the Maha Gujrat Movement for a separate Gujrat state and became the founder president of the Maha Gujrat Janata Parishad; between 1957 and 1972 he was a member of the Lokshava. See *DNB*, vol. IV, pp. 454–6.

Appendix II
The Composition of the BPCC, 1939

President: Subhas Chandra Bose (Calcutta).
Secretary: Ashrafuddin Ahmad Chowdhury (Comilla).

Members: (according to their affiliations)

Anushilan ex-state detenus

Trailakhya Chakrabarti (Mymensingh); Ramesh Acharyya (Dacca); Pratul Ganguly (Dacca); Rabindra Sen Gupta (Dacca).

Anushilan ex-detenus

Dhiren Mukherjee (Calcutta); Makhan Sen (Calcutta); Jnan Majumdar (Mymensingh); Nihar Mukherjee (Murshidabad); Chatrapati Ray (Murshidabad); Pratap Rakshit (Chittagong); Atin Ray (Tippera).

Jugantor ex-state detenus

Sarat Chandra Bose (Calcutta); Paran Chandra Das (Faridpur).

Jugantor ex-detenus

Amar Bose (Calcutta); Kali Mukherjee (Calcutta); Khagen Dasgupta (Jalpaiguri); Satyapriya Banerjee (Rajshahi); Kalipada Bagchi (Rangpur); Suren Sarkar (Pabna); Mohendra Sen (Bogra); Atul Kumar (Malda); Jatindra Bhattacharjee (Faridpur); Satindra Nath Sen (Barisal); Bipin Ganguly (Calcutta); Lalit Barman

(Comilla); Khagendra Nath Chatterjee (24 Parganas); Tarak Banerjee (Nadia); Jnanendra Swami (Chittagong); Gopal Halder (Noakhali); Basanta Majumdar (Tippera).

Sri Sangha ex-detenus

Akhil Ray (Dacca); Lila Nag (Dacca).

Bengal Volunteers Group: ex-detenus

Satya Bhusan Gupta (Calcutta).

Ananda Bazar Group

Suresh Majumdar (Calcutta).

Congress

J. C. Gupta (Calcutta); Hemanta Basu (Calcutta); Purusattam Ray (Calcutta); Haren Ghosh (Howrah); Basanta Das (Midnapore); Kishori Chatterjee (Khulna); Kali Narayan Singha (Murshidabad); Haripada Chatterjee (Nadia); Haren Ghosh Chowdhury (Noakhali); Kamini Dutta (Tippera); Mrs Hemprava Majumdar (Tippera).

Source: IOR, L/PJ/5/144, Chief Secretary's (Government of Bengal) report for the first half of June, 1939.

Appendix III
14-Point Election Manifesto of the KPP, Declared in the 1936 Dacca Session

1   Abolition of the zamindari system (permanent settlement) without compensation.
2   Establishment of proprietory rights of the cultivators in the land.
3   Reduction of land rent by fixing a maximum rate for each class of land.
4   Annulment of landlord's right of pre-emption.
5   Abolition of *nazar salami* (fees exacted by the landlords from various categories of cultivators on succeeding to property or on introducing the new rent collectors or on receiving a lease by a cultivator) and criminal punishment for all illegal exactions, such as *abwab* (illegal exaction from the cultivators on top of rents to meet zamindar's expenses incurred, for instance, for his daughter's wedding).
6   Solution of the problem of agricultural indebtedness of cultivators by constituting Debt Settlement Board and giving long-term loans at more than 4 per cent interest per annum.
7   Restriction of jute cultivation and fixation of the minimum price of jute.
8   Resuscitation of dead and dying rivers and improvement of agriculture, trade, commerce and sanitation.
9   Establishment of one hospital in each *thana* (local police station).
10   Full self-government in Bengal.
11   Introduction of compulsory and free education.
12   Reduction of cost of administration.
13   Fixation of minister's salary at Rs1000 per month.
14   Repeal of all repressive laws and release of all prisoners.

Source: The Star of India, Calcutta, 12 September 1936.

Notes

Introduction

1 R. Ray, 'Social conflict and political unrest in Bengal' (unpublished PhD thesis, University of Cambridge, 1972), p. 42.

2 Partha Chatterjee 'Caste and politics in west Bengal', in Gail Omvedt ed., *Land, Caste and Politics in Indian States* (Delhi, 1982), p. 1.

3 Report on the census of Nadia, 1891, p. 10, quoted in Asok Sen, *Vidyasagar and His Elusive Milestone* (Calcutta, 1979), p. 40.

4 Anil Seal, *The Emergence of Indian Nationalism* (Cambridge, 1968), p. 73. Gordon Johnson, 'Chitpavan Brahman and politics in western India in the late nineteenth and twentieth centuries', in E. Leach et al., *Elites in South Asia* (Cambridge, 1970), p. 117.

5 J. F. Hillikar, 'The creation of a middle class as a goal of educational policy in Bengal', in C. H. Philips et al., *Indian Society and the Beginning of Modernization, 1830–50* (London, 1976), p. 33.

6 Report of the Bengal District Administration Committee, 1915, p. 176.

7 *Bangadoot*, 13 June 1829, cited in S. N. Mukherjee, 'Class, caste and politics in Calcutta, 1815–38', in E. Leach et al., *Elites in South Asia* (Cambridge, 1970), p. 53.

8 Bhavanicharan Bandapadhyay, *Kalikata Kamalaya* (Bengali) (Calcutta, repr., 1343 (1936)), pp. 8–13.

9 Ibid., p. 31.

10 J. C. Jack, *Economic Life of a Bengal District* (Oxford, 1916), p. 89.

11 A. H. M. Nooruzzaman, 'Rise of Muslim middle class' (unpublished PhD thesis, University of London, 1964), pp. 237–9.

12 Report of the Bengal Land Revenue (Floud) Commission, 1940, vol. 1, p. 335.

13 N. C. Chaudhuri, *An Autobiography of an Unknown Indian* (New York, 1951), p. 377.

14 IOR, L/PO/3, extract from a daily report of the Director of Intelligence Bureau, Home Department, Government of India (hereafter GI), New Delhi, 10 February 1927.

15   Ibid.
16   Foreword by Tridib Chaudhury, in B. Bhattacharyya, *Origins of the RSP: from National Revolutionary Politics to Non-Conformist Communism* (Calcutta, 1982), pp. 5–8.
17   Ibid., p. 5.
18   Jadugopal Mukherjee, *Biplabi Jiboner Smriti* (Bengali) (Calcutta, 1982), p. 398.
19   Our Aims published in *The Statesman*, 23 December 1931.
20   Ibid.
21   Subhas Chandra Bose, *Collected Works* (hereafter *CW*) (Bengali), vol. 11 (Calcutta, 1980), pp. 96–7.
22   Bidyut Chakrabarty, 'Bengal Congress and the peasantry, 1928–38', *South Asia Research* 5.1 (May 1985).
23   Gordon Johnson, 'Partition and agitation and Congress: Bengal, 1904–8', *Modern Asian Studies* (hereafter *MAS*), 7.3 (1973), p. 577.
24   For a comparative study of these two organizations, see Pradyut Ghosh, 'Organizational structure of a revolutionary society: Anushilan Samiti, 1901–18', *Bengal Past and Present* (July–December 1978).
25   Report of the *Sedition Committee*, 1918 (Calcutta, 1919), pp. 101–2.
26   Mazaffar Ahmad, *Amar Jiban O Bharater Communist Party* (Calcutta, 1971), p. 432.
27   Men like Abdullahel Baqui of Dinajpur, Maniruzzaman Islamabadi of Chittagong, Akram Khan of 24 Parganas, Shamsuddin Ahmad of Kusthia and Ashrafudin Ahmad Chowdhury of Tippera were recruited to the provincial Congress hierarchy. See Partha Chatterjee, 'Some considerations on the making of the 1928 Bengal Tenancy (Amendment) Act', occasional paper, Centre for Studies in Social Sciences, Calcutta, p. 10. Harun or Rashid, 'The Bengal Provincial Muslim League, 1906–47' (unpublished PhD thesis, University of London, 1983), p. 49. Rajat Ray, 'Masses in Politics', *Indian Economic and Social History Review* (hereafter *IESHR*) 11.4 (December 1974), pp. 343–410.
28   See appendix I for Tamijuddin Khan's biographical sketch.
29   Tamijuddin Khan Memoirs (Tss), available by courtesy of Mrs M. N. Huda of Dacca.
30   U. Das, Bengal Pact, in *Bengal Past and Present*, pp. 99, 188, January–December, 1980. 'To a large group of congressmen, the Pact was a scheme of distribution of loaves and fishes according to population. Any unity based on this understanding could not last long because of the inherent limitations of concessional Pact.' See Bhupati Majumdar (oral transcript), Nehru Memorial Museum and Library (NMML), p. 21. Even Muslims were opposed to it. Abdullah Suhrawardy, for instance, told C. R. Das, 'you have given so many concessions to the Muslims that tomorrow they will say that all the

Muslims must grow beards. I refuse to grow beards. You are playing into the hands of religious fanatics.' See Suren Ghosh (oral transcript), NMML, p. 182.

31 Tamijuddin Khan Memoirs, op. cit., p. 13.
32 Tonish Diana Millie, 'The failure of national integration in Bengal, 1921–37' (unpublished PhD thesis, University of Pennsylvania, 1981), p. 203. J. H. Broomfield, *Elite Conflict in a Plural Society, Twentieth Century Bengal* (Berkeley, Calif., 1968), p. 279.
33 OL, MSS EUR F.160. Lutton Collection, Lutton to Oliver, 23 July, 1924. Bhupati Majumdar (oral transcript), NMML.
34 Partha Chatterji, 1928 Amendment Act, op. cit., p. 9.
35 Jadugopal Mukherji, *Biplabi Jibaner Smriti* (Bengali) (Calcutta, 1982), p. 479.
36 'Masses in politics: the non-cooperation movement in Bengal', in *IESHR* 11.4 (December 1974), p. 369.
37 Abul Mansur Ahmad, *Amar Dekha Rajnitir Panchas Bachhar* (Bengali) (Dacca, 1968), pp. 52–3.
38 H. Tinker, *The Foundations of Local Self-Government in India, Pakistan and Burma* (London, 1954), p. 149.
39 J. H. Broomfield, *Elite Conflict in a Plural Society*, op. cit., p. 279.
40 Jadugopal Mukherji, *Biplabi Jibaner Smriti*, op. cit., p. 418.
41 *Dictionary of National Biography*, vol. III (Calcutta, 1974), p. 531.
42 Bhupati Majumdar (oral transcript), NMML, p. 119.
43 Bimalanda Sasmol *Swadhinatar Fanki* (Bengali) (Calcutta, 1969), pp. 310–12; J. Gallagher, 'Congress in Decline, Bengal: 1930–39', *MAS* 7.3 (1973), p. 597.
44 Suren Ghosh (oral transcript), NMML, op. cit. p. 172.
45 Jadugopal Mukherji, *Biplabi Jibaner Smriti*, op. cit., p. 454.
46 Suren Ghosh (oral transcript), op. cit., p. 172.
47 Jadugopal Mukherji, *Biplabi Jibaner Smriti*, op. cit., p. 454.
48 NAI, Home-Poll, File No. (F.N. hereafter) 45/1/1933. Decision in a meeting at the Governor House on 6 January 1933, attended by W. D. R. Prentice, R. N. Reid, H. J. Twynam, Sir Henry Haig, M. J. Hallet and I. M. Stephenson (DPI).
49 Tamijuddin Khan, Memoirs, op. cit., p. 35.
50 Muzzafar Ahmed, *Prabandha Sankalan* (Bengali) (Calcutta, 1970), p. 86.
51 Tamijuddin Khan, Memoirs, op. cit., p. 37.
52 Tamijuddin Khan, ibid., p. 39.
53 WBSA, Government of Bengal (hereafter GB) Poll, 516/1926, District Magistrate, Mymensingh quoted in A. N. Moberly, Chief Secretary, Government of Bengal to H. C. Haig, Home Secretary, Government of India (GI hereafter), dated 4 November, 1926. Subhas Bose in his letter to Motilal Nehru expressed concern in this development: 'The

effect of communal feeling has been amply demonstrated in the recent district local elections in East Bengal. In the election in Mymensingha held about a year ago, out of 22 members, not a single Hindu has been returned in spite of the existence of the joint electorate. This is practically the case in Chittagong, Noakhali, Tippera, Barisal and other districts.' Bose to Motilal, 12 July 1930. See AICC papers, 4/1928 (Part II).

54 Abul Mansur Ahmed, *Amar Dekha Rajnitir Panchas Bachhar*, op. cit., p. 61.

55 Abul Mansur Ahmad, *Amar Dekha Rajnitir Panchas Bachhar*, op. cit., pp. 5–6, 12–13.

56 Jatindra Nath De, 'The history of the Krishak Praja Party: a study of changes in classes and inter-community relations in agrarian Bengal, 1937–47' (unpublished PhD thesis, University of Delhi, 1980), p. 226.

57 Abul Mansur Ahmad, *Amar Dekha Rajnitir Panchas Bachhar*, op. cit., pp. 98–9.

58 Humaira Momen, *Muslim Politics in Bengal: a Study of the KPP and the Elections of 1937* (Dacca, 1972), pp. 46–7.

59 WBSA, 56/1936, Report from the Chittagong Commissioner to the Chief Secretary, Government of Bengal, 7 August 1936.

60 Haroon Rashid, 'The Bengal Provincial Muslim League, 1906–47' (unpublished PhD thesis, University of London, 1983), p. 11.

61 IOR, R/3/2/2, John Anderson, Bengal Governor to Linlithgow, 8 February 1937.

62 Bidyut Chakrabarty, 'The 1932 Communal Award and its implications in Bengal', *MAS* 23.3 (1989).

63 See appendix III: the KPP Election manifesto, *The Star of India*, 12 September 1936.

64 IOR, R/3/2/2, Anderson to Linlithgow, 9 March 1937.

65 Shila Sen, *Muslim Politics in Bengal* (New Delhi, 1976), pp. 118–19.

66 Partha Chatterjee, 'Bengal politics and Muslim masses, 1920–47', *Journal of Commonwealth and Comparative Studies* 20.1 (March 1982), p. 14.

67 IOR, R/3/2/64, Bengal Governor to the Governor-General of India, 5 November 1939.

68 Amalendu De, 'Fazlul Haq and his reaction to two-nation theory, 1940–47', *Bengal Past and Present* 13.2 (January–April, 1974).

69 WBSA, Home-Poll 30/1940, Report from the Chittagong Commissioner to the Chief Secretary, GB, 4 May 1939.

70 WBSA, Home-Poll 242/1939, Report from the Chittagong Commissioner to the Chief Secretary, GB, 4 May 1939.

71 *India and Communism*, Government of India, Calcutta, 1935, p. 234.

72 Gopal Halder, Foreword, in Jadugopal Mukherjee, *Biplabi Jibaner Smriti*, op. cit., p. 10.

73 *India and Communism*, op. cit., p. 238.
74 Ibid., p. 239.
75 WBSA, Home-Poll 345/1931, Sl. no. 18 (Part II), 'An appreciation of the political situation in Bengal'.
76 *Communism in India*, Government of India, Calcutta, 1927, p. 139.
77 G. Adhikari, *Documents on the History of the CPI*, vol. III (C) (New Delhi, 1982), p. 275.
78 WBSA, Home-Poll 148/1927, 'Report on Jute Mill situation', 24 Pargana's District Magistrate to the Chief Secretary, 7 August 1927.
79 Dipesh Chakrabarty, 'On deifying and defying authority: managers and workers in the jute mills of Bengal, 1890–1940', *Past and Present* (August 1983), pp. 144–5.
80 G. Adhikari, *Documents on the History of the CPI*, op. cit., p. 278.
81 WBSA, Home-Poll 245(1–5)/1931, Chittagong Commissioners' note on the Krishak Samiti, no date.
82 Sugata Bose, 'Agrarian economy and politics in Bengal, 1919–47', (unpublished PhD thesis, University of Cambridge, 1983), pp. 217–18.
83 WBSA, Home-Poll 18/1940–41, a brief summary of the political events in Bengal during the year 1939, Government of Bengal, Calcutta, 1940, p. 9.
84 Badrudding Umar, *Chirosthayee Bandabaste Banglar Krishak* (Bengali) (Dacca, 1974), pp. 53–4.
85 A brief summary of the political events in Bengal during the year 1937, Government of Bengal, Calcutta, 1938, pp. 8–9.
86 Resolution adopted at the 1936 Lucknow meeting of the Kishan Sabha; see M. A. Rasul, *A History of the Kisan Sabha* (Calcutta, 1974), p. 5.

Chapter one

1 Hugh Toye, *The Springing Tiger* (London, 1959); D. Singh, *The Rebel President* (Lahore, 1942); L. Gordon, *Bengal: the Nationalist Movement, 1876–1940* (New York, 1974).
2 IOR, L/PJ/7/792, 'parliamentary notice', 30 April 1936, 'Jail history of Bose'; IOR, R/3/2/21, report from Deputy Commissioner of Police, Special Branch, 1 February 1941. He was detained on eight occasions: arrested in December 1924 and sentenced for six months simple imprisonment; detained in October 1924 and released by September 1927 for reasons of health; arrested in January 1930 and sentenced to nine months imprisonment; arrested in January 1931 for seven days; detained again on 27 January 1931 for six months; arrested in January 1932 and released to come to Europe for treatment; imprisoned in April 1936 for three months; arrested in

July 1940 and released in December 1940.

3   IOR, R/3/2/25, Governor, Central Provinces to Bengal Governor, Tgm, 19 July 1940.

4   CSASC, Tegart Papers, 'Terrorism in India', a speech delivered before the Royal Empire Society, 1 November 1932, p. 13.

5   CSASC, Carter Papers, pp. 1–2.

6   IOR, L/PJ/7/793, Zetland's answer to the question raised by Lord Kinnoull in the House of Lords, 1 December 1936.

7   Ibid., J. W. Taylor of the British Consulate (Vienna) to the Foreign Office, 25 April 1936; see also, *The Daily Herald*, London, 21 May 1936.

8   Subhas Bose *Indian Struggle* (hereafter *IS*) (Bombay, 1964), pp. 300–1.

9   Subhas Bose, 'Anti-Imperialism and *Samyabad*', London Speech of 1933 in *The Fundamental Questions of Indian Revolution* (Calcutta, 1970), pp. 1–32.

10 IOR, L/PJ/7/792, Bose's interview in Budapest, 9 May 1934.

11 Subhas Bose, 'What is revolution', TSS (by courtesy of Sisir Bose of the Netaji Research Bureau, Calcutta).

12 IOR, L/PJ/7/792, R. S. Peel, Secretary to the Judicial and Public Department, to the Secretary of State (hereafter ss), Tgm, 15 June 1936.

13 Subhas Bose, *Collected Works* (hereafter *CW*), vol. 1, Bose's letter to his mother, pp. 127–48. According to the editor, these letters were written in 1912–13.

14 Ibid., p. 144; see also, Nanda Mukherjee, *Vivekananda's Influence on Subhas* (Calcutta, 1977).

15 *CW*, vol. I, op. cit., p. 136.

16 Ibid., p. 69.

17 Ibid., p. 71.

18 Hugh Toye, *The Springing Tiger* (London, 1959), p. 17.

19 Subhas Bose, *CW*, vol I, p. 75.

20 D. K. Roy, *Netaji: the Man. Reminiscences* (Bombay, 1966), p. 10.

21 Subhas Bose, *CW*, vol. I, p. 80.

22 CSASC, Oaten Papers, p. 42.

23 Ibid.

24 Ibid., p. 43.

25 Ibid., p. 45.

26 Ibid., p. 46.

27 Subhas Bose, *CW*, vol. I, p. 77.

28 CSASC, Oaten Papers, p. 46.

29 D. K. Roy, *Netaji: the Man*, op. cit., p. 25. For details of the report of the Committee appointed for investigation, see Subhas Bose, *CW*, vol. I, pp. 254–66.

30 Ibid., p. 257.

31 Subhas Bose, *CW*, vol. I, p. 73.

32 Ibid., p. 86.
33 Ibid., pp. 88, 90–2.
34 Ibid., p. 33.
35 Subhas Bose *CW*, vol. I, Bose to Hemanta Sarkar, 26 August 1919, p. 94.
36 Ibid., p. 94.
37 Ibid.
38 Ibid., p. 95.
39 Ibid., p. 99.
40 Information by courtesy of Dr D. M. Thompson, Master (1982–), Fitzwilliam College, Cambridge.
41 Subhas Bose, *CW*, vol. I, pp. 103–4.
42 D. K. Roy, *Netaji: the Man*, op. cit., p. 30.
43 Ibid., p. 117; see also M. V. Sharma ed., *The Right Man in the Right Place: S. C. Bose, President, Haripura Congress* (Lahore, 1938), p. 10.
44 Subhas Bose, *CW*, vol. I, Bose to Sarat Bose, 23 April 1921, p. 232.
45 Ibid., p. 233.
46 Ibid., Bose to C. R. Das, 2 March 1921, p. 217.
47 *CW*, vol. 1, p. 210.
48 Ibid., Bose's letter to C. R. Das, 2 March 1921, p. 217.
49 Sarat Bose, Cahru Chandra Ganguly and Hemanta Sarkar wrote to Bose in Cambridge. See *CW*, vol. 1, pp. 207–37.
50 N. G. Jog, *In Freedom's Quest: a biography of Subhas Chandra Bose* (Bombay, 1969), p. 13.
51 Subhas Bose, *Indian Struggle, 1920–34* (hereafter *IS*) (London, 1964), p. 54, see notes.
52 Ibid., p. 55.
53 A. Rumbold, *Watershed in India, 1914–22* (London, 1979), p. 269.
54 For a background study, see R. A. Gordon, 'Non-cooperation and Council Entry, 1919–20', *Modern Asian Studies* (hereafter *MAS*) 7.3 (July 1973), pp. 443–73.
55 *Indian Annual Register* (hereafter *IAR*), vol. I, 1922, C. R. Das's 1922 Gaya presidential address, pp. 182–7.
56 P. C. Roy, *Life and Times of C. R. Das* (London, 1927), p. 88.
57 IOR, MSS/EUR/C235, Tegart Biography, p. 231.
58 Chapter 2.
59 *Dainak Azad*, 1 February 1924. At this stage, since the majority of the revolutionary terrorists were in prison, there was no significant difficulty for Das in regulating their politics.
60 CSASC, Tegart Papers, p. 16.
61 WBSA, 16/1924, Note on the connection between the revolutionary parties and the Swaraj Party in Bengal.
62 IOR, L/PJ/7/793, 'Jail history of Bose'.
63 *Indian Annual Register*, vol. I, 1926, p. 84.
64 *Indian Quarterly Register* (hereafter *IQR*), vol. I, 1926, pp. 85, 100(a).

65   Subhas Bose, *CW*, vol. III, Bose to Sarat, 30 June 1926, p. 314.
66   WBSA, 16/1924, 'Note on the connection between the revolutionary parties and the Swaraj Party in Bengal'.
67   *IQR*, vol. I, 1926, p. 89.
68   Tamijuddin Khan Memoirs (TSS) (available by courtesy of Mrs M. N. Huda of Dacca), p. 25.
69   Hemanta Dasgupta *Subhas Bose* (Calcutta, 1946), p. 96.
70   NMML, AICC, APl/1928, Motilal to Bose, 18 June 1928.
71   Jawaharlal Nehru, *Collected Works*, vol. III (New Delhi, 1972), Nehru's press statement 22 May 1928.
72   *Ganavani*, 30 February 1929.
73   *IAR*, vol. I, 1928, p. 398.
74   Recommendation of the All Parties Conference, Report, AICC, Allahabad, no date, chapter 7, p. 100.
75   Subhas Bose, 'Towards Complete Independence', in S. A. Ayer ed., *Selected Speeches* (hereafter *SS*), Publication Division, Ministry of Information and Broadcasting, Government of India, 73rd edn (Delhi, 1974), pp. 56–7.
76   In a telegram to Mrs Basanti Das, widow of C. R. Das, Bose attributed the formation of the Congress Democratic Party to the 'tyranny of the majority'. See D. Singh, *The Rebel President* (Lahore, 1942), p. 75.
77   NMML, AICC, G39/1930, Youth Movement in India.
78   Subhas Collected Works (Bengali), vol. III, Bose's speech of 24 September 1930, p. 22.
79   Subhas Bose, 'Students and politics', speech delivered at the students' conference (Lahore, 1929), in *SS*, op. cit., p. 50.
80   Subhas Bose, 'Role of Youth Movement', speech delivered at the third session of all India Youth Congress, 25 December 1928, in *SS*, op. cit., pp. 42–5.
81   *Amrita Bazar Patrika* (hereafter *ABP*), 7 December 1928.
82   *ABP*, 27 December 1928.
83   IOR, L/PJ/7/80, Home Department Government of India (hereafter GI) to the Secretary of State for India (hereafter SS), Tgm. 30 March 1931.
84   Subhas Bose, 'After Gandhi-Irwin Pact', in *SS*, op. cit., p. 58.
85   Ibid., pp. 58–9.
86   Subhas Bose, *The Fundamental Question of Indian Revolution* (Calcutta, 1970), pp. 1–32.
87   Subhas Bose, 'The 1933 London address', in *The Fundamental Question of India's Revolution*, ibid., pp. 1–32.
88   '*Samya* means equality, *samyabadi* means one who believes in equality ... The idea of *samya* is a very old Indian concept – first popularized by Buddha 500 hundred years before Christ. I therefore prefer this name to the modern names now popular in Europe.' Bose to Mrs K.

Kurti, 23 February 1934, quoted in K. Kurti, *Subhas Chandra Bose: As I Knew Him* (Calcutta, 1966), p. 59.

89   CSASC, Taylor Papers, TSS, p. 4.

90   *Manchester Guardian*, 13 May 1933.

91   Ibid.

92   IOR, L/PJ/7/792, Subhas Bose's interview in Budapest on 9 May 1934.

93   IOR, L/PJ/7/793, British Embassy, Rome to the Foreign Office, 29 January 1935.

94   IOR, L/PJ/7/792, note on the activities of S. C. Bose from the British Legation, Sofia, 10 June 1934.

95   *ABP*, 17 May 1936.

96   IOR, L/PJ/7/792, note by M. Clawson of the India Office, 15 December 1932.

97   Ibid.

98   Ibid., note by Clawson, 7 February 1933.

99   Ibid., note by Clawson, 15 December 1932.

100 Lother Frank, 'India's ambassador abroad', in S. K. Bose ed., *A Beacon Across Asia: a Biography of S. C. Bose* (Delhi, 1973), pp. 46–68.

101 IOR, L/I/1/1315, an article by Bose written in Karlsbad, 21 July 1935 (published in *Contemporary India*, a Lahore Quarterly), pp. 317–26.

102 NAI, Wood Collection, no. 12, Bose to Mrs Wood, 21 December 1935.

103 Lother Frank, 'India's ambassador abroad', S. K. Bose ed., *A Beacon Across Asia: a Biography of S. C. Bose*, op. cit., p. 60.

104 IOR, L/I/1/1315, excerpts from *Mein Kampf*.

105 *ABP*, 15 March 1936.

106 F. Kurti, *Subhas Chandra Bose: As I Knew Him*, op. cit., p. 42.

107 CSASC, Bor Papers, TSS, p. 8.

108 M. Hauner, *India in the Axis Strategy* (London, 1981), p. 672.

109 IOR, L/I/1/1315, *Chicago Tribune*, 30 November 1937.

110 IOR, R/3/2/25, telegraphic correspondence between the Bengal Governor and Viceroy on events leading up to the arrest of Subhas Bose, June–August 1940.

111 *Advance*, 12 December 1938.

112 Phil Johannes H. Voigt, 'Relation between the Indian National Movement and Germany, 1870–1945', a pamphlet published by the Information Bureau of the Consulate General of the GFR, no date, p. 14.

113 IOR, L/PS/12/107, British Embassy, Rome to the Foreign Office 11 February 1935, mentioning reply of Mussolini in response to a vote of thanks.

114 Ibid., British Embassy, Rome to the Foreign Office, 22 December 1933.

115 Hugh Toye, *The Springing Tiger*, op. cit., pp. 41–4.

116   IOR, L/PJ/7/792, British Embassy, Rome to the Foreign Office, 1 February 1935. See also, L/I/1/1315, *Sunday Mercury*, Ireland, 9 January 1938, Bose insisted that India should support Japan's onslaught against the white peril in the east.

117   Ibid. Bose later identified Japan as the British of the East, see K. Kurti, *Subhas Bose: As I Knew Him*, op. cit., p. 59.

118   J. Nehru, 'Fascism and communism', in *Nehru on Socialism* (New Delhi, 1964), pp. 48–9.

119   Subhas Bose, *IS*, op. cit., p. 431.

120   Interview with R. P. Dutt, January 1938, see *Crossroads* (hereafter *CR*), op. cit., p. 30.

121   Subhas Bose, 'Fifty-first presidential address at Haripura', (Allahabad, 1938), p. 12.

122   Ibid., p. 10.

123   Ibid., p. 15.

124   Subhas Bose, *The Mission of Life* (1933) (Calcutta, 1953), p. 88.

125   Subhas Bose, 'Haripura address', 1938, op. cit., p. 15.

126   Subhas Bose, 'Presidential address at the Midnapore youth conference on 29/12/1929', in Subhas Bose *The Mission of Life*, op. cit., pp. 213–14.

127   Subhas Bose, *SS*, op. cit., p. 71.

128   Subhas Bose, *CW*, vol. 1, pp. 7–11.

129   Subhas Bose, 'Haripura address', 1938, p. 10.

130   NAI, Wood Collection, no. 12, Bose to Mrs Wood, 11 May 1937.

131   Ibid., 9 September 1937.

132   IOR, L/I/1/1315, *The Tribune*, 28 January 1938.

133   Ibid.

134   Subhas Bose *The Fundamental Questions of Indian Revolution*, op. cit., p. 81.

135   *Hindustan Times*, 8 March 1946.

136   Subhas Bose, 'Free India and her problems', Bulletin issued by the Netaji Research Bureau, 1961, p. 7.

137   *ABP*, 4 February 1936.

138   Subhas Bose, 'Haripura address', 1938, pp. 11–12.

139   Ibid., see also *CR*, p. 12.

140   Subhas Bose's speech to the BPCC session, held at Vishnupur on 30 January 1938, quoted in M. V. Sharma, *The Right Man at the Right Place*, op. cit., p. 28.

141   NMML, AICC, G/81/1937, Mohan Kapur to Nehru, 24 September 1937, 'The Congress president should be elected from Bengal'. See also the list included in the above file recommending the names.

142   Sankari Prasad Basu, *Suhbas Chandra O National Planning* (Bengali) (Calcutta, 1981), pp. 74–91.

143   AICC, P5/1938, Gandhi to Nehru, 3 June 1938.

144 S. Sarkar, *Popular Movements and Middle Class Leadership in Late Colonial India: Perspectives and Problems of a History From Below* (Calcutta, 1983); and also D. Taylor, 'The crisis of authority in the Indian National Congress, 1936–9', in B. N. Pandey ed., *Leadership in South Asia* (Delhi, 1977).

145 Pattabhi Sitaramayya, *History of the Indian National Congress, 1935–47*, vol. II (New Delhi, 1969), p. 104.

146 Ibid., p. 105.

147 Ibid., p. 105.

148 Ibid.

149 *IAR*, vol. I, 1939, p. 44.

150 *ABP*, 27 January 1939.

151 Nehru to Bose, 3 April 1939 in J. Nehru, *A Bunch of Old Letters* (Bombay, 1958), p. 346.

152 K. Kurti, *Subhas Chandra Bose: As I Knew Him*, op. cit., p. 29.

153 *Hindustan Standard* (hereafter *HS*), 27 January 1939.

154 *HS*, 28 January 1939.

155 *HS*, 28 January 1939.

156 *ABP*, 27 January 1939.

157 IOR, L/I/1/1116, P. C. Joshi, *The Communist Party: its Policy and Work in the War of Liberation*, CPGB (September 1942), p. 30.

158 Tagore was quoted in a letter from Anil. K. Chanda to Nehru, 28 November 1938, J. Nehru, *A Bunch of Old Letters*, op. cit., pp. 299–300.

159 Pattabhi Sitaramayya, *History of the Congress*, vol. II, op. cit., p. 111.

160 Nehru's press statement of 23 February 1939, quoted in *IAR*, vol. I, 1939, p. 49.

161 D. Taylor, 'The crisis of authority', in B. N. Pandey ed., *Leadership in South Asia*, op. cit., pp. 327–33.

162 *Kaiser-I-Hind* (published from Bombay), 25 January 1939.

163 *The Lahore Tribune*, 27 January 1939.

164 IOR, L/PJ/5/144, FR(2) (January 1939), Bengal.

165 *IAR*, vol. I, 1939, p. 46.

166 Ibid., p. 48.

167 Ibid., p. 49.

168 *Prabashi* (Bengali), miscellaneous subjects, 38(2), IV–VI, 1939, p. 900.

169 *IAR*, vol. I, 1939, pp. 343–4.

170 Ibid.

171 *Prabashi* (Bengali), miscellaneous subjects, 38(2), IV–VI, 1939, p. 900.

172 S. Sarkar, *Modern India, 1885–1947* (New Delhi, 1984), p. 373.

173 NMML, Jawaharlal Nehru Papers (hereafter JNP), Part I/VIII, Gandhi to Subhas 10 April 1939.

174   Gandhi to Bose 30 March 1939, in J. Nehru, *A Bunch of Old Letters*, op. cit., p. 357.

175   *IAR*, vol. I, 1939, p. 52.

176   NMML, JNP, Part I/VIII, Subhas to Gandhi, 17 April 1939.

177   Nehru to Gandhi, 17 April 1939, in J. Nehru, *A Bunch of Old Letters*, op. cit., pp. 369–71.

178   Gandhi to Bose, 2 April 1939, in Subhas Bose, *Crossroads* (hereafter *CR*), p. 160.

179   IOR, R/3/2/14, Linlithgow to R. N. Reid, 13 May 1939.

180   *The National Front*, 19 March 1939.

181   JP quoted in Ashim Chaudhuri, *Socialist Movement In India, the Congress Socialist Party, 1937–47* (Calcutta, 1980), p. 110.

182   NMML, MN Roy Papers, M. N. Roy to Bose, 1 February 1939. Jibanlal Chattapadhyay's letter of 29 October 1939 corroborates the refusal.

183   NMML, AICC, G20/Part III/1939, Bose's letter of resignation, no date.

184   Rajendra Prasad, *Autobiography* (Bombay, 1957), p. 486.

185   Bose explained the genesis in his speech at Shraddhananda Park on 3 May 1939, see *SS*, p. 100–3.

186   Subhas Bose, 'All power to the people', a Forward Bloc pamphlet, 1940, p. 27.

187   Yusuf Meherally ed., *Towards Struggle* (Bombay, 1946), pp. 137–8.

188   NMML, MN Roy Papers, M. N. Roy to Amarendranath Chatterjee, 1 December 1939.

189   M. N. Roy to Nehru 5 July 1939, Tgm, published in *HS*, 9 July 1939.

190   Pattabhi Sitaramayya, *History of the Congress*, vol. II, op. cit., p. 115.

191   See chapter 4.

192   Rajendra Prasad, *Autobiography*, op. cit., p. 489.

193   Bose's explanatory letter was quoted in Pattabhi Sitaramayya, *History of the Congress*, vol. II, op. cit., p. 116.

194   NMML, AICC, P5/Part II/1939, Working Committee's decision of 11 August 1939, signed by Rajendra Prasad.

195   CSASC, Edgar Hyde Papers, p. 37.

196   NMML, Suren Ghosh Oral Transcript, p. 99.

197   Madhu Limaye, 'Netaji: a Reappraisal', *The Illustrated Weekly of India* 15–21 (January, 1984), p. 15.

198   D. Taylor, 'The crisis of authority in the Indian National Congress, 1936–39', in B. N. Pandey ed., *Leadership in South Asia* (Delhi, 1977), pp. 329, 331.

199   Nehru to Bose, 4 February 1939, in J. Nehru, *A Bunch of Old Letters*, op. cit., p. 309.

200   N. C. Chaudhuri, 'Subhas Chandra Bose', *The Illustrated Weekly of India*, op. cit., p. 19.

Chapter two

1 Partha Chatterjee, 'Some considerations on the 1928 Bengal Tenancy (Amendment) Act', occasional paper no. 30, Centre for Studies in Social Sciences (Calcutta, 1980), p. 10.
2 Shila Sen, *Muslim politics in Bengal*, op. cit., p. 53; U. Das, 'The Bengal Pact, 1924, *Bengal Past and Present* (January–June, 1980).
3 S. Sarkar, *The Swadeshi Movement in Bengal, 1903–8*, op. cit., pp. 422–4.
4 Ibid.
5 Sarat Chatterjee, *Swadesh O Sahitya* (in Bengali) (Calcutta, 1973), pp. 57–8.
6 *Ananda Bazar Patrika*, 25 July 1924.
7 *The Mussalman*, 25 July 1924.
8 Partha Chatterjee, 'Some considerations on 1928 Bengal', op. cit., p. 13.
9 Amalesh Tripathy, *The Extremist Challenge*, op. cit.; Hiren Chakrabarty, 'Government and Bengal terrorism, 1912–18', *Bengal Past and Present* (July–December, 1971), pp. 165–81.
10 Partha Chatterjee, 'Some considerations on 1928 Bengal Tenancy Act', op. cit., p. 9.
11 Subhas Chandra Bose, *Collected Works* (hereafter *CW*), vol. III, (Calcutta, 1980), p. 354.
12 IOR, L/PJ/7/793, a departmental note signed by R. S. Peel, Chief Secretary (hereafter CS), 24 November 1936; IOR, MSS/EUR/C235, Tegart Biography, p. 231.
13 An exploration of the theme will be attempted in chapter 4.
14 IOR, L/PO/49(ii), names of the Bose-appointed Congress Executive; IOR, L/PJ/5/144, CS report for the first half of June, 1939: 'Congress in Bengal is completely dominated by the terrorists ... and the doctrine of violence as opposed to non-violence or constitutional action is daily being more widely advocated.'
15 J. H. Broomfield, 'The forgotten majority', D. A. Low ed., *Soundings in South Asia*, op. cit.
16 See Bidyut Chakrabarty, 'The Communal Award of 1932 and its implications in Bengal', *MAS* 23.3 (1989).
17 See chapter 1.
18 IOR, L/PJ/5/144, R. N. Reid, Bengal Governor to Linlithgow, 27 April 1939.
19 IOR, V/9/1289, vol. LIV, No. 2, 1939, Bengal Legislative Assembly debate, speech of S. P. Mookherjee in the Legislative Assembly, p. 182.
20 Ibid. Nawab Khaja Habibullah Bahadur of Dacca while introducing the bill justified the enactment, p. 19.

21   Ibid., speech of A. K. Fazlul Haq, 6 March 1939, p. 189.
22   Sarat Bose's speech in the Legislative Assembly, Sisir Bose ed., *The Voice of Sarat Bose* (Calcutta, 1979), p. 93.
23   IOR, V/9/1289, speech of S. P. Mookherjee, op. cit., p. 182.
24   Ibid., speech of Nausher Ali, 27 February 1939, p. 35.
25   Ibid., speech of Maulvi Abu Hossain Sarkar, 27 February 1939, p. 30.
26   Ibid.
27   The Bengal Legislative Acts, 1939.
28   IOR, R/3/1/13, J. A. Herbert, Bengal Governor (hereafter Herbert) to Linlithgow, 7 March 1940.
29   Subhas Bose, editorial, *Forward Bloc, CR*, p. 295.
30   *HS*, 28 February 1940.
31   Sisir Bose ed., *CR*, p. 296.
32   *HS*, 28 February 1940.
33   *HS*, 30 March 1940.
34   IOR, R/3/2/13, FR, first half of February, 1940.
35   IOR, R/3/1/13, J. A. Herbert to Linlithgow, 7 March 1940.
36   Subhas Bose, editorial, *Forward Bloc* in Sisir Bose ed., *CR*, pp. 296–7.
37   IOR, R/3/1/13, Herbert to Linlithgow, 20 March 1940.
38   *Forward*, vol. III, no. 7, March 9, 1940.
39   *HS*, 3 April 1940.
40   *The Modern Review* 67.4 (April 1940), pp. 392–3.
41   *HS*, 17 April 1940.
42   IOR, Eur F/125/40, Linlithgow papers, Herbert to Linlithgow, 22 April 1940.
43   IOR, R/3/2/22, H. J. Twynam's (CS), report for the second half of April, 1940.
44   IOR, Eur F/125/40, Herbert to Linlithgow, 22 April 1940.
45   Ibid.
46   Sisir Bose ed., *CR*, p. 310.
47   Abul Mansur Ahmad, *Amar Dekha Rajnitir* (in Bengali), op. cit., p. 195.
48   IOR, EUR F/125/40, Herbert to Linlithgow, 22 April 1940.
49   IOR, R/3/2/25, Report of D. A. Brayden, Central Intelligence Officer (hereafter Brayden), 1 July 1940.
50   *HS*, 19 April 1940.
51   *Forward*, 13, 20 April 1940.
52   *Forward*, 14, 27 April 1940.
53   *Advance*, 19 April 1940.
54   *The Modern Review* 67.5 (May 1940).
55   IOR, R/3/2/25, Bengal Governor to the Viceroy, 3 June 1940.
56   IOR, Eur F/125/1940, Herbert to Linlithgow, 22 April 1940.
57   IOR, R/3/2/17, Nazimuddin quoted in Braydon to W. N. P. Jenkins, Deputy Director, Intelligence Bureau, Home Dept, Government of

India, Simla, 16 July 1940.

58 NAI, Home-Poll/148/40, Central Intelligence Report, Calcutta, 7 December 1940.

59 IOR, R/3/2/19, B. C. Chatterjee to Laithwaite, 3 January 1941.

60 IOR, R/3/2/25, Brayden's report, 1 July 1940, op. cit.

61 Subhas Bose, 'Toward a communal unity', Sisir Bose ed., *CR*, p. 286.

62 IOR, R/3/1/13, op. cit. The Governor wrote that 'there has been persistent information since then of negotiations with a view to extending the scope of his cooperation, and there has been talk of a pact by which Subhas and some others would be brought in to an enlarged Bengal cabinet.'

63 IOR, Mss Eur/F/125/39, op. cit. FR, first half of August, 1939.

64 Jinnah-Bose correspondence, Sisir Bose ed., *CR*, op. cit., pp. 37–46.

65 In his discussion with Abul Mansur Ahmad he admitted this. See Abul Mansur Ahmad, *Amar Dekha Rajnitir*, op. cit., p. 136.

66 IOR, MSS Eur/F/125/39, FR, first half of August, 1939; Raghunandan Saran to Nehru, 14 October 1939, *A Bunch of Old Letters*, op. cit., p. 389.

67 Raghunandan Saran to Nehru, 14 October 1939, in *A Bunch of Old Letters*, ibid.

68 AICC, P5/Part 1/40, Bose to Rajen Dev, 7 October 1939.

69 Raghunandan Saran to Nehru, 14 October 1939, *A Bunch of Old Letters*, op. cit., p. 389. IOR, R/3/1/13, Herbert to Linlithgow, 27 April 1940. 'The Governor was scared when the pact was signed because as a result of which (a) Subhas will be able to keep his fingers on some of the resources of the Calcutta Corporation and (b) the Muslim leadership took a risk in trying to outwit so clever and slippery an opponent.'

70 *The Modern Review* 67.5 (May 1940), p. 286. *The Modern Review* criticized the move on the part of Bose on the ground that it implies 'support to Muslim League theory of two nations and therefore partition as well'.

71 IOR, R/3/1/13, Herbert to Linlithgow, 3 January 1940.

72 R. C. Banerjee, 'The Holwell Monument', *The Modern Review* 68.2 (August 1940).

73 S. C. Bose, 'Holwell must go', *Forward Bloc*, 29 July 1940.

74 IOR, R/3/2/25, Herbert to Linlithgow, 4 July 1940.

75 *HS*, 3 June 1940; *ABP*, 3 July 1940.

76 IOR, R/3/2/25, Tgm, Bengal Governor to Viceroy, 4 July 1940.

77 Ibid.

78 IOR, R/3/2/17, Brayden to W. N. P. Jenkins, 16 July 1940.

79 Ibid.

80 IOR, R/3/2/25, Herbert to Linlithgow, 4 July 1940.

81 Ibid.

82 Ibid.
83 IOR, R/3/2/17, Brayden to Jenkins, 16 July 1940.

Chapter three

1   When C. R. Das died in 1925 Bose was in prison and he was released in 1927.
2   Both J. M. Sengupta and B. N. Sasmol, the two formidable contenders for provincial leadership, had strong political bases in Chittagong and Midnapore respectively.
3   Chapter 2.
4   S. Bose, 'The Kishoreganj riot', *MAS* op. cit.; Partha Chatterjee, 'Agrarian relations and communalism', R. Guha ed., *Subaltern Studies*, vol. I, op. cit.
5   See chapter 1.
6   See chapter 1.
7   See chapter 1.
8   An explanation of this has been sought in chapter 1.
9   The role Subhas Bose played during the passage of the Bengal Tenancy (Amendment) Act, 1928.
10 The Fawcus Committee Report, 1940, vol. I, p. 80.
11 The Finlow Committee Report, 1934, vol. I, part I, p. 81.
12 The Census of India, 1931, vol. V, part I, p. 275.
13 The Finlow Committee Report, 1934, vol. I, p. 77.
14 A K. Bagchi, *Private Investment in India, 1900–39* (Cambridge, 1972), p. 195.
15 A. Z. M. Iftikar, 'The industrial development of Bengal 1930–39' (unpublished PhD thesis, University of London, 1978), p. 141.
16 A. K. Bagchi, *Private Investment*, op. cit., p. 136.
17 Ibid.
18 A. Z. M. Iftikhar, 'The industrial development of Bengal', op. cit., p. 141.
19 IOR, V/26/670/29, memorandum on the labour conditions in Bengal prepared for the Royal Commission on Labour, p. 21.
20 The Finlow Committee Report, 1939, op. cit., p. 146.
21 Azizul Haq's report in the Finlow Committee Report, p. 146.
22 A. Z. M. Iftikhar, 'The industrial development of Bengal', op. cit.. p. 348.
23 A. K. Bagchi, *Private Investment*, op. cit., p. 126.
24 Royal Commission on Labour (hereafter RC on Labour), evidence, vol. V, part I, p. 271.
25 Ibid., p. 261.
26 Ibid., vol. V, part II, p. 119.

27 Ibid., vol. V, part I, p. 127.
28 A. J. Mackenzie, 'British Marxists and the Empire: anti-imperialism in theory and practice' (unpublished PhD thesis, University of London, 1978), p. 163.
29 Centre for South Asian Studies, Cambridge (hereafter CSASC), E. Benthall's diary (1920–9), 10 September 1929.
30 IOR, L/PJ/12/2, FR, first half of August, 1929.
31 Ibid., FR(2), 1929.
32 Bengal Legislative Council proceedings, official report, 33rd session, 5–9 August, 1929, Calcutta, 1930, B. C. Roy's speech, p. 287.
33 Ibid.
34 Ibid., Mr Laird's comment in the Council, p. 292.
35 Ibid., T. Lamb's comment in the Council, 9 August 1929, p. 303.
36 Ibid., B. C. Roy's comment in the Council, 9 August 1929, p. 288.
37 Ibid., Jogesh Chandra Gupta's comment in the Council, 9 August 1929, pp. 293–4.
38 A. K. Bagchi, *Private Investment*, op. cit., p. 144.
39 RC on Labour, evidence, vol. v, part I, Bengal, p. 128.
40 Kalidas Bhattacharyya, 'Strikes in jute mills', in *Ganavani*, 5 July 1928, pp. 9–10.
41 Bengal Legislative Council Proceedings, op. cit., T. Lamb's comment, p. 302.
42 IOR, V/26/670/29, memorandum on the labour conditions in Bengal, op. cit., p. 21; the 1921 Census corroborates the Commission's characterization. The jute industry employed 90.06 per cent of the total jute workers in Bengal and 46.86 per cent of the total work force were employed in textile, non-textile, tea plantations and collieries.
43 Bengal Legislative Council Proceedings, McAlpin's comment in the Council, op. cit., p. 297.
44 Ibid., H. S. Suhrawardy's comment in the Council, p. 304.
45 CSASC, E. Benthall's diary, op. cit., 10 September 1929.
46 Ibid., Laird to Benthall, 18 September 1928.
47 RC on Labour, evidence, vol. I, part I, Bombay Presidency, London 1931, p. 117.
48 IOR, L/PO/73 (ii), report on the strikes of Indian railways.
49 Report on the Committee on Industrial Unrest, supplement to the Calcutta Gazettee, 22 June 1921, pp. 1258–9, 1261, quoted in S. Gourlay, *Bengal Working Class, 1875–1922* (unpublished PhD thesis, University of London, 1983), p. 194.
50 Panchanan Saha, *The History of the Working Class Movement in Bengal* (New Delhi, 1978), pp. 110–13.
51 Jawaharlal Nehru to Bose, 24 January 1929, see Jawaharlal Nehru *Selected Works*, vol. IV (New Delhi, 1973), p. 269.
52 Bengal Council Proceedings, Subhas Bose's comment in the Council,

9 August 1929, op. cit., p. 300; IOR, L/PJ/12/2, FR(2) October, 1929.

53   IOR, L/PO/73(ii), strike of Indian railways.

54   Ibid.

55   Ibid.

56   These strikes will be discussed below.

57   *Liberty*, 11 October 1931.

58   Panchanan Saha has confirmed the role of the communists, like Gopendra Chakrabarti, Sibnath Banerji, Dharani Goswami and Kiran Chandra Mitra, in the above strike. See Panchanan Saha, *The History of the Working Class Movement*, op. cit., p. 93.

59   *Liberty*, 17 August 1929.

60   Subhas, *Selected Works* (Bengali), vol. I (Calcutta, 1978), pp. 124–5, 175.

61   *Liberty*, 17 August 1929.

62   *ABP*, 7 July 1931.

63   RC on Labour, evidence, vol. I, part I, Bombay Presidency, op. cit., p. 169.

64   S. Sarkar, *Popular Leadership and Middle Class Movement in Late Colonial India*, Centre for Studies in Social Sciences (Calcutta, 1983), p. 56.

65   Richard Newman, *Workers and Unions in Bombay, 1918–29: a Study of Organization in the Cotton Mills*, Australian National University monograph series (Canberra, 1981), p. 247.

66   *Liberty*, 6 July 1931.

67   *ABP*, 7 July 1931.

68   Ibid.

69   *Liberty*, 6 July 1931.

70   Subhas Bose, *Indian Struggle* (hereafter *IS*), London, p. 233.

71   *ABP*, 7 July 1931.

72   'The communist menace', *Liberty*, 11 July 1931.

73   IOR, L/PJ/12/25, FR(1 and 2), November, 1931, Bengal.

74   Bose stated, 'obviously such organization [as Trade Union Congress and Kishan Sabha] should not appear as a challenge to the National Congress which is the organ for capturing political power. They should therefore be inspired by Congress ideals and work in close co-operation with the Congress.' See *Selected Speeches* (hereafter *SS*), op. cit., p. 83.

75   *Liberty*, 6 August 1931.

76   Sukumal Sen, *Working Class of India, 1870–1970* (Calcutta, 1977), p. 314.

77   J. Nehru, *Autobiography* (London, 1941), p. 199.

78   IOR, L/PO/73(ii), B. Shiva Rao's press statement. The split occurred as N. M. Joshi, F. Bakhal, V. V. Giri and Shiva Rao himself decided to break away from the AITUC. They opposed the

resolutions boycotting the RC on Labour, the annual international conference at Geneva, and the affiliation of the Trade Union Congress to the Pan-pacific secretariat at San Francisco. They refused to be associated with the International Federation of Trade Unions. See also, B. Shiva Rao, *The Industrial Workers in India* (London, 1939), p. 154.

79 IOR, L/PJ/12/2, FR(1), April, 1929, Bengal.
80 Bimal Ghosh, a member of the Bengal Volunteers, in his memoirs, stated this: see Narayan Ganguli and Suddhasatwa Bose ed., *Ardha-Satabdi* (Bengali) (Calcutta, 1960). (I owe this reference to Dr Tapan Raychaudhuri of St Antony's College, Oxford.) IOR, L/PJ/12/3, FR(1) January for Bihar and Orissa, in a public meeting the speakers condemned this attitude of Bose.
81 Panchanan Saha, *History of the Working Class*, op. cit., p. 105.
82 IOR, L/PJ/12/2, FR(1), January, 1929, Bengal.
83 Subhas, *Selected Works* (Bengali), vol. III, op. cit., p. 114.
84 N. Mitra ed., *Indian Annual Register*, 1927, vol. II, p. 71.
85 NMML, Purushattamdas Thakurdas Papers (hereafter PTP), PT 42(ii), Purushattamdas Thakurdas to N. M. Mazumdar, 7 June 1929.
86 Ibid., G. D. Birla to Thakurdas, 30 July 1929.
87 See below.
88 Subhas *Selected Works* (Bengali), vol. III, op. cit., p. 114.
89 PTP, PT 42; Bose was quoted in a letter of Ibrahim Rahimtoala to G. D. Birla, 9 July 1929.
90 *Liberty*, 1 December 1929.
91 IOR, L/PO/73; Viceroy to the Secretary of State (Tgm), 4 February 1931. 'At the Nagpur congress, a large body seceded from the Trade Union Congress on the ground that policy of the congress was fundamentally opposed to the genuine interests of the working class, as shown in the resolutions, among other matters, to boycott Whitley Commission; to affiliate Congress to the League against Imperialism; not to send delegates on behalf of India to future sessions of the International Labour Conference at Geneva; and in rejecting the Round Table Conference in addition to Congress's adoption of a resolution in favour of independence'. Shiva Rao's letter of 31 December 1929 (quoted earlier) confirms this.
92 J. Nehru, *Autobiography*, op. cit., p. 199.
93 NMML, AICC, 16/1929, Nehru's press statement, 20 September 1929.
94 AICC, 12/1929, Bhupendra Nath Dutta to Nehru, 24 October 1929.
95 Ibid., Nehru to R. S. Ruikar, 29 October 1929.
96 IOR, L/PJ/12/2, FR(1) September, 1929, *Liberty*'s news was quoted

97   Subhas Bose, *IS*, op. cit., p. 167.
98   Subhas Bose, *SS*, p. 62.
99   IOR, V/26/670/31, J. R. Dain, Deputy Commissioner, Singbhum district, 'Memorandum on Labour Dispute in Jamshedpur', 1920 to 1930. This is the document where the entire TISCO strike situation has been extensively covered. Though it is an official version and the author is aware of its limitations (being a review of the events from one angle), the information supplied is of intrinsic value.
100 Ibid., p. 13.
101 *The Statesman*, 19 March 1920.
102 RC on Labour, main report, p. 129.
103 *ABP*, 20 March 1920.
104 *ABP*, 25 July 1922.
105 NAI, Meerut Conspiracy Case, file no. 31/3213, 'An appeal of the Jamshedpur Labour Association' (hereafter JLA), 1924, p. 1.
106 Ibid.
107 RC on Labour, main report, p. 122.
108 Ibid.
109 *ABP*, 20 October 1922.
110 Sukumal Sen, *Working Class of India*, op. cit., p. 210.
111 AICC, R1/1929, Andrews to Motilal, 7 July 1924.
112 Ibid., 'About the formation of a Labour Association in Tata: a note', no date.
113 Ibid.
114 Notes at the meeting of the Conciliation Committee held at Jamshedpur, 20 August 1924, File no. 16, Jamshedpur Labour Situation, Conciliation Committee, TISCO, Bombay, p. 20, quoted in E. M. Lavalle, 'Confrontation within a confrontation: Subhas Bose and the 1928 steel strike', in J. R. Mclane ed., *Bengal in the 19th and 20th Centuries*, Asian Studies Centre, Michigan State University, East Lansing (Michigan, 1975), p. 173.
115 Gandhi *Collected Works*, vol. XVIII, New Delhi, Government of India, 1963, no page number, quoted in ibid., p. 174.
116 IOR, J. R. Dain's memorandum, op. cit., no name was given but Dain's report mentions that they were Bengali babus.
117 IOR, J. R. Dain's report, 'Memorandum', op. cit.
118 NAI, Meerut Conspiracy Case, file no. 32/3213, 'A note'.
119 *Forward*, 21 March 1928.
120 *ABP*, 4 May 1928.
121 *Foward*, 1 July 1928.
122 *Bombay Chronicle*, 20 July 1928.
123 IOR, L/PJ/12/1, FR(1), February, 1928, Bihar and Orissa.
124 *ABP*, 11 April 1928, press statement of C. F. Andrews.
125 *ABP*, 19 March 1928.

126 Ibid.
127 See appendix I for Homi's biographical sketch.
128 M. Homi, 'Representation to the Tariff Board, 1924', TSS, 1923, quoted in Lavalle, 'Confrontation within a confrontation', op. cit., p. 175.
129 *ABP*, 18 March 1928.
130 Ibid.
131 IOR, L/PJ/12/1/, FR(2), May, 1928, Bihar and Orissa.
132 Ibid.
133 IOR, V/67/670/31. Dain, 'Memorandum', op. cit., p. 25.
134 NAI, Home-Poll, file no. 18/11/1928. Jamshedpur Strike Situation.
135 IOR, V/67/670/31, Dain, 'Memorandum', op. cit., p. 25.
136 Ibid.
137 NAI, Meerut Conspiracy Case, file 32/3213, 'A note', op. cit.
138 Sukumal Sen, *Working Class of India*, op. cit., p. 271.
139 P. Lakshman, *Congress and the Labour*, op. cit., p. 55.
140 IOR, V/67/670/31, Dain, 'Memorandum', op. cit., p. 27. The strike started on 18 April and ended on 13 September 1928.
141 Ibid., p. 25.
142 *ABP*, 2 June 1928.
143 *ABP*, 12 June 1928.
144 NMML, Purushuttamdas Thakurdas Papers (hereafter PTP), file no. 42(2), N. B. Saklatvala's, chairman, TISCO Board of Directors, terms of settlement, 4 July 1928.
145 *ABP*, 1 July 1928.
146 Ibid.
147 *ABP*, 25 July 1928.
148 AICC, R1/1929, Bose to Motilal, Tgm, 11 August 1928.
149 Ibid., Motilal to Bose, Tgm, 13 August 1928.
150 NAI, Meerut Conspiracy Case, file no. 32/3213, Homi's straight talk with Subhas Bose (printed), Hamshedpur, 30 November 1928.
151 Ibid.
152 AICC, R1/1929, Samaldas to Bose, 17 August 1928.
153 Ibid., G. L. Mehta to Samaldas, 21 August 1928.
154 IOR, V/26/670/31, Dain's 'Memorandum', op. cit., p. 25.
155 *ABP*, 20 August 1928.
156 *ABP*, 5 September 1928. Homi's statement was quoted in Bose's press statement of 4 September 1928.
157 NAI, Meerut Conspiracy Case, file no. 32/3213. The terms of settlement (signed by Subhas Bose and C. A. Alexender, the TISCO managing director) was published on 12 September 1928.
158 Subhas Bose, *Indian Struggle* (hereafter *IS*) (London, 1964), p. 154.
159 NAI, Meerut Conspiracy Case, file 32/3213, Homi's straight talk to Bose, op. cit.

160 Ibid., 'The Jamshedpur Labour dispute', published by the JLA, no date.

161 Ibid., Homi and Saklatvala's discussion for a settlement, 10 August 1928.

162 *Forward*, 14 September 1928.

163 *Forward*, Bose's press statement.

164 *ABP*, 16 September 1928.

165 IOR, L/PJ/12/1, FR(2), September, 1928, Bihar and Orissa.

166 IOR, V/67/670/31, Dain, 'Memorandum', op. cit., p. 36.

167 *ABP*, 20 November 1928.

168 IOR, L/PJ/12/1, FR(1), December, 1928, Bihar and Orissa.

169 Ibid.

170 NAI, Meerut Conspiracy Case, file, 32/3213, note by P. K. Peterson, TISCO managing director.

171 IOR, L/PJ/12/3, FR(1), March, 1929, Bihar and Orissa.

172 IOR, V/26/670/31, Dain's 'Memorandum', op. cit., p. 38.

173 AICC, G94–99/1929, Bakar Ali Mirza, 'Golmuri Strike, a brief account', op. cit., p. 1.

174 Ibid., AITUC Bulletin, op. cit., p. 1.

175 Ibid.

176 NMML, AICC G94–99/1929: AICC Bulletin, op. cit.

177 Ibid.

178 AICC, G71/1929, Nehru's note on the strike, no date.

179 AICC, G94–99/1929, AITUC Bulletin, op. cit.

180 IOR, L/PJ/12/3, FR(1), April, 1929, Bihar and Orissa.

181 AICC, G92–99/1929, AITUC Bulletin, op. cit.

182 AICC, G71/1929, Nehru's note, op. cit.

183 AICC, G92–99/1929, Bakar Ali Mirza's account, op. cit.

184 Ibid., AITUC Bulletin, op. cit.

185 Dain explained how the new hands were easily available: 'A number of them were men who had taken their compensation and left TISCO after 1928. Some of them were men who at some time or other had been employed in Tinplate but had saved little money and returned for a time to the fields, as Indian workmen often do.' See IOR, V/26/670/31, Dain, 'Memorandum', op. cit., p. 40.

186 AICC, G94–99/1929, Bakar Ali Mirza's account, op. cit.

187 IOR, V/26/670/31, Dain, 'Memorandum', op. cit., pp. 39–40.

188 Ibid., 2235 new hands and 1012 old hands.

189 AICC, G94–99/1929, Bakar Ali Mirza's account, op. cit.

190 AICC, G95/1929, H. K. Briscoe, CS to the government of Bihar and Orissa to the secretary, Golmuri Tinplate Workers' Union, 6 June 1929.

191 *ABP*, 7 July 1929.

192 AICC, G95/1929, Mitra to Nehru, 14 July 1929.
193 Ibid., Nehru to Mitra, 2 June 1929.
194 Ibid., Mitra to Nehru, 14 June 1929.
195 Ibid., Mitra to Nehru, 27 June 1929.
196 Ibid., Nehru to Bakhale, 1 July 1929.
197 Ibid., Mitra to Nehru, 2 August 1929.
198 Ibid., Mitra to Nehru, 15 July 1929.
199 AICC, G71/1929, Nehru to Bose, 21 August 1929. See also Nehru's press statement, 'An open letter to the Shaw and Wallace Company' (managing agent for the Tinplate company), *ABP*, 21 August 1929.
200 Ibid., Prasad to Nehru, 23 August 1929.
201 Ibid.
202 IOR, V/26/670/31, Dain, 'Memorandum', op. cit., p. 42.
203 *Liberty*, 7 July 1929.
204 Ibid., 1 August 1929.
205 Ibid., 23 August 1929.
206 Ibid.
207 Ibid., 7 September 1929.
208 IOR, L/PJ/12/3, FR(2), November, Bihar and Orissa.
209 IOR, L/PJ/12/14, FR(1), March, 1930, Bihar and Orissa.
210 *The Statesman*, 23 September 1921. See also NAI, Meerut Conspiracy Case, file 32/3213, JLA Bulletin, 21 September 1931.
211 See above.
212 NAI, Meerut Conspiracy Case, file 32/3213, Bose to P. K. Alexander, TISCO managing director, 29 October 1928.
213 Dipesh Chakrabarty, 'Sasipada Banerjee: first Bhadralok contact with the working class in Bengal', *IHR* 2.2 (July 1976), p. 356.
214 Ibid., p. 358.
215 See above.
216 G. D. Birla, *In the Shadow of Mahatma: a Personal Memoir* (Calcutta, 1953).
217 NMML, PTP, PT 42(2), N. M. Majumdar to Purushattamdas Thakurdas, 22 May 1929.
218 Ibid., Ibrahim Rahimtoola to G. D. Seth, Secretary, JLA, no date.
219 NAI, Meerut Conspiracy Case, file, 32/3213, JLA Bulletin, 12 September 1928.
220 NMML, PTP, PT 42(2), G. D. Birla to Purushattamdas Thakurdas, 16 July 1929.
221 Subhas Bose, *Selected Speeches*, Government of India, p. 33.
222 *ABP*, 3 May 128, editorial.

Chapter four

1   J. Gallagher, 'Congress in decline: Bengal, 1930–39' *Modern Asian Studies* (hereafter *MAS*) 7.3 (1973), p. 589; see also Anil Seal, 'Imperialism & nationalism in India', ibid., p. 336.

2   IOR, L/PJ/7/242. Terrorism in Bengal, printed for the Cabinet (May 1932), p. 3.

3   Ibid., p. 1.

4   Subhas Bose, Presidential Speech, Haripura, in *Crossroads*, (hereafter *CR*), Netaji Research Bureau, Calcutta, 1971, pp. 10, 22–3; NMML, Yaznik Papers, Bose to Yaznik, 17 April 1936.

5   Subhas Bose appreciated unequivocally the sacrifice of the terrorists who died after the Writers' Building shooting episode. He refused to characterize them as 'misguided' because 'they wanted freedom not merely following the Congress programme but, if need be, they wanted freedom at any price and by any means. *Liberty*, 11 December 1930.

6   IOR, L/PJ/7/242, brief note on the alliance of Congress with terrorism in Bengal, p. 8.

7   Ibid., p. 9.

8   IOR, L/PJ/5/145, CS', GB, report for the first half of June 1939.

9   Ibid.

10   WBSA Home-Poll 9/1939: Chief Secretary's Fortnightly Report for the first half of October 1939.

11   *Sanibarer Chhiti* (Saturday's Letter), a Bengali weekly, edn 3.1 (Aghrahayan, 1336), p. 910; Same (Bhadra, 1336), p. 326.

12   Tomilson has shown in general terms how 'the extension of the organization and campaign to enrol members was often linked to these elections', B. R. Tomlinson, *The Indian National Congress and the Raj, 1929–42: the Penultimate Phase* (London, 1976), p. 87.

13   *Amrita Bazar Patrika* (hereafter *ABP*), 17 October 1923, quoted in J. Gallagher, 'Congress in Decline', *MAS*, op. cit., p. 594.

14   NMML, AICC papers, G25-26/1934, AICC report on the controversy of 'Bengal AICC membership'.

15   Ibid.

16   NMML, AICC, G120/1929, complaint signed by Prafulla Ghosh, J. C. Gupta, Monoranjan Banerjee, Probhat K. Ganguli, Kshitish Ch. Gupta, and Nirmal Chandra Datta, no date.

17   NMML, AICC, G120/Part 1/1929, J. Nehru to the secretary, Chittagong DCC, 8 November 1929.

18   NMML, AICC, G120/Part I/1929, anonymous letter addressed to the secretary, BPCC, 14 June 1929.

19   NMML, AICC, G120/1929, complaints from Darjeeling and Sylhet, 17 November 1929.

20 NMML, AICC, G120/1929, complaint from Sylhet DCC to the BPCC, 16 November 1929.
21 NMML, AICC, G120/1929, letter of B. C. Roy to J. Nehru, 26 November 1929, p. 2; AICC, G120/Part I/1929, letter from Akhil Chowdhury to Pattavi, 24 November 1929 – Akhil Chowdhury was asked by Sengupta (who later admitted) to lodge a complaint to Pattavi.
22 Ibid., p. 3.
23 NMML, AICC, G120/1929, complaint from Chittagong, 4 November 1929.
24 Ibid.
25 West Bengal State Archives (hereafter WBSA), Home-Poll 139/1932, revolutionary movement and examples of their propaganda in Bengal. Home Department Bulletin, 1932.
26 NMML, AICC, G25-26/1934, report entitled Bengal AICC membership, p. 2.
27 NMML, AICC, G120/Part I/1929, J. Nehru's reply to the Chittagong DCC, 4 November 1929.
28 NMML, AICC, G120/1929, letter of J. Nehru to Bhupendranath Datta, 13 December 1929.
29 NMML, AICC, G120/1929, Motilal's Award, p. 1.
30 NMML, AICC, G120/Part I/1929, Telegram from Motilal to Subhas Bose, 23 November 1929.
31 NMML, AICC, G25-26/1934, Bengal AICC membership, op. cit.
32 NMML, AICC, G25-26/1934, Sengupta to Motilal, 5 December 1929.
33 NMML, AICC, G120/1929, letter from Hem Chandra Ghosh, Raj Kumar Chakrabarty, Nalini Mohan Roy Chowdhury, Basanta Kuma Majumdar to the Secretary, AICC, no date, p. 2.
34 Ibid., pp. 2–3.
35 NMML, AICC, G25-26/1934, Bengal AICC membership, op. cit., p. 3.
36 NMML, AICC, G120/Part I/1929, letter of Bose to the President AICC, 27 December 1929.
37 Ibid., p. 3.
38 Ibid., p. 2.
39 Forward, *Liberty* of 9 December 1929.
40 NMML, AICC, G120/Part I/1929, telegram from Bose to J. Nehru, 7 December 1929.
41 NMML, AICC, G120/Part I/1929, telegram from Sengupta to Motilal, 8 December 1929.
42 NMML, AICC, G120/1929, letter from S. K. Mitra, J. C. Gupta to the President, AICC, 13 December 1929.
43 NMML, AICC, ibid., report of the AICC-appointed inspector, p. 3.

44   NMML, AICC, ibid., letter of S. K. Mitra and J. C. Gupta, op. cit., p. 5.
45   Ibid., p. 5.
46   NMML, AICC, ibid., Motilal's assessment of Bengal affairs, no date, p. 5.
47   NMML, AICC, ibid., p. 3.
48   NMML, AICC, G25-26/1934, Bengal's affairs, p. 2.
49   NMML, AICC, ibid., Motilal's Award.
50   NMML, AICC, G25-26/1929, Bengal AICC membership, p. 1.
51   NMML, AICC, G120/Part II/1931, letter from Purna Chandra Das to Vallabhbhai Patel, President, AICC, 9 April 1931.
52   Ibid., memorandum to the Congress President, no date, by Sris Chandra Datta, Sures Chandra Majumdar, Khirode Chandra Deb, Paresh Lal Shome, J. C. Gupta, Binode Behari Chakrabarti, Prafulla Chandra Ghosh (content and file number indicate that it was sent in 1929).
53   NMML, AICC, P5/Part I/1937, letter of Hara Dayal Nag to J. Nehru, 10 October 1937.
54   IOR, L/PJ/12/25, FR, first half of December 1931.
55   NMML, AICC, G120/Part II/1930, letter of B. C. Roy to Nehru, 27 March 1930; Jadugopal Mukherji too held Corporation politics responsible for all troubles within the Congress. See Jadugopal Mukherji, *Biplabi Jinaner Smriti* (Bengali), (Calcutta, 1982), p. 418.
56   IOR, L/PJ/12/25, FR, first half of September 1931.
57   NMML, AICC, G120/Part I/1930, *Advance*, (12 February 1920), Representatives of the City Congress League were as follows: (1) Benoy Kumar Bose, Secretary, Central Calcutta CC; (2) Hemanta Basu, North Calcutta CC; (3) Paritosh Banerjee, South Calcutta CC; (4) Madhusudan Das Barman, Bara Bazar CC; and (5) Satyanarayan Chatterjee, 24 Parganas CC.
58   NMML, AICC, G120/Part I/1930, *Advance* (2 March 1930).
59   NMML, AICC, G120/Part I/1930, letter of J. Nehru to Bose, 5 April 1930.
60   NMML, AICC, G120/Part I/1930, Nehru's note on the conflict in Congress circles in Bengal, 29 March 1930.
61   NMML, AICC, ibid., letter of Hari Kumar Chakrabarty, secretary, BPCC to J. Nehru, 15 March 1930.
62   *Liberty*, 20 March 1930.
63   NMML, AICC, G120/Part II/1930, letter of B. C. Roy to Nehru, 27 March 1930.
64   Ibid.
65   NMML, AICC, G120/Part I/1930, letter of Hari Kumar Chakrabarty to Nehru, 15 March 1930.
66   NMML, AICC, G120/Part II/1931, letter of K. S. Roy to Vallabhbhai Patel, 25 May 1931, p. 2.

67 *Liberty*, 5 September 1931.
68 IOR, L/PJ/12/25, FR, first half of September 1931.
69 *ABP*, 5 September 1931 and *Advance*, 5 September 1931, for Sengupta's Election Manifesto.
70 NMML, AICC, P6/Part I/1927–31, telegram of Bose to Vallabhbhai Patel, 8 September 1931.
71 NMML, AICC, P15/1931, Letter of B. C. Roy to Patel, 7 September 1931.
72 NMML, AIC, G120/Part II/1920, letter of B. C. Roy to Nehru, 27 March 1930.
73 NMML, AICC, ibid., letter from Nandalal Roy to Patel, 11 September 1931.
74 The election dispute will be dealt with in the following section.
75 NMML, AICC, ibid., letter of Bose to M. S. Aney, 17 September 1931; letter of K. S. Roy to M. S. Aney, 8 September 1931.
76 NMML, AICC, ibid., letter of M. S. Aney to Patel, 17 September 1931.
77 NMML, AICC, ibid., report signed by Patel, 11 September 1931.
78 NMML, AICC, ibid., letter of Patel to Sengupta, 11 September 1931.
79 NMML, AICC, ibid., M. S. Aney to Patel, 17 September 1931.
80 IOR, L/PJ/12/25 FR, first half of September 1931; *Advance*, 5 September 1931.
81 NMML, AICC, P6/Part I/1927–31, telegram from Bose to Patel, 10 September 1931.
82 NMML, AICC, G120/Part II/1931, letter of K. S. Roy to Patel, 25 May 1931.
83 *Liberty*, 5 September 1931.
84 IOR, L/PJ/12/25, FR, second half of May 1931.
85 *Liberty*, 5 September 1931; NMML, AICC, G120/Part II/1931, K. S. Roy to Patel, 25 May 1931.
86 NMML, AICC, G120/Part I/1930, Nehru's note on the conflict in Congress circles in Bengal, 7 March 1930.
87 *Liberty*, 4 June 1931.
88 *Advance*, 17 July 1931.
89 NMML, AICC, G120/Part I/1931, resolution of the Working Committee contained in a letter of Nehru to the secretary, BPCC, 12 June 1931.
90 NMML, AICC, G120/Part II/1931, Patel's letter to Pulin Behari Ghosh, 15 May 1931.
91 NMML, AIC, G120/Part I/1930, Nehru's note: Conflict in Congress crisis in Bengal.
92 NMML, AICC, P6/Part II/1927–31, the composition of the BPCC for 1929, 1930 and 1931 was as follows: president: Subhas Chandra Bose; vice-presidents: (1) Satyendra Ch. Mitra and (2) Maulana

Muhammad Akram Khan; secretary: K. S. Roy; assistant secretaries: (1) Lal Mohan Ghosh, (2) Siris Kumar Chowdhury and (3) Maulvi Shamsuddin Ahmed; Treasurer: B. C. Roy.

93 NMML, AICC P6-P12/1927–31, letter of J. Nehru to K. S. Roy, 15 August 1929, p. 3.

94 NMML, AICC, G120/Part II/1931, letter of Nehru to Subhas Bose, 18 May 1931.

95 Ibid., letter of Subhas to Nehru, 27 May 1931.

96 *Advance*, 24 May 1931.

97 NMML, AICC, P6-P12/1927–31, letter of Sengupta to J. Nehru 15 August 1929.

98 NMML, AICC, G120/Part II/1931, letter of Bose to Nehru, 27 May 1931; the BPCC published the figure in *Liberty* too. See *Liberty*, 25 May 1931.

99 NMML, AICC, G120/Part I/1931, telegrams from 26 districts during the months of April, May and June of 1930.

100 NMML, AICC, P6-P12/1927–31, letter of Nehru to K. S. Roy, 15 August 1929.

101 NMML, AICC, G120/Part II/1931, this file contains complaints from the DCCS.

102 NMML, AICC, G120/Part II/1931, letter from Haripada Bhattacharjee, secretary, Jessore DCC to the secretary, AICC, 30 May 1931.

103 NMML, AICC, G120/Part II/1931, memorandum from Mymensingh signed by 26 people, no date; complaints from Barisal, signed by 8 DCC members, 28 May 1931. AICC, P6-P12/1927–31, letter from the secretary, Chittagong DCC, to the secretary, AICC, 22 May 1931. AICC, G120/Part I/1931, memorandum from Comilla DCC to the AICC, 8 June 1931; Telegram from the secretary, Faridpur DCC, to the Congress president, 8 June 1931.

104 NMML, AICC, 13/1929, letter from Kshitish Dasgupta to Sengupta, 30 January 1931.

105 Ibid.

106 *Advance*, 26 May 1931.

107 NMML, AICC, G120/Part I/1931, telegram from Sengupta to Patel, 6 June 1931.

108 NMML, AICC, P6/Part II/1927–31, letter from Syed Mahmud, general secretary, AICC, to the secretary, BPCC, 6 March 1931.

109 *ABP*, 18 August 1931, Bose's letter to the editor of *ABP* concerning the BPCC election dispute.

110 NMML, AICC, P6/Part I/1927–31, telegram from Patel, Congress President, to the secretary, BPCC, 11 July 1931.

111 NMML, AICC, P6/Part I/1927–31, ibid.

112 NMML, AICC, G86/KW (1)/1930, letter from Hari Kumar Chakrabarty, secretary BPCC, to the secretary AICC, 11 April 1930.

113 *ABP*, 22 April 1931, Kshitish Dasgupta's letter to the Editor, *ABP*.
114 *Advance*, 18 March 1930.
115 WBSA, F.N. 345/1931, SL. no. 18/Part II, opinion of S. H. H. Mills, Deputy Commissioner of Police, Special Branch, Calcutta, no date.
116 NAI, Home-Poll, F.N. 146/1931, telegram from the Home department, GI, to the UP government, 6 May 1931.
117 IOR, Halifax Collection, MSS, Eur/C 152/24, Stanley Jackson, Governor of Bengal, to Lord Irwin, Governor-General, India, 9 January 1930.
118 NMML, AICC, 1 P6-P12/1927–31, letter of B. C. Roy to Motilal, 11 April 1930.
119 *ABP*, 7 June 1931, A. Chakrabarty's letter to the editor, *ABP*.
120 *ABP*, 31 May 1931, an open letter to Sengupta and Bose.
121 NMML, AICC, G1/1931, Nehru's report on the Progress of civil disobedience, quoted in Sumit Sarkar, *Modern India* (Delhi, 1983), p. 289.
122 NMML, AICC, G86/1930, letter of Birendranath Guha, secretary, BCCD, to the AICC, 6 November 1930.
123 Ibid., 'A brief account of the civil disobedience movement in Bengal', report from Comilla (Salt Campaign), part I (1930).
124 NMML, AICC, G86/KW II/1930, letter of Hari Chakrabarty, secretary, BPCC to the Secretary, AICC, 11 April 1930.
125 NAI, Home-Poll, F.N. 248/1930, letter of J. Peddie, DM, Midnapore, to W. S. Hopkyns, CS, GB, 12 June 1930.
126 NMML, AICC, G/86/1930, 'A brief account of civil disobedience in Bengal', 1930, part II, p. 1. The underground newspaper, *The Challenge*, contains information relating to no-tax campaign.
127 Ibid., *The Challenge*, 15 September 1930.
128 Tanika Sarkar has shown how the government tried to utilize the 'Pirs' to dissociate the Muslim peasantry from the civil disobedience campaign. See Tanika Sarkar, Communal Riots in Bengal in M. Hasan ed., *Communal and Pan-Islamic Trends in Colonial India* (Delhi, 1981), p. 289.
129 NMML, AICC, G86/KWII/1930, letter of Hari Kumar Chakrabarty to the Congress President, 11 April 1930.
130 Tanika Sarkar, 'First phase of civil disobedience in Bengal 1930–31', in *Indian Historical Review* (hereafter *IHR*), 4.1 (July 1977), p. 90.
131 NMML, AICC, P6/Part I/1927–31 letter from M. N. Dutta, secretary, Flood Relief Committee, to Patel, President, AICC, 12 September 1931.
132 *Advance*, 19 August 1931.
133 *ABP*, 22 August 1931.
134 *ABP*, 25 August 1931.
135 *The Statesman*, 29 August 1931.
136 *Liberty*, 8 September 1931.

137 NMML, AICC, P6/Part I/1927–31, telegram from Sengupta to Patel, 25 August 1931.

138 Ibid., telegram from Bose to Patel, 30 August 1931.

139 Ibid., Reply of Patel to Bose, 31 August 1931.

140 Ibid., Nehru's letter to Bose, 4 September 1931.

141 NMML, AICC, G120/Part I/1931, letter from Jnanendra Mohan Sarkar, President, Murshidabad DCC, to Nehru, GS, AICC, 2 September 1931.

142 WBSA, Home-Poll, F.N. 345/1931 (SL. no. 18/Part II), note on the relief operation by the DM, Mymensingh, 30 August 1931. *The Statesman* also advertised for the rival Committee, see the edition of 29 September 1931.

143 NMML, AICC, G120/Part I/1931, letter of Jnanendra Mohan Sarkar, op. cit., 2 September 1931.

144 NMML, AICC, G/120/Part I/1931, Aney Award, p. 3.

145 *ABP*, 22 September 1931.

146 NMML, AICC, G/120/Part I/1931, Aney Award, op. cit., p. 5.

147 Ibid., p. 6.

148 NMML, AICC, G/120/Part I/1931, Nehru's (GS) letter to the secretary, BPCC, 30 October 1931.

149 Ibid., p. 10.

150 Ibid., p. 11.

151 Ibid., p. 12.

152 Ibid., p. 13.

153 Ibid., list of Aney-appointed executive and the BPCC executive in 1928, 1929 and 1930.

154 *ABP*, 27 September 1931.

155 NMML, AICC, P15/1931, telegram from Patel to Aney, 25 September 1931.

156 NMML, AICC, P15/1931, letter from Satis Chandra Sarkar, member of the BPCC to Aney, no date. See also AICC P6/Part I/1927–31, Bengal's record: a report written by an anonymous author. In this the Aney report was criticized for being favourable to Sengupta.

157 NMML, AICC, P15/1931, letter from Satis Chandra Sarkar (see above).

158 IOR, L/PJ/12/25, FR, second half of September 1931.

159 WBSA, FN345/1931/SL no. 18 (Part II), note by S. H. H. Mills, Deputy Commissioner of Police, Special Branch, Calcutta.

160 IOR, L/PJ/12/25, FR, first half of December 1931. Resolution was: 'Time has come for the resumption of Satyagraha for the achievement of complete independence.' Apart from this general resolution, four specific resolutions were adopted demanding: (1) the intensive boycott of all British goods; (2) the boycott of all

banks, insurance companies and steamship companies and other concerns controlled by the British, and the boycott of Anglo-Indian newspapers; (3) the boycott of foreign clothes; and (4) the prohibition of liquor and intoxicating drugs.

161 *Liberty*, 13 December 1931.
162 R. Ray, *Urban Roots of Indian Natinalism* op. cit., p. 170.
163 NMML, AICC, P6/Part II/1936, a note entitled Bengal Congress Affairs, no date.
164 NMML, AICC, G25/1934–35, Complaints from Kshitish Dasgupta to the General Secretary, AICC, 10 January 1935 (enclosing a list of 25).
165 NMML, AICC, P6/Part II/1936, a note, op. cit., p. 2.
166 NMML, AICC, G25/1934–35, letter from D. C. Chakrabarty, member of the BPCC (writing on behalf of twenty-five BPCC members) to Syed Mahmud, secretary, AICC, 11 November 1934. 'To us this course [allowing both groups of Bengal congressmen equal representation in the AICC] offers the only smooth way out of the present tangle.'
167 Ibid., p. 2.
168 NMML, AICC, P6/P2/1936, letter of Subhas Bose to Suresh Chandra Majumdar, secretary, BPCC, 7 July 1935.
169 NAI, Rajendra Prasad Papers (hereafter RPP), IV/1936, Bose to Sures Majumdar, 29 July 1935.
170 Ibid., K. S. Roy to Nehru, 28 March 1936.
171 *ABP*, 15 July 1935.
172 NMML, AICC, P6/Part 2/1936, a note, op. cit., p. 2.
173 NMML, AICC, letter of K. S. Roy to the President, AICC, 2 December 1935.
174 NMML, AICC, ibid., letter of Rajendra Prasad to J. Nehru, 10 May 1936.
175 Ibid., p. 3.
176 Ibid.
177 Ibid.
178 NMML, Jawaharlal Nehru Papers (hereafter JNP), Subhas Bose to Nehru from Austria, 13 December 1937. Though written in 1937, Bose referred to what happened in 1936.
179 NMML, AICC, P6/P2/1936, a report, op. cit., p. 3.
180 NMML, AICC, G25/1934–35, note of Kshitish Dasgupta, op. cit.
181 NMML, AICC, P6/P2/1936, Prasad's Award.
182 Ibid., p. 1.
183 NMML, AICC, P6/Part I/1936, representation from the BPCC to the Working Committee, AICC, signed by Suresh Majumdar, secretary, BPCC, 14 June 1936.
184 NMML, AICC, P6/P2/1936, Prasad's Award, op. cit.

185 Ibid.
186 NMML, AICC, P6/Part I/1936, copy of the Resolution adopted by the BPCC, 1 June 1936.
187 NMML, AICC, P6/Part I/1936, Working Committee resolution, 2 July 1936.
188 NMML, AICC, P6/Part II/1936, report by the scrutineer's to the AICC, 2 August 1936.
189 Ibid., letter of K. S. Roy to J. Nehru, 8 August 1936.
190 NMML, AICC, P6/Part I/1936, memorandum by the BPCC, 14 June 1936; AICC, P6/Part II/1936, Bengal Congress Affairs, op. cit., p. 5.
191 NAI, RPP, I/1936, summary report of the informal talks held between Bengal friends and Prasad, 19 March 1936.
192 NMML, AICC, P6/Part I/1936, report of the discussion held at the Working Committee meeting, 15 March 1936.
193 It is surprising to find that both the BPCC members and those outside opposed the idea of AICC dominance in provincial matters. See AICC, P6/Part II/1936, Bengal Congress Affairs, op. cit., p. 7; AICC, P6/Part I/1936, memorandum from the BPCC signed by Sures Majumdar, secretary BPCC, 14 June 1936.
194 NMML, AICC, P6/Part 1/1936, a letter to J. Nehru from a nameless Congress worker, no date.
195 Ibid.
196 Ibid.
197 Ibid.
198 Ibid., p. 3.
199 NMML, AICC, G58(II)/1936, a complaint from sixteen members of the Primary Congress Committee of Tippera to the President, 3 April 1937.
200 See chapter 1.
201 IOR, L/PJ/5/144, FR, first half of March, 1939.
202 NAI, Home-Poll FN/18/3/1939, note by the Chief Secretary Bengal, 22 April 1939.
203 Ibid.
204 Ibid.
205 *The Statesman*, 13 August 1939.
206 NMML, AICC, P5/1939, letter from K. S. Roy, Amarkrishna Ghosh, Arun Chandra Guha, Raj Kumar Chakrabarty, Abinash Chandra Bose, Benoyendranath Palit to the Congress President, 31 July 1939.
207 Ibid., see the copy of the notice annexed with the above letter.
208 NAI, RPP, 3/B/39, letter of Prafulla Ghosh to Prasad, 20 July 1939.
209 Ibid., B. C. Roy to Patel, 17 July 1939.
210 NMML, M. N. Roy Papers (hereafter MNRP), letter of M. N. Roy

to Amarendranath Chakrabarty, 24 July 1939.

211 *ABP*, 27 July 1939.

212 *Hindustan Standard* (hereafter *HS*), 27 July 1939, list of the office bearers. President: Subhas Bose; Vice-presidents: Rajen Deb, Hem Prava Majumdar; Moulvi Golam Mohiuddin Khan, Bepin Behari Ganguly and Sures Chandra Banerjee; Secretary: Maulvi Ashrafuddin Ahmed Chowdhury; Assistant Secretaries: Kalipada Bagchi, Krishna Kumar Chatterji, Sudhansu Bose, Gopal Halder, Panchu Gopal Bhadury; Treasurer: J. C. Gupta.

213 *ABP*, 27 July 1939.

214 Ibid.

215 NMML, AICC, P5/1939, letter of K. S. Roy and others to the Congress President, 31 July 1939.

216 *ABP*, 30 July 1939.

217 NMML, AICC, P5/IV/1939–40, letter of Ashrafuddin Ahmed Chowdhury, secretary, BPCC to the Congress President, no date.

218 NMML, AICC, P5/1939, letter of K. S. Roy and others to the Congress President, 31 July 1939, pp. 3–7.

219 NMML, P5/IV/1939–40, complaints from Murshidabad, Noagon, Jessore, Netrokona, Mymensingh, Jamalpur and Balurghat.

220 *HS*, 7 July 1939.

221 *HS*, 7 July 1939 and 9 July 1939.

222 NAI, RPP, 3/B/39, letter of B. C. Roy to Patel, 17 July 1939.

223 NMML, AICC, P5/1939, Prasad's press statement, 10 August 1939.

224 NMML, AICC, P5/1939, AICC, note on the defiance and insubordination of the Executive Council of the BPCC, p. 1.

225 Subhas's statement on disciplinary action (dated 19 August 1939) in *CR*, pp. 200–1.

226 NMML, AICC, P5/1939, section IV, Bengal Congress Election Tribunal, p. 3.

227 NMML, AICC, P5/Part I/1939–40, the copy of the resolution adopted on 25 August 1939.

228 Ibid.

229 *ABP*, 31 August 1939.

230 Ibid.

231 Ibid.

232 *HS*, 31 August 1939.

233 *ABP*, 31 August 1939. In the meeting Somnath Lahiry, an active member of the CPI, defended the resolution and condemned the working Committee for being 'autocratic'.

234 *HS*, 31 August 1939, Joint statement of K. S. Roy and Prafulla Ghosh.

235 *HS*, 1 September 1939, Bose's press statement relating to the assault.

236   NMML, AICC, P5/Part II/1939–40, letter of Prasad to Kripalani, 1 January 1940.
237   NMML, AICC, P5/Part II/1939–40, defiance and insubordination of the Executive Council of the BPCC, p. 4.
238   NMML, JNP, Part I/VIII, letter of Sarat Bose to the Congress President, 21 January 1940.
239   NMML, AICC P5/1939, defiance and insubordination, op. cit., p. 4.
240   Ibid.
241   Ibid., letter of K. S. Roy to the Congress President, 30 September 1939.
242   Ibid., complaints from Murshidabad, Jessore and Mymensingh.
243   Ibid., letter of K. S. Roy to the Congress President, 30 September 1939.
244   Ibid., defiance and insubordination, op. cit., p. 4.
245   NMML, AICC P5/Part I/1939–40, copy of the resolution adopted by the Executive Council of the BPCC on 30 October 1939.
246   NMML, AICC, P5/1939, Rajendra Chandra Deb was elected President of the BPCC on 30 October 1939.
247   *HS*, 31 October 1939.
248   *HS*, 8 January 1940, this edition published the correspondence between Sarat Bose and the Congress High Command relating to the 'Fund Problem'. Copy of the resolution adopted on 15 October 1939 is enclosed in Maulana Azad's letter to Sarat Bose, 27 October 1939.
249   Ibid., letter of Prasad to Sarat Bose, 12 November 1939.
250   Ibid., Maulana Azad's letter to Sarat Bose, 16 November 1939.
251   Ibid., Resolution adopted on 23 November 1939.
252   NMML, AICC, AR6/1931, audit report signed by audit inspector, AICC, 14 October 1931.
253   Ibid.
254   Ibid., letter of Nehru 20 October 1931.
255   Ibid., letter of Nehru to the BPCC secretary, 14 November 1931.
256   *HS*, 8/1/1940, resolution adopted between 19 and 23 of November, 1939.
257   Ibid., Azad acknowledged the receipt of the money in his reply (of 27 November 1939) to Sarat Bose.
258   Ibid., Sarat Bose's letter to Azad, 26 November 1939.
259   Ibid.
260   Ibid., Nehru's letter of 30 November 1937 was quoted in this edition.
261   NMML, JNP, Part I/VIII, letter of Sarat Bose to the Congress President, 21 January 1940.
262   *ABP*, 1 January 1940.
263   *HS*, 8 January 1940, Sarat Bose's letter, 26 November 1939.
264   Ibid.

265 NMML, JNP, Part I/VIII, letter of Sarat Bose to Nehru, 21 January 1940.

266 *HS*, 8 January 1940, op. cit., letter of Sarat Bose to Prasad, 14 December 1939.

267 Ibid., letter of Prasad to Sarat Bose, 15 December 1939.

268 Ibid., letter of Sarat Bose to Maulana Azad, 18 December 1939.

269 Ibid., letter of J. B. Kripalani to Sarat Bose, 21 December 1939.

270 Ibid., letter of Prasad to Sarat Bose, 23 December 1939.

271 NMML, AICC, P5/1939, defiance and insubordination, op. cit., Prasad's statement, p. 3.

272 NAI, RPP, 3/B/1939, letter of Prasad to Nehru on the Congress Fund in Bengal, 18 December 1939.

273 NMML, AICC, P5/1939, defiance and insubordination, op. cit.

274 NAI, RPP, III/1940, summary of the audit report submitted to Prasad, 30 December 1939, pp. 3–5.

275 *HS*, 31 December 1939, Ashrafuddin's defence of the accounts of the Congress fund, as kept by the BPCC.

276 NAI, Home-Poll, 139–40, a note by the Home Department on the Congress Fund and property.

277 Ibid.

278 NAI. RPP, III/1940, audit report, op. cit., p. 5.

279 *HS*, 9 January 1940.

280 NMML, AICC, P5/Part II/1939–40, BPCC resolution transferring Rs10,000 to Subhas Bose on 30 December 1939.

281 *ABP*, 1 January 1940, Working Committee Resolution on 31 December 1939.

282 NMML, AICC P5/Part II/1939–40, Resolution accepted by the Executive Council of the BPCC at its meeting held on 5 January 1940.

283 Ibid.

284 *HS*, 24 January 1940, report of the subcommittee.

285 NMML, AICC, P5/II/1939–40, resolution passed by the Executive Council of the BPCC, 30 December 1939.

286 *ABP*, 6 January 1940.

287 Ibid., press statement.

288 *HS*, 2 January 1940, J. C. Gupta's press statement.

289 Ibid., BPCC resolution authorizing Sarat Bose to hold the brief for the BPCC.

290 NMML, AICC, P5/II/1939–40, resolution of Executive Council of the BPCC, 5 January 1940.

291 NMML, AICC, P5/II/1939–40, letter of Nehru to Prasad, 7 January 1940.

292 *Sangarsh*, 7 January 1940 (Hindi Weekly of the CSP), Jayprakash's statement.

293   NMML, MNRP, letter of Jibanlal Chattapadhyay to M. N. Roy, 13 January 1940.
294   Ibid., M. N. Roy to Jibanlal, 15 January 1940. This letter is a copy of an earlier letter sent by Roy to Jibanlal (dated 9 January 1940).
295   *ABP*, 6 January 1940, press statement of Sures Chandra Banerjee.
296   NMML, MNRP, letter of Jibanlal to Roy, 13 January 1940.
297   Ibid.
298   *ABP*, 6 January 1940, Prasad's press statement.
299   NMML, AICC, P5/Part LL/1939–40, copy of the circular signed by Ashrafuddin Ahmed Chowdhury, secretary to the BPCC.
300   NMML, AICC, P5/Part II/1939, telegram from Sarat Bose to Prasad, 30 January 1940.
301   Ibid., reply from Prasad to Sarat Bose, 30 January 1940.
302   Ibid., telegram from Sarat Bose to Prasad, 31 January 1940.
303   Ibid., letter of Prasad to Sarat Bose, 1 February 1940.
304   Ibid., letter of Prasad to Sarat Bose, 8 February 1940.
305   *ABP*, 26 February 1940.
306   NMML, AICC, P5/Part II/1939, resolution of the Working Committee, 29 February 1940, signed by Maulana Azad, the Congress President.
307   *ABP*, 30 February 1940, see also *HS*, 30 February 1940.
308   NMML, JNP, Part I/VIII, resolution of the Executive Council of the suspended BPCC, 30 February 1940.
309   NMML, Sahajanand Papers, Sahajanand's (leader of the All-Indian Kishan Sabha) press statement.
310   J. P's statement, 5 February 1940, Muzaffar Ahmad was quoted in this edition.
311   NMML, MNRP, letter of M. N. Roy to the secretary of the Radical Congressmen, 19 June 1940.
312   NMML, AICC, P5/II/1940, letter of Arun Chandra Guha to the general secretary, AICC, 7 May 1940.
313   Ibid., letter of S. M. Ghosh, president, official BPCC, to the Congress President, 16 August 1940.
314   NMML, AICC, P5/1939–40, BPCC resolution adopted on 7 January 1940.
315   See chapter 1.
316   Sixth Quinquenniel Report on the Progress of Education in Bengal (hereafter QRPEB), pp. 91–2, quoted in B. R. Khan, 'Some aspects of society and politics in Bengal, 1927–36' (unpublished PhD thesis, University of London, 1979), pp. 172–3.
317   Ibid.
318   Edward Shils, 'Students, politics and universities in India', in Philip G. Altbach ed., *Turmoil and Transition* (Higher Education and Student Politics in India), p. 2.

319 Subhas Bose, *Indian Struggle* (hereafter *IS*) (London, 1964), p. 65; see also H. Mitra ed., *Indian Annual Register* (hereafter *IAR*) (1921), p. 246.

320 WBSA, Home-Poll, F.N. 139/1931, report of DPI on the activity of students during the civil disobedience, 2 November 1931.

321 Eighth QRPEB, p. 131, quoted in B. R. Khan, 'Some aspects of society and politics in Bengal, 1927–34', op. cit., p. 187.

322 B. R. Khan, 'Some aspects of society and politics in Bengal, 1927–34', op. cit., p. 187.

323 Sixth QRPEB, pp. 90–1, quoted in B. R. Khan, 'Some aspects of society and politics in Bengal, 1927–34', ibid., p. 188.

324 WBSA, Home-Poll (confidential), F.N. 441/1929, a short note on the youth association in Bengal by F. J. Lowman, Deputy Inspector General of Police, GB, June, 1929.

325 IOR, L/PJ/6/1947, letter of Charles Tegart, Police Commissioner to the CS, GB, 4 February 1928.

326 *The Statesman* of 7 February 1928 and 4 March 1928.

327 NMML, Suren Ghosh, oral transcript, p. 18.

328 WBSA, Home-Poll, F.N. 441/1929, Lowman, op. cit.

329 Ibid.

330 WBSA, Home-Poll (confidential), F.N. 345/1931, SL. no. 18/Part II, note by S. H. H. Mills, Deputy Commissioner of Police, Special Branch, Calcutta.

331 NMML, AICC, G120/Part II/1931, annual report of the Third Session, 1929–30.

332 IOR, L/PJ/12/2, FR, second half of September 1929.

333 NMML, AICC, G120/Part II/1931, annual report of the ABSA, pp. 4–5.

334 Ibid., p. 5.

335 NMML, AICC, G120/Part I/1931, report of Mymensingh Conference.

336 IOR, L/PJ/12/25, FR, second half of April 1931.

337 Ibid.

338 NMML, AICC, G120/Part II/1931, memorandum from Mymensingh signed by 26 primary Congress members (no date) to the AICC.

339 *ABP*, 9 June 1931, press statement of Sj. Sachindranath Mitra of ABSA.

340 WBSA, Home-Poll (confidential), F.N. 345/1931, SL. no. 18, Part II, Report of Deputy Commissioner Police, Special Branch, op. cit.

341 WBSA, Home-Poll (confidential) F.N. 345/1931, SL. nos 1–17, report of the DM, Mymensingh to the Commissioner, Dacca Division, 19 June 1931.

342 WBSA, Home-Poll (confidential) F.N. 139/1932, a pamphlet

entitled, 'To the young political workers'.

343 Myron Weiner, *The Politics of Scarcity* (Chicago, 1962), p. 163.

344 Ibid., p. 164.

345 Abul Mansur Ahmad, *Atmakatha* (Bengali) (Dacca, 1978), p. 108–14.

346 IOR, L/PJ/12/36, FR, second half June 1932.

347 *The Statesman*, 16 July 1930.

348 At the second All-Bengal Muslim Students Conference held at Mymensingh in June 1935, Additional District Superintendent of police was present as a guest. See *Star of India*, 2 September 1935.

Glossary

abhijata bhadralok   aristocrat

ahsan manzil   a beautiful building

apni   the term of respect for a senior or relatively unknown person in conversation

Baidya   name of a caste associated with the medical profession

bargadar   share-cropper

bhadralok   gentleman

caliph   ruler of Turkey and religious leader

chhillim   cone-shaped earthen container of tobacco for smoking placed on the perpendicular cylinder of a *hooka*

Chitpavan Brahmans   a type of Brahman in Maharashtra

dhyana   meditation

farash   knee-high platform covered with *sataranj* or sheets

grihastha bhadralok   those having income both from land and a profession

hartal   strike

hooka   smoking pipe

hookum   order

jihad   holy war, or effort to establish the supremacy of Islam

jotedar   large landowner, holding rights of either intermediate tenure or mere tenancy, sometimes having tenants under him and often engaging in money-lending or grain trading

kachhari   zamindar's administrative block

Kayastha   writer caste

khoraki   a maintenance grant to workers while not working

kisan   peasant

krishak samitis   peasant organizations

madhyabitta sreni   middle class

madrassah   a school of Islamic learning

mahajan   money-lender

maulana a title given to a person respected for learning in Islamic theology

maulvi a learned man in Islam

panchayats village administration

piri low wooden stool

praja tenant

pranayama breathing exercise

raiyat or *ryot* cultivator who held lands from landlords subject to certain conditions

samiti organization

sampanna praja well-off cultivators

samya equality

samyabada egalitarianism

samyabadi one who believes in equality

sataranji a carpet made of cotton

sikhshitya madhyabitta sreni educated middle class

tui a pronoun used either to show disrespect or to express familiarity and love

ulema expert in Islamic training

vishayi bhadralok those having income from a profession

Selected Bibliography

Unpublished sources

Private papers

India Office Library, London

Anderson (Bengal Governor, 1932–7) Papers Mss Eur F 207 and Mss Eur
  D 806.
Linlithgow (Viceroy of India, 1936–43) Papers, Mss Eur F 125.
Templewood (Secretary of State for India, 1931–5) Papers, Mss Eur E
  240.
Willingdon (Governor-General of India, 1931–6) Papers Mss Eur F 93.
Brabourne (Bengal Governor, 1937–9) Papers, Mss Eur F 97.
Zetland (Secretary of State for India, 1935–40) Papers, Mss Eur D 609.
Reid (Acting Bengal Governor, 1938–9) Papers, Mss Eur E 278.

Nehru Memorial Museum and Library, New Delhi

All-India Congress Committee Papers, 1926–40.
All-India Hindu Mahasabha Papers, 1931–40.
All-India Trade Union Congress Papers, 1928–40.
S. P. Mukherjee Papers.
Jawaharlal Nehru Papers.
B. C. Roy Papers.
M. N. Roy Papers.
N. R. Sarkar Papers.
Sahajanand Sarswati Papers.
Indulal Yaznik Papers.

Centre for South-Asian Studies, Cambridge

Baker Papers.
Bell Papers.

Benthall Papers.
Carter Papers.
Dash Papers.
Oaten Papers.
Taylor Papers.
Tegart Papers.
Tottenham Papers.

National Archives of India, New Delhi

V. J. Patel Papers.
Rajendra Prasad Papers.
Bholanath Roy Papers.
Wood Collection.

Dacca

Tamijudin Khan Memoirs (Tss) available by courtesy of Mrs M. N. Huda
   of Dacca University.

Government records

India Office Library

Files of Bengal Governor's Secretariat, 1938–40, R/3/2.
Private Office Papers, L/PO.
Records of the Information Department, L/I/1.
Records of the Public and Judicial Department, L/PJ.

National Archives of India

Meerut Conspiracy Case Files.
Record of the Home Political Department, 1925–40.

West Bengal State Archives, Calcutta

Records of the Home Political (Confidential) Department, 1926–40.

Bangladesh Secretariat Record Room, Dacca

Police Department, 'B' Proceedings, 1928–34.
Home Political Department, 'B' Proceedings, 1935–40.
Revenue Department 'B' Proceedings, 1928–40.

Oral transcripts

Nehru Memorial Museum and Library

Satis Dasgupta; R. P. Dutt; S. M. Ghosh; Padam Kant Malaviya; Bhupati Majumdar; Anil Baran Roy; Neillie Sengupta; Promode Sengupta.

Published records

Reports

Sedition Committee (Rowlatt), 1918.
Calcutta University (Sadler) Commission, 1917–19.
Report of the Working of the Reformed Constitution of Bengal, 1921–7, Calcutta, 1928.
Bengal Unemployment Enquiry (Meek) Committee, 1922–4.
Proceedings of the All Parties Conferences, 1928, Allahabad, no date.
Proceedings of the Bengal Legislative Council, 1928–31.
Bengal Provincial Banking Enquiry (De) Committee, 1929–30.
Royal (Whitley) Commission of Labour, 1929–31.
Indian Franchise (Lothian) Committee, 1931–32.
Bengal Jute Enquiry (Finlow) Committee, 1933.
Bengal Jute Enquiry (Fawcus) Committee, 1938–9.
Bengal Land Revenue (Floud) Commission, 1938–40.
Famine Inquiry (Woodhead) Commission, 1944–5.
Census of India, 1901, 1911, 1921, 1931 and 1941.
Census of Bengal, 1872, 1891, 1901, 1911, 1921, 1931, 1941 and 1951.

Newspapers

Advance (English), Calcutta.
Amrita Bazar Patrika (English), Calcutta.
Ananda Bazar Patrika (Bengali), Calcutta.
Azad (Bengali), Calcutta.
Forward (English), Calcutta.
Ganavani (Bengali), Calcutta.
The Mussalman (English), Calcutta.
The Star of India (English), Calcutta.
The Statesman (English), Calcutta.

Unpublished doctoral theses

Bandyapadhyay, Gitasree, 'Constraints in Bengal Politics, 1921–41: Gandhian Leadership', University of Calcutta, 1980.

Bose, Sugata, 'Agrarian Society and Politics in Bengal, 1919–47', University of Cambridge, 1983.

Dasgupta, Swapan, 'Local Politics in Bengal: Midnapore, 1921–32', University of London, 1980.

De Jatindra, Nath, 'The History of the KPP of Bengal, 1929–47: A study of Changes in Class and Inter-Community Relations in the Agrarian Bengal', University of Delhi, 1977.

Iftikhar-ul-Awwal, A. Z. M., 'The Industrial Development of Bengal, 1900–39', University of London, 1978.

Karim, A. K. M., 'The Modern Muslim Political Elite in Bengal', University of London, 1964.

Khan, Bazlur Rahaman, 'Some Aspects of Society and Politics in Bengal, 1927–36', University of London, 1979.

Mackenzie, A. J., 'British Marxists and Empire: Anti-Imperialism in Theory and Practice, 1920–45', University of London, 1978.

Millie, Tonish Diana, 'The Failure of National Integration in Bengal, 1921–37', University of Pennsylvania, 1981.

Norruzzaman, A. H. M., 'Rise of Muslim Middle Class as a Political Force', University of London, 1964.

Park, R. L., 'The Rise of Militant Nationalism in Bengal: A Regional Study of Indian Nationalism', University of Harvard, 1951.

Rashid, Harun-or, 'The Bengal Provincial Muslim League, 1906–47', University of London, 1983.

Ray, Rajat, 'Social Conflict and Political Unrest in Bengal, 1875–1908', University of Cambridge, 1973.

Sarkar, Tanika, 'National Movement and Popular Protest in Bengal, 1928–34', University of Delhi, 1980.

Articles

Addy, Premen and Azad, Ibne, 'Politics and culture in Bengal', *New Left Review* 79 (May–June 1973).

Alavi, Hamza, 'Peasant classes and primordial loyalties', *Journal of Peasant Studies* (hereafter *JPS*) 11.4 (December 1974).

Argov, Daniel, 'Moderates and extremists: two attitudes towards British rule in India', St Antony's (Oxford) paper, no. 18, no date.

Arnold, David, 'Gramsci and peasant subalternity in India', *JPS* 2.4 (July 1984).

Awwal-ul, Ifthikar, 'The problem of middle class educated unemployment in Bengal, 1912–42', *Indian Economic and Social History Review* (hereafter *IESHR*) 19 (January–March 1982).

Bagchi, Amiya, 'Reflections on patterns of regional growth in India during the period of British rule', *Bengal Past and Present* 95.180, part 1 (January–June 1976).

Baker, C. J., 'The Congress at the 1937 elections at Madras', *Modern Asian Studies* (hereafter *MAS*) 10.4 (1976).

Banaji, Jairus, 'The comintern and Indian nationalism', in K. N. Panikkar ed., *National and Left Movements in India*, Vikas Publications (Delhi, 1980).

Banerjee, R. C., 'The Hollwell Monument', *Modern Review* (herafter *MR*) 68.2 (August 1940).

Basu, Aparna, 'Growth of education and Muslim separatism, 1919–39', in B. R. Nanda, *Essays in Modern Indian History*, Oxford University Press (hereafter OUP) (Delhi, 1980).

Behl, Vinay, 'Tata Iron and Steel Company te sramik andolan, 1920–28' (Bengali), *Anya Artha* (July 1976).

Bhaduri, Amit, 'The evolution of land relations in eastern India under British rule', *IESHR* 17 (January–March 1976).

Bhattacharyya, Jnanabrata, 'An examination of leadership entry in Bengal peasant revolts', *Journal of Asian Studies* (hereafter *JAS*) 37.4 (1978).

Bose, S., 'Industrial unrest and labour unions in Bengal, 1920–24', *Economic and Political Weekly* (hereafter *EPW*) 16.44–6 (November 1981).

Bose, Sugata, 'The roots of communal violence: the case of Kishoreganj riot 1930', *MAS* 16.3 (July 1982).

Brenan, Lance, 'The illusion of security: the background of separatism in UP' *MAS* 18.2 (1984).

Broomfield, J. H., 'The regional elite: a theory of modern Indian history', *IESHR* 3.3 (September 1966).

——, 'The forgotten majority: the Bengali Muslims', in D. A. Low ed., *Soundings in Modern South Asian History* (London, 1968).

Chakrabarti, Hiren, 'Government and Bengal terrorism, 1912–18', *Bengal Past and Present* (July–December 1971).

Chakrabarti, L., 'Emergence of an industrial labour force in a dual economy – British India', *IESHR* 15.3 (1978).

Chakrabarty, Bidyut, 'Bengal Congress and the peasantry, 1928–38' *South Asia Research* 5.1 (May 1985).

——, 'The 1932 Communal Award and its implications in Bengal', *MAS*, 23 March 1989.

Chakrabarty, Dipesh, 'Sasipada Banerjee: first bhadralok contact with the working class in Bengal', *IHR* 2.2 (January 1976).

——, 'Communal riots and Labour: Bengal's Jute Millhands in the 1890s', *Past and Present* 91 (May 1981).

——, 'Conditions for knowledge of working class conditions: employers government and the jute workers of Calcutta, 1890–1940', in Ranajit

Guha ed., *Subaltern Studies* 2, OUP (Delhi, 1983).

——, 'On deifying and defying authority: managers and workers in the jute mills of Calcutta, circa 1890–1940', *Past and Present* 100 (August 1983).

Chatterjee, Partha, 'Bengal: rise and growth of a nationality', *Social Scientist* 4.1 (August 1975).

——, 'Agrarian relations and politics in Bengal: some considerations on the making of the Tenancy Act Amendment 1928', Occasional Paper 30, Centre for Studies in Social Sciences, Calcutta (hereafter CSSSC) (September 1980).

——, 'Agrarian relations and communalism in Bengal, 1926–35' in Ranajit Guha ed., *Subaltern Studies I: Writings On South Asian History* (OUP, Delhi, 1982).

——, 'Agrarian structure in pre-partition Bengal', in Asok Sen et al., *Three Studies on the Agrarian Structure in Bengal, 1850–1947* (OUP, Calcutta, 1982).

——, 'Bengal politics and Muslim masses, 1920–47', *Journal of Commonwealth and Comparative Politics* 20.1 (March 1982).

——, 'Caste and politics in west Bengal' in Gail Omvedt ed., *Land Caste and Politics in Indian States* (Authors' Guild, Delhi, 1982).

——, 'Spontaneity and organization in peasant movements in Bengal', in W. H. Morris-Jones et al., *Political Violence* (Institute of Commonwealth Studies, London, 1982).

——, 'The colonial state and peasant resistance in Bengal, 1920–47', Occasional Paper 55, CSSSC (January 1983).

Chatterjee, R., 'C. R. Das and the Chandpur strike of 1921', *Bengal Past and Present*, (May–August and September–Decembeer, 1974).

Chaturvedi, H. K. 'On jute industry in Bengal', *Marxist Miscellany* 7 (1946).

Chaudhuri, Benoy, 'Agrarian economy and agrarian relations in Bengal, 1859–1885', in N. K. Sinha ed., *The History of Bengal, 1757–1905* (University of Calcutta, Calcutta, 1967).

——, 'The process of depeasantization in Bengal and Bihar', *Indian Historical Review* (hereafter *IHR*) 2.1 (July 1975).

——, 'Eastern India' in Dharma Kumar ed., *The Cambridge Economic History of India*, vol. 2 (Orient Longman, New Delhi), 1984.

Chaudhuri, Nirad C., 'Subhas Chandra bose – his legacy and legend', *Pacific Affairs* 26.4 (December 1953).

——, 'Subhas Chandra Bose', *The Illustrated Weekly of India*, 76.38 (September 1955).

Das, Ujjalkanti, 'The Bengal Hindu–Muslim Pact, *Bengal Past and Present* 99.188 (January–June 1980).

Dasgupta, Ranajit, 'Factory labour in eastern India: sources of supply, 1855–1946', *IESHR* 13.3 (September 1976).

——, 'Structure of the labour market in colonial India', *EPW* 17, 44, 45, 46 (special number) (1981).

De Amalendu, 'Fazlul Haq and his reaction to the two-nation theory', *Bengal Past and Present* (January–April 1974).

Dutta, J. M. 'Communalism in the Bengal administration', *MR* 49.2 (February 1931).

——, 'The real nature of Muhammedan majority in Bengal', *MR* 49.6 (February 1931).

——, 'The electorate in Bengal', *MR* 49.6 (June 1931).

Gallagher, John, 'Congress in decline: Bengal 1930–9', *MAS* 7.3 (1973).

Ghosh, Pradyut, 'Organizational structure of a revolutionary secret society: Anushilan Samiti, 1901–18', *Bengal Past and Present* (July–December 1978).

Ghosh, Shyamali, 'Fazlul Haq and Muslim politics in pre-partition Bengal', *International Studies* 13.3 (July–September 1974).

Gordon, Leonard, 'Bengal's Gandhi: a study of regionalism politics and thought', in D. Kopf ed., *Bengal Regional Identity*, Asian Studies Centre, Michigan State University, Michigan, East Lansing, 1969).

——, 'Ambivalence toward authority: a theme in the political biography of Subhas Chandra Bose', paper presented to the postgraduate seminar, Institute of Commonwealth Studies (1971).

Gordon, Richard, 'Non-Co-operation and council entry, 1919–20', *MAS* 7.3 (1973).

Goswami, Omkar, 'Agriculture in Slump: the peasant economy in east and north Bengal in the 1930s', *IESHR* 21.3 (July–September 1984).

Greenough, Paul, 'Indulgence and abundance as an Asian peasant values: a Bengali case in point', *JAS* 42.4 (August 1983).

Haithcox, J. P., 'Left-wing unity and the Indian nationalist movement: M. N. Roy and the CSP', *MAS* 3.1 (1969).

Haldar, Gopal, 'Bengal situation', *MR* 51.1 (January 1932).

——, 'Revolutionary terrorism in Bengal', in A. C. Gupta ed., *Studies in Bengali Renaissance*, The National Council of Education (Jadavpur, 1958).

Hardiman, David, 'The Indian faction: a political theory examined', in Ranajit Guha ed., *Subaltern Studies*, vol. I (OUP, Delhi, 1982).

Jalal Ayesha and Seal Anil, 'Alternative to partition: Muslim politics between the wars', *MAS* 15.3 (1981).

Johnson, Gordon, 'Partition, agitation and Congress: Bengal 1904–8', *MAS* 7.3 (1973).

Krishna, Gopal, 'The development of Indian National Congress as a mass organization, 1918–23', *JAS* 25.3 (May 1966).

Lavalle, E. M., 'Confrontation within confrontation: Subhas C. Bose and the 1928 steel strike', in J. Maclane ed., *Bengal in the 19th and 20th*

Centuries, Asian Studies Centre, Michigan State University (Michigan, East Lansing, 1975).

Limaye, Madhu, 'Subhas Chandra Bose', *Illustrated Weekly of India*, 15–21 January 1984.

Mahatab, P. C. 'Bengal's nobles in politics, 1911–19', *Bengal Past and Present* (July–December 1977).

Mcpherson, K., 'The Muslim of Madras and Calcutta: agitational politics in the early 1920s', *South Asia* 5 (Decemer 1975).

Metcalf, Barbara, 'Nationalist Muslims in British India: the case of Hakim Ajmal Khan', *MAS* 19.1 (February 1985).

Mukherjee, S. N., 'Class, caste and politics in Calcutta, 1815–38', in E. Leach et al., *Elites in South Asia* (Cambridge University Press (hereafter CUP) Cambridge, 1975).

——, *'Bhadralok* in Bengali language and literature', *Bengal Past and Present* 95.181 (July–December 1976).

Nugent, Helen M., 'The Communal Award: the process of decision making in South Asia', *South Asia*, New Series, 2.1 and 2 (March–September 1979).

Rahim, Enayetur, 'Subhas Bose and Bengal politics, 1939–40', *Oracle* 3.2 (April 1981).

Ray, Rajat, 'The crisis of Bengal agriculture, 1870–1927', *IESHR* 10.3 (1973).

——, 'The dynamics of continuity in rural Bengal under British imperialism', *IESHR* 10.2 (1973).

——, 'Masses in politics: the Non-Co-operation movement in Bengal, 1920–22', *IESHR* 11.4 (December 1974).

—— and Ratna, Ray, 'Zamindars and *jotedars*: study of rural politics in Bengal', *MAS* 9.1 (1975).

——, 'Political change in British India', *IESHR* 14.4 (October–December 1977).

——, 'Three interpretations of Indian nationalism', in B. R. Nanda ed., *Essays in Modern Indian History* (OUP, Delhi, 1980).

Ray, Ratna, 'Landlords and peasants: a historiographical view of rural Bengal from pre-colonial to colonial times', *Peasant Studies* 11.4 (1984).

Raychaudhuri, Tapan, 'Indian nationalism as animal politics', *The Historical Journal* 22.3 (1979).

Rothermund, D., 'Constitutional reforms and national agitation in India, 1900–50', *JAS* 21.4 (August 1962).

——, 'Depression of the 1930s', *IESHR* 18.1 (January–March 1981).

Saha, K. B., 'Middle class unemployment in Bengal', *Calcutta Review* 13 (December 1924).

Sanyal, Hitesranjan, 'Arambager jatiatabadi andolan, 1921–1927', (Bengali) *Anya Artha* 6 & 7 (September–October and November–December 1974).

——, 'Social mobility in Bengal: its sources and constraints', *IESHR* 2.1 (July 1975).

——, 'Dakshin-paschim Banglay jatiatabadi andolan' (Bengali) 1, 2, & 3, *Chaturanga* 38 (1 and 3) and 39 (1) (1976–7 and 1977–8).

——, 'Congress movements in the villages of southwest Bengal', in Alice Thorner et al., *Asie du Sud: Traditions et Changements* (Editions du CNRS, Paris, 1979).

Sarkar, Sumit, 'Logic of Gandhian nationalism: civil disobedience and Gandhi-Irwin Pact, 1930–1', *IHR* (July 1976).

——, 'The conditions and nature of subaltern militancy: Bengal from Swadeshi to Non-Cooperation', Occasional Paper on 'History and Society', Nehru Memorial Museum and Library (1983).

Sarkar, Tanika, 'The first phase of civil disobedience movement in Bengal, 1930–31', *IHR* 4.1 (July 1977).

——, 'A study of three communal riots in Bengal, 1930–31', in Mushirul Hasa ed., *Communal and Pan Islamic Trends in Colonial India* (Vikas Publishers, Delhi, 1981).

Seal, Anil, 'Imperialism and nationalism in India, *MAS* 7.3 (1973).

Smalley, Alan, 'The colonial state and agrarian structure in Bengal', *Journal of Contemporary Asia* 13.2 (1983).

Taylor, David, 'The crisis of authority in the Indian National Congress, 1936–39', in B. N. Pandey ed., *Leadership in South Asia* (Vikas Publishers, Delhi, 1977).

Books

Ahmad, Abul Mansur, *Amar Dekha Rajnitir Panchas Bachhar* (Bengali) (Nowroje Kitabistan, Dacca, 1968).

——, *Atmakatha* (Bengali) (Khosroj Kitabmahal, Dacca, 1978).

Ahmad, Imtiaz ed., *Caste Among the Muslims* (Delhi, 1973).

Ahmad, Mazaffar, *Prabandha Sankalon* (Bengali) (National Book Agency, Calcutta, 1970).

——, *Amar Jiban O Bharater Communist Party* (Bengali) (National Book Agency, Calcutta, 1971).

Ahmad, Mukhtar, *Trade Unionism and Labour Disputes in India* (Madras, 1935).

Ahmad, Rafiuddin, *The Bengal Muslims, 1871–1906: a Quest for Identity* (OUP, Delhi, 1981).

Argov, Daniel, *Moderates and Extremists in the Indian Nationalist Movement, 1883–1920* (London, 1967).

Ayer, S. A., *Selected Speeches of Subhas Chandra Bose* (Publication Divisions, Ministry of Information and Broadcasting, Government of India, New Delhi, 1974).

Azad, Maulana, *India Wins Freedom* (Orient Longman, Calcutta, 1959).
Bagchi, Amiya Kumar, *Private Investments in India, 1900–39* (CUP, Cambridge, 1972).
Bamford, P. C., *History of the Non-Cooperation and Khilafat Movements* (Government of India Press, Calcutta, 1925).
Banerjee, Anil Chandra, *The Agrarian System of Bengal*, vol. 2 (K. P. Bagchi and Company, Calcutta, 1981).
Bauner, R. van, M. ed., *Aspects of Bengali History and Society* (University Press, Hawii, 1975).
Bhattacharyya, Buddhadeva, et al., *Satyagrahas in Bengal, 1921–39* (Minerva Publications, Calcutta, 1977).
——, *Origins of the RSP: From National Revolutionary to Non-Conformist Marxism* (Publicity Concern, Calcutta, 1982).
Birla, G. D., *In the Shadow of Mahatma: a Personal Memoir* (Orient Longman, Calcutta, 1953).
Biswas, Kalipada, *Jukta Banglar Sesh Adhyay* (Bengali) (Orient Book Company, Calcutta, 1966).
Bose, Mihir, *The Lost Hero* (Quartet Books, London, 1982).
Bose, Nirmal, *Modern Bengal* (Berkeley, California, 1959).
——, *The Structure of Hindu Society* (Sangam Books, New Delhi, 1976).
Bose, Subhas Chandra, *Collected Works* (Bengali), vols I, II, III, IV (Jayasree Prakashani, Calcutta, 1979, 1980, 1981).
——, *Collected Works*, vols I, II, III, IV (Netaji Research Bureau, Calcutta, 1980, 1981, 1982).
Broomfield, J. H., *Elite Conflict in a Plural Society: Twentieth-Century Bengal* (University of California Press, Berkeley, 1968).
Brown, Judith, *Modern India: the Origins of an Asian Democracy* (OUP, Delhi, 1985).
Chakrabarti, D. and Bhattacharyya C., *Congress' Policy on Communal Award* (Congress Nationalist Party, Calcutta, 1939).
Chakrabarty, Dipesh, *Rethinking Working Class History: Bengal 1890–1940* (Delhi, Oxford University Press, 1989).
Chandra, Bipan, *Rise and Growth of Economic Nationalism in India: Economic Policies of Indian Leadership, 1880–1905* (New Delhi, 1966).
Chatterjee, Bhola, *Aspects of Bengal Politics in the early Nineteen-Thirties* (Calcutta, 1969).
Chatterjee, Partha, *Bengal, 1920–47: the Land Question*, vol. I (K. P. Bagchi, Calcutta, 1984).
Chattopadhyay, Sarat Chandra, *Swadesh Sahitya* (Bengali) (Sriguru Library, Calcutta, 1933).
Chaudhuri, Nirad C., *An Autiobiography of Unknown Indian* (New York, 1951).
——, *The Continent of Circe* (Chatto and Windus, London, 1965).
Chirol, Valentine, *Indian Unrest* (Macmillan and Company, London, 1910).

Franda, Marcus, *Radical Politics in West Bengal* (MIT Press, Cambridge, Mass., 1971).

Giri, V. V., *Labour Problems in Indian Industry*, 3rd edn (Asia Publishing House, New York, 1972).

Gordon, Leonard, *Bengal: the Nationalist Movement, 1876–1940* (Columbia University Press, New York, 1974).

Guha, Ranajit ed., *Subaltern Studies*, vols I, II (OUP, Delhi, 1982 and 1983).

——, *Elementary Aspects of Peasants Insurgency in Colonial India* (OUP, Delhi, 1983).

Gupta, M. N., *Land System of Bengal* (University of Calcutta, Calcutta, 1940).

Haithcox, J. P., *Communism and Nationalism in India: M. N. Roy Comintern Policy* (Princeton University Press, Princeton, 1971).

Haque, M. Azizul, *A Plea for Separate Electorate in Bengal* (Calcutta, 1931).

——, *The Man Behind the Plough* (Book Company, Calcutta, 1939, repr. Dacca, 1980).

Hardiman, David, *Peasant Nationalists of Gujrat, Kheda District, 1917–34* (OUP, Delhi, 1981).

Hauner, Milan, *India in the Axis Strategy* (German Historical Institute, London, 1981).

Hopkins, A. G. and Dewey, C. eds, *The Imperial Impact* (University of London, 1978).

Islam, M. Mufakharul, *Bengal Agriculture, 1920–47: a Quantitative Analysis* (CUP, Cambridge, 1978).

Jalal, Ayesha, *The Sole Spokesman: Jinnah, the Muslim League and the Demand for Pakistan* (Cambridge University Press, Cambridge, 1985).

James, Robert Rhodes, *Memoirs of a Conservative: J. C. C. Davidson's Memoirs and Papers, 1910–37* (Weidenfeld and Nicolson, London, 1969).

Kohli, Atul, *The State and Poverty in India: the Politics of Reform* (Cambridge University Press, Cambridge, 1987).

Kurti, K., *Subhas Chandra Bose As I Knew Him* (Firma K. L. Mukhopadhyay, Calcutta, 1966).

Lakshmanam, P., *Congress and Labour Struggle* (AICC, Allahabad, 1947).

Laushy, David, *The Bengal Terrorists and Their Conversion to Marxism: Aspects of Regional Nationalism in India, 1905–42* (Firma K. L. Mukhcpadhyay, Calcutta, 1975).

Leach, E. R. et al., *Aspects of Caste in South India, Ceylon and North-West Pakistan* (CUP, Cambridge, 1979).

Lebra, Joyce, *Jungle Alliance* (D. Moore, Singapore, 1972).

Low, D. A. ed., *Soundings in Modern South Asian History* (Weidenfeld, London, 1968).

—— ed., *Congress and the Raj, Facets of the Indian Struggle: 1917–47* (Heinemann, London, 1977).

Majumdar, S. N., *In Search of a Revolutionary Ideology and Revolutionary*

Programme: a Study in the Transition from National Revolutionary Terrorism to Communism (Peoples' Publishing House, New Delhi, 1979).

Marquand, David, *Ramsay Macdonald* (Jonathan Cape, London, 1977).

Meherally, Yusuf ed., *Towards Struggle* (Padma Publications, Bombay, 1946).

Misra, B. B., *The Indian Middle Classes* (OUP, London, 1961).

Momen, Humaira, *Muslim Politics in Bengal: a Study of the Krishak Praja Party and the Elections of 1937* (OUP, Dacca, 1972).

Mukherjee, Jadugopal, *Biplabi Jibaner Smriti*, repr. (Bengali) (Academic Publishers, Calcutta 1982).

Mukherjee, Nanda, *Netaji Through German Lense* (Jayasree Prakashani, Calcutta, 1970).

Mukherjee, Radhakamal, *Land Problems of India* (Longman, London, 1933).

Nehru, Jawaharlal, *A Bunch of Old Letters* (Asia Publishing House, Bombay, 1958).

Orr, G. H., *The War of Springing Tiger* (London, 1975).

Page, David, *Prelude to Partition: the Indian Muslims and the Imperial System of Control, 1920–1932* (OUP, Delhi, 1987).

Rao, B. Shiva, *The Industrial Workers in India* (George Allen and Unwin Ltd, London, 1939).

Ray, Prithwis Chandra, *Life and Times of C. R. Das* (OUP, London, 1927).

Ray, Rajat, *Urban Roots of Indian Nationalism* (Vikas Publications, New Delhi, 1979).

Roskil, Stephen, *Hankey: Man of Secrets*, vol. II (1919–31) (Collins, St James, London, 1972).

Roy, D. K., *Netaji – The Man: Reminiscences* (Bharitiya Vidya Bhavan, Bombay, 1966).

Rumbold, Algernon, *Watershed in India, 1914–22* (The Athlone Press, London, 1979).

Saha, Panchanon, *History of Working Class Movement in Bengal* (Peoples' Publishing House, New Delhi, 1978).

Sarkar, Sumit, *The Swadeshi Movement in Bengal, 1903–8* (Peoples' Publishing House, New Delhi, 1973).

——, *Modern India* (Macmillan and Company, New Delhi, 1983).

——, *Popular Movements and Middle Class Leadership in Late Colonial India: Perspectives and Problems from a History from below* (Centre for Studies in Social Sciences, Calcutta, 1983).

Seal, Anil, *The Emergence of Indian Nationalism, Competition and Collaboration in the late Nineteenth Century* (CUP, Cambridge, 1968).

Sen, Asok, *Iswar Cahndra Vidyasagar and his Elusive Milestones* (Ruddhi India, Calcutta, 1977).

—— et al., *Three Studies on the Agrarian Structure in Pre-Partition Bengal* (OUP, Calcutta, 1982).

Sen, Shila, *Muslim Politics In Bengal* (Impex India, New Delhi, 1976).

Sen, Sukumal, *Working Class of India: History of Emergence and Movement, 1830–1970* (K. P. Bagchi and Company, Calcutta, 1977).

Shamsuddin, Abul Kalam, *Atit Diner Smriti* (Bengali) (Nowroje Kitabistan, Dacca, 1968).

Sitaramiah, B. Pattabhi, *History of the Indian National Congress*, vols 1 and 2 (Chand Publishers, New Delhi, 1969).

Thomas, K. P., *Dr B. C. Roy* (WBPCC, Calcutta, 1955).

Toye, Hugh, *Subhas Chandra Bose: the Springing Tiger* (Cassell, London, 1959).

Umar, Badruddin, *Chirasthayi Bandobaste Bangladesher Krishak* (Bengali) (Maola Brothers, Dacca, 1974).

Washbrook, D. A., *The Emergence of Provincial Politics: the Madras Presidency, 1870–1920* (OUP, Delhi, 1970).

Zetland, *Essayez: Memoirs of Lawrence of Marquess of Zetland* (London, 1956).

Index

Lightning Source UK Ltd.
Milton Keynes UK
UKHW020429280921
391301UK00004B/106

9 781350 186576